CONCISE NEWSWRITING

CONCISE
NEWSWRITING

John Hohenberg

Professor Emeritus, COLUMBIA UNIVERSITY

Communication Arts Books
HASTINGS HOUSE, PUBLISHER

CONCISE NEWSWRITING

Copyright © 1987 by John Hohenberg

Hastings House, Publishers,
New York, Ltd.

Library of Congress Catalog Card Number: 87-81298

ISBN: 0-8038-9304-3

Distributed to the trade by:
Kampmann & Company, Inc.
New York, New York

Printed in the United States of America

Designed by Irving Perkins Associates

10 9 8 7 6 5 4 3 2 1

CONTENTS

PREFACE

EDUCATION FOR JOURNALISM has come a long way. Early on, there was a mystical belief among hard-nosed professionals that journalists were born, not made. It was a symptom of a profoundly anti-intellectual attitude that still hangs on here and there, even today.

And yet, as early as 1888, the notion was challenged at the University of Pennsylvania by an editor, Eugene M. Camp of the *Philadelphia Times,* in a paper entitled, "Journalists: Born or Made?" The ever-aggressive Joseph Pulitzer, successful publisher of newspapers in St. Louis and New York City, was so attracted to the idea of a special education for journalists that he wrote to Camp:

"I see no reason why a chair of journalism, filled by a man of real character, could not be made beneficial . . . I have thought seriously upon this subject, and think well of the idea, though I know it is the habit of newspapermen to ridicule it. . . ."

The battle has long since been fought and won. In spite of every effort by the scoffers to limit the development of education for journalism, it is now soundly established both in principle and purpose in the United States and many other countries.

From a few struggling institutions that included Pulitzer's Columbia Journalism School, the movement to give journalists a decent education has developed a momentum all its own. Today, hundreds of American universities have colleges, schools, and departments

of journalism. Moreover, in many a secondary school, beginners'
courses are now available.

No matter what strategy the opponents of journalism education
may use, it is too late to turn the clock back. Nor will it do to argue,
as some do, that a broad liberal arts education is better than training
for journalism at the university level. Graduates with liberal arts
degrees can't absorb the special requirements of journalism merely
by breathing the air, as Eugene M. Camp pointed out a hundred
years ago.

It is primarily because of the broad acceptance of journalism education that I have been encouraged to produce this textbook for
beginners at every level. I believe it will fill a need not covered
by most existing texts, which are addressed mainly to young professionals.

In centering this book on instruction in concise newswriting, I
am aware that good reporting and editing are equally important. I
have taken due account of all three. However, it is my belief based
on experience that the principal need at the beginners' level is for
instruction in the difficult art of writing well under pressure.

This can't be done by resort to journalistic clichés or blueprint
forms of news stories; nor can it be done by substituting the routine
writing of most liberal arts classes. Writing for all forms of journalistic
media really is different, as the beginner quickly discovers.

Learning to write gracefully under pressure is mainly what marks
off journalism students from others whose classes are adapted to
more leisurely forms of writing. There are other differences as well.
Journalists, for one, must be familiar with the laws and other general
practices governing their work. And, equally important, they must
be sensitive to the political, economic, and social problems of their
times.

In designing a textbook on writing for journalism, the first problem
is to decide what to do about the manifold forms the media have
taken—daily and weeky newspapers, weekly news magazines,
monthly specialized magazines of comment, radio, TV, cable, wire
services, syndicates, feature services, and public relations.

I have chosen to begin with the general writing practices of daily
newspapers and wire services because they are basic to most other
forms of journalism. The appearances differ, it is true, but the fun-
damentals are identical, as will be seen in the instructional material
about the newer aspects of journalism in the latter part of this work.
Still another consideration is the usual trend of most beginners to

gravitate toward wire services and print journalism at the outset of their careers.*

The thirty-two chapters in this book have been divided equally as follows: Part I: Writing Basic News; Part II: Writing in the Public Interest; Part III: Specialized Journalism.

Instead of selecting often dated published or broadcast material for illustrative purposes, I have chosen, for the most part, to present realistic writing problems based upon simulated incidents. Where such instructional detail is illustrated with copyrighted material, the originating organization in all cases is credited. For instructors who use the manual that goes with this work, the suggestions for classroom discussions and assignments originate mainly from my own experience.

The text as a whole is designed to cover an academic year's instruction in journalism. The three parts divide naturally for classes under the quarter system, but it will be seen that the material can easily be arranged to fit the semester system as well. As for the writers' handbook in the Appendix, students are advised to consult it frequently. A dictionary and a grammar handbook will be useful, too. I know of no shortcuts to good writing.

Finally, let me thank my academic colleagues among the faculties of the colleges and universities where I have taught for their support and encouragement over the years. And, as always, I owe particular gratitude to my wife, JoAnn F. Hohenberg, for her patience and her forbearance as well as her much-appreciated help.

JOHN HOHENBERG

Aquebogue, New York

---

* Of about five thousand students who have been in my classes at various American colleges and universities, I recall only one major instance of a student who began in broadcast journalism and transferred with great success to print. Many went just the other way.

PART I
WRITING BASIC NEWS

1

News Makers

A HOARSE-VOICED STRANGER on a mean street proclaims the virtues of a dangerous, habit-forming drug to a gullible teen-ager and makes a sale. . . .

A weary scientist, working in a cluttered lab, tests an antidote to the deadly disease called AIDS (Acquired Immune Deficiency Syndrome). . . .

A watchman sees a telltale ribbon of steam escaping from a sensitive area in an atomic power plant and sounds the alarm. . . .

These are the signs and sounds of some of the news makers in our time.

The Sources of the News

The war on illicit drugs, the crusade for public health, and the effort to make atomic energy safe are all part of a different kind of news in the latter part of this century. Call it the "new journalism."

It is the news that deeply affects our society. To be sure, there are many other kinds of news in more traditional patterns. From the president of the United States to the public information offices at Police Headquarters, we receive such an outpouring of other kinds of news daily that it is difficult to absorb.

This intelligence, coming atop all else, therefore complicates the problems of journalists in this era. Theirs never has been a simple job. Today, the pressures on them are even more intense.

The ever-widening sources of the news call for clear thinking and clear writing. There is also a compelling need for conciseness, close attention to detail, and the capacity to deal with the unexpected. It is no longer sufficient to define the ingredients of the news as accuracy, interest, and timeliness. Explanation is required, too.

All too often, the news that comes to us, even from strange and varied sources, can deeply affect a community. There was a time, for example, when a proposal in Congress to put a heavy tax on foreign imports would not have created much of a stir. But today, in a seaport where three thousand new jobs have been created to handle a bumper import of foreign automobiles, such news can stir grave concern.

Nor are the problems of war and peace easy to define in this era.

It was only a little more than a generation ago that our nation was electrified by an eight-word radio broadcast that cut into a quiet Sunday in early December and forever changed our world: "Air raid Pearl Harbor . . . this is no drill. . . ."

We knew then that we had been plunged into World War II. We have sought in vain ever since for the kind of peace we thought we had earned through the victory of our armed forces in that war. Instead, we have faced the enmity of our erstwhile ally, the Soviet Union, which supported our enemies in both the Korean and Vietnam wars and remains a threat to us in the latter years of this century.

Thus, in the depth of the cold war, we have become all too familiar with another kind of news—the news that deals with national security.

It may not have been a great consideration earlier in this century when we felt relatively safe between our two-ocean barrier. But today, with the development of atomic warfare and the "Star Wars" defenses against ballistic missiles, we know that there is now no place to hide. Our national security, consequently, becomes of the first importance not only in the nation's capital but in the smallest communities in every part of the land.

Nor does the broadening of the categories of news end there. In this century, we have developed different legal guidelines for our society that make us markedly more diverse in our relations with minorities.

It came about in part because in 1955 a black woman, Rosa Parks, refused to give her seat on a bus to a white man in Montgomery, Alabama, as required by local law. From that simple act, certainly not a part of conventional news patterns at the time, there flowed a pattern of legal decisions that created virtual desegregation in the United States.

Beyond our borders, the movement to break down barriers against black people has also given impetus to our national policies that deal with the apartheid principle in the Union of South Africa. It was not something that Rosa Parks could have foreseen when she decided against giving her bus seat to a white man.

Our news patterns have expanded in other areas as well.

Many of us anticipated that our country's wealth and strength in a world of shifting values would bring us new friends. That has been the case among the Japanese, our enemies in World War II, and some oil-rich nations such as Saudi Arabia from which we receive substantial oil imports.

But we also made new enemies who have used terror tactics to strike deeply into the heart of our land by holding some of our citizens abroad as hostages. We had paid little attention to Iran, for example, until its revolutionary government kidnaped Americans in 1979 and we failed to free them in an air raid that foundered. Nor had many Americans even heard of the dictator of Libya, Muammar el-Khadafi, before our bombers attacked his country in 1986.

Such actions did not stop terrorism. Indeed, among Arab activists who used terror tactics against us because of our support of the state of Israel, it became a part of their campaign to seize Americans as hostages in the Middle East to advance their cause. In so doing, they brought fear to many an American city and town where families mourned their loved ones.

The point cannot be made too strongly: as is shown by these examples and many more that are based on societal developments toward the end of this century, we cannot limit our definition of what news is and how it is created.

Within the memory of many journalists who still practice their profession, it was once sufficient to say to newcomers, "News is anything that makes you say, 'Gee whiz, I didn't know that!' " Alas, the Gee Whiz school of journalism scarcely covers the massive changes that have come about in our land and elsewhere through the evolution of our society. Would anybody except possibly a few zealots have exclaimed, "Gee whiz!" because Rosa Parks refused to give her bus seat to a white man? Or because a teen-ager bought some crack, a dangerous form of cocaine, from a drug trafficker?

No, it just isn't good enough as a definition of news. In fact, almost any definition in these times is risky because new concepts of news are being formulated by events month after month, year after year. However, as an interim definition, it could be said that anything which interests or affects large numbers of people in our society may be considered as news.

The problem for us remains that there isn't space enough in all but the very largest and richest newspapers and magazines to publish and explain the great volume of such material daily. And as far as the broadcast media are concerned, the commercial networks and their affiliates can scarcely afford to devote that much time to news in depth except for specials and documentaries. That holds true, as well, for cable and its various offshoots.

The creation of the video display terminal (VDT), the computer, and all the other marvels of the electronic age can scarcely solve this problem either now or in the future. For no matter how interested average readers or viewers may be in the day's events, their attention spans are limited by the time they can spare. And that, too, is something that must be taken into account by the beginning journalist in this era.

Early in this century, what passed for news among most of the media could be supplied cheaply and in volume merely by stationing a reporter at Police Headquarters and one or two more to cover the courts in most cities. That kind of news provided a daily grist of violence, sex, crime, and punishment which in theory, at least, attracted a mass audience.

In any event, although police and court news still must be produced and written about, that cannot constitute the be-all and end-all of the daily news report for any responsible segment of the media, print or electronic. Such news, however, may serve as an illustration of how a relatively simple news account originates and at least one way in which it may be written.

Handling Basic News

The scene is the newsroom of the *Central City Leader,* a P.M. newspaper in a large midwestern city. Mack Roberts, a recent journalism graduate at State University, is awaiting his first assignment.

However, instead of sending him out, an assistant city editor calls to him, "Roberts, take Jim Hadley on two."

Roberts locates and punches the number 2 button on a small telephone panel and hears a drawling voice in his earphones as he prepares to take notes:

"This is Hadley at Police Headquarters. Just got a police slip on an overnight robbery at the home of an eighty-five-year-old woman. Here's the name, Mary McTaggart (and it is spelled out), of 6818 Beverly Road. She lives there with her daughter, Agnes Leonard, a sixty-year-old widow. The cops say a burglar got in the house around 2:30 A.M. by prying open a downstairs window, pulled a gun on the two women in an upstairs bedroom, and got away with $30.50. Not much of a story, except that when I phoned to check the facts with the old lady, she said she tricked the thief into passing up a $35,000 ring. It was one her late husband gave her and it was on her dresser, but when the thief picked it up, the old lady said, and you can use this as a quote, 'That's not worth the bother. It's only glass and it brings bad luck.' Well, he believed her, because he passed it up, took the money from her purse, and got away. The old lady's husband, Fred McTaggart, a realtor, died four years ago. Nobody was hurt. Any questions?"

There were no questions.

Being well-trained, Roberts also knows better than to bother the city desk with instructions on how to write such a small, routine piece. He begins on his VDT (video display terminal):

> A burglar took $30.50 at gunpoint early today from an 85-year-old woman after awakening her in her bedroom at 6818 Beverly Road.
> The woman, Mrs. Mary McTaggart, widow of a local realtor, Fred McTaggart, managed to trick the intruder into passing up a $35,000 ring. . . .

Roberts stops. It isn't very good and he knows it. The woman at the next desk, Sally Ward, realizing that he is a beginner and be-fuddled, glances at what he has written and murmurs, "The second graf is your lead." Instinctively, Roberts knows she is right. He begins again:

> An 85-year-old widow tricked an armed robber into passing up a $35,000 ring early today, limiting the theft to $30.50 in cash.
> "That's not worth the bother," Mary McTaggart said she told the thief as he picked up the ring in her bedroom at 6818 Beverly Road. "It's only glass and it brings bad luck." The ring was a gift from the woman's husband, Fred McTaggart, a realtor who died four years ago. Instead, the intruder took the cash from Mrs. McTaggart's purse. Police said he broke into the house by prying open a downstairs window.
> A 60-year-old widowed daughter, Agnes Leonard, was in the bedroom with her mother at the time. Both women were unharmed.
>
> end

This time, when Sally Ward glances over at the finished story, she nods and smiles. "You'll do," she says. "Let it go." When the copy comes up at the city desk, her judgment is sustained. The story is passed without change because it stresses the unusual, includes all relevant facts and sources, and is briefly and quickly told.

That is how routine basic news is written.

Working Against TV

Not long afterward, Sally Ward is summoned to talk to the city editor, Joe Stoddard. By that time, Roberts has learned that she is a reporter with a dozen years' service at the *Leader* and is a specialist in news of medicine and science. When she returns, she consults a notebook and dials a number on her telephone.

Seeing young Roberts watching her, she smiles and says, "It's just a telephone interview, no big deal."

Subsequently, he learns that the press agent for the Catlin Clinic, the most important medical research group in the area, has called a news conference for 2:00 P.M. with its director, Dr. Hans Bergin, who has just been awarded the Nobel Prize in Medicine. It is Sally Ward's job to do a telephone interview with Dr. Bergin for the late edition of the *Leader*. As she explains:

"If we wait until the news conference, we can only make a squib for the late edition. And by that time, KTLT-TV will have used the whole news conference live directly from Catlin Clinic and we'll look foolish. So the boss says to talk to Dr. Bergin now and I think Bergin will do it for me. . . ."

Sally's luck is good. She is on the phone with the Nobel laureate for more than a half hour, but she evidently isn't prepared to write when she hangs up. Instead, she sits before her VDT in a brown study.

Finally, without explanation, she leaves her desk and confers earnestly with the city editor who assigned her to the telephone interview. When she returns, she seems assured and smiling. "Didn't know how they wanted to play the story," she explains. "Mine will be separate from the Nobel Prize announcement, which makes it a lot easier to tell."

Now she confronts her VDT with confidence. Just before she begins writing, Roberts takes a chance on asking about something that has been bothering him: "How do you know what to lead with?"

"That was my problem," she replies. "If the announcement from Norway and the interview were to be combined, it would be bound to make for a wordy beginning. But once the wire desk and the city desk straightened everything out, I knew what I had to do. The lead has to be on cancer."

Roberts tries to be blasé. "More antismoking propaganda?"

"Heavens, no, Bergin's talked so much about not smoking that it's old stuff. But this time, I think, he's given me something that's new, bless his heart."

With that, her fingers fairly fly over the VDT keyboard. And now and then, as Roberts peeks at what comes up on the VDT, he sees that she is moving an interesting but concisely written piece:

BERGIN

Dr. Hans Bergin celebrated his Nobel Prize award today by predicting that early warning tests for cancer soon will be practical.

In a telephone interview with the *Leader,* shortly after the Nobel announcement in Norway, the director of the world-famous Catlin Clinic said:

"I am confident that our new tests will give many people an early warning that they are susceptible to cancer."

On the basis of such tests, Dr. Bergin forecast, it may be possible to institute either scientific treatment or changes in personal habits, perhaps both, that will help prolong the lives of victims of some types of cancer.

"But please don't think of this as a cure for cancer," he urged. "We are a long way from that right now, although I still hope some day that it will come about."

Dr. Bergin stressed his familiar warning against smoking once again. He said that people inclined toward cancer were, in effect, "pronouncing a death sentence on themselves" by puffing away at cigarettes. . . .

It doesn't take Sally long to finish her piece, although it runs close to a column in length. Nor does anybody come around to congratulate her on the exclusive interview or the professional manner in which she has handled it. Such things are taken for granted in the nation's newsrooms.

By the time of the 2:00 P.M. news conference with Dr. Bergin at the Catlin Clinic, the *Leader* is on the street with Sally's interview as well as the Nobel Prize announcement—a wire service story filed in Oslo. As Sally predicted, the local TV station, KTLT, does a live newscast of the proceedings that very largely repeats what has been reported in her interview.

It is not often nowadays that the print media can compete with the spontaneity of the electronic media, but this is one way in which it is done. By and large, because of the nature of their operations, reporters for broadcast and cable have inherited the first telling of the news when their organizations find it important enough to use at once.

New Methods and Old

The contrast between the two types of news here illustrated is self-evident, as is the difference in the way they are handled. This is modern journalistic practice and it makes sense. While some readers may be amused by the old lady's guile in saving her valuable ring, the story really isn't very important and should not be told at length. However, there can be no argument about the importance of the science story, both the Nobel Prize announcement in Norway and the way the *Leader's* reporter gained a significant interview with the recipient. Too many people still fall victim to cancer.

This is the rationale for judging the news as well as those who make it and report it. If we have broadened our concept of what news is to fit today's needs, however, it isn't because everybody in the profession has agreed that it is necessary. Even today, there are publications and broadcasters who still believe that police stuff, sex, and violence are the keys to successful journalism. But responsible news organizations operate quite differently.

In practicing the new journalism, the first lesson is to serve the public interest. All else that we do flows from that basic standard of the profession.

The Routine of Journalism

Like every other profession, journalism has its share of mechanical routines. The first one for every beginner is copy preparation. Whether the writer uses a VDT or a typewriter, copy must be prepared in a precise way. And while it varies in some details from one newspaper to another, with entirely different formats for the broadcast media, the way Mack Roberts handled his first story for the *Central City Leader* is fairly standard for print (see fig. 1).

Roberts's piece is called a "short," as distinct from longer stories, such as the one Sally Ward wrote, which is called a "spread."

In preparing copy for a short, the main idea is to try to keep it on a single sheet of copy paper or a comparable space on a VDT. The

Roberts rewrite   Hadley, Police HQ

ROB

An 85-year-old widow tricked an armed robber into passing
up a $35,000 ring early today, limiting the theft to $30.50 in
cash.

"That's not worth the bother," Mary McTaggart said she told
the thief as he picked up the ring in her bedroom at 6818 Beverly
Road. "It's only glass and it brings bad luck."

The ring was a gift from the woman's husband, Fred McTaggart,
a realtor who died four years ago. Instead, the intruder took the
cash from Mrs. McTaggart's purse. Police said he broke into the
house by prying open a downstairs window.

A 60-year-old widowed daughter, Agnes Leonard, was in the
bedroom with her mother at the time. Both women were unharmed.

end

FIG. 1   *Copy preparation for a "short." The example illustrates
the appearance of Roberts's first piece for the Central City News.*

writer's name goes at the top, upper left, with the source next to it. An inch or so below is the name of the story, ROB, a one-word slug, which also will identify the headline when it is written. The short then begins as indicated below the slug with sharply indented paragraphs and short sentences. It is double-spaced (some news organizations use triple-spacing to make the copy easier to edit) and finishes on the page with the word "end" at the bottom to show it is complete.

A "spread," which runs to two or more pages, follows this general pattern for newspapers. However, if later developments make changes necessary, there are accepted ways of preparing the copy both for newspapers and wire services, as will be illustrated in the third section of this book. For the electronic media, particularly television, where the written word must be coordinated with visuals, the process becomes more complicated, as illustrated in the third section of this book.

The point cannot be overstressed. While copy preparation is purely mechanical, it is a necessary part of the journalistic process and must be done carefully. Otherwise, the work of the most skilled writers may become unmercifully scrambled.

2

On Writing News

TOO MANY RULES are the bane of writers of all descriptions. In journalism, that is particularly true because there are two definitions of style: 1) the manner in which an individual writer uses language, and 2) the way a news organization wants its writers to work. Obviously, the two may be in conflict and confusion can sometimes result.

For that reason, there is a useful bit of advice for all editors and broadcast news directors at the beginning of the *New York Times's Manual of Style and Usage,* which ought to be taken to heart: "The rules should encourage thinking, not discourage it. A single rule might suffice: 'The rule of common sense will prevail at all times.'"

Would that it were so!

Organizing a News Story

Fortunately, not all style books have a tendency to inhibit. In Ernest Hemingway's earliest days as a reporter on the *Kansas City Star,* he was much impressed with the first paragraph in the *Star's* style book of instructions for writers: "Use short sentences. Use short first paragraphs. Use vigorous English, not forgetting to strive for smoothness. Be positive, not negative."

After winning both the Nobel and Pulitzer Prizes for his work,

Hemingway told an interviewer: "Those were the best rules I ever learned for the business of writing. I've never forgotten them. No man with any talent, who feels and writes truly about the things he is trying to say, can fail to write well if he abides by them."*

For journalists, the advice is sound; for other writers, despite Hemingway's enthusiasm for the *Kansas City Star*'s style book, the results are not always as satisfactory. America's greatest dramatist, Eugene O'Neill, another Nobel and Pulitzer laureate, failed as a young reporter on his hometown paper, the *New London Day* in Connecticut, partly because he couldn't abide writing short, simple sentences.

As for broadcast journalism, its outstanding figure in the early days of television, Edward R. Murrow, had his "hard news" written for him at CBS by Jesse Zousmer, who followed the rules. As another broadcasting colleague explained, "Murrow's diction and articulation may have been exemplary, but his spelling was always suspect and his pronunciation of proper names a little shaky."**

Leaving aside these great ones and their foibles, we already have seen that even a newcomer to journalism, in writing his first short, is subject to the mechanical rules of copy preparation. For experienced professionals, that becomes second nature in the handling of spreads as well. In addition to the instructions for doing shorts, a spread ends a page of copy or a "take" (section) of a VDT on a paragraph; also, that the addition of the word "-more-" indicates there is another page to come. All pages after the first page of a spread carry the slug of the story and the page number as indicated, with copy beginning directly under the slug.

The "end" mark, of course, comes at the conclusion of the story.

The Forms of the News Story

If copy preparation for shorts and spreads were all that a beginner had to worry about, life in the newsroom would be a breeze. But there are other considerations that must be taken into account by journalists at the outset of their careers and not all of them are purely mechanical. For example, deadlines must be met.

Although the news story is scarcely an art form, it does follow

*As quoted by Charles A. Fenton in "The Apprenticeship of Ernest Hemingway," published in 1954.
**Alexander Kendrick, *Prime Time* (Boston: Little Brown 1969), pp. 303–304.

certain recognizable patterns, however loosely they may be adhered to.

To start with, there are two main divisions of news. These are known to the trade as *hard news,* events of the moment that must be given immediate circulation, and *feature news,* which includes almost everything else except interpretive and editorial material.

Hard news covers all kinds of events from a presidential news conference to a holdup in the next block. Feature news depends almost entirely on what a particular audience is interested in, which could be anything from a profile of a politician or a love goddess to an account of an interesting new hobby.

Specialized subjects such as campaigns against illicit drugs or other threats to public health and investigations of political corruption may turn out to be either hard news or features, depending on what reporters are able to disclose. As for interpretive material, which could take the form of an article or series in print or a documentary in television, its use depends entirely on the nature of the event it attempts to explain.

To proceed with the format for hard news, which is as a general rule the simplest and the easiest to understand:

The story almost automatically divides itself in the writing into two parts, the lead and the body. For usage in the print media, mainly newspapers and wire services, the lead generally consists of a short sentence summarizing an event and the time it occurred—today, last night, yesterday, etc.

The body gives the documentation for the lead—a quote or a source—plus other relevant details in the order of descending importance so that the story can easily be trimmed from the bottom.

The whole is told in the past tense. Wherever there are quotations, special notice is given to them by making them separate paragraphs but quotes seldom are used by themselves as a lead.

Throughout, the principle followed by most journalists is to use short, simple sentences, vigorous verbs, few adjectives, and no editorial comment in any guise. With the exception of first-person stories written by victims of a catastrophe, or other events lending themselves to personal observation, hard news is told in the third person.

The critical beginner, who has ambitions as a writer, no doubt will ask, "What distinguishes one piece of journalistic writing from another if the patterns for hard news are so much alike and the restrictions on a writer's style are so rigid?"

Admittedly, the question is difficult to answer. And yet, in the hands of a skilled writer, news style can be enormously effective. One needn't be another Ernest Hemingway to write simply and effectively about an event in which large numbers of people are interested.

From Peter Arnett's reports for the Associated Press from Vietnam to Red Smith's sports pieces in the *New York Times,* and from Ernie Pyle's stories about his beloved "goddamned infantry" to Karen Elliott House's financial reporting in the *Wall Street Journal,* the files of the Pulitzer Prizes show that this kind of writing can be distinctive and meaningful.

It doesn't help much for beginners to sulk, groan, or write with their elbows, because these wouldn't measurably change the system. Nor are the limitations in the electronic media any less stringent; if anything, because writers for radio and TV must always be aware that their news reportage is to be heard, not read, their job is more difficult than that of writers for print.

There have been a few changes over the years in what is expected of writers for all forms of journalism. These are not revolutionary, it is true, being aimed mainly at creating a better understanding of the news of the day among a mass audience.

For example, at the turn of the century, it was an article of faith that every hard news story—even the leads—should reflect the "five Ws and H," that is, the *who, when, where, what, why, and how* of events. That rule was cumbersome and frequently unnecessary. And the newspapers of the early part of the century reflected it in their often tortured prose. Not all the five Ws and H were needed in every news account, and some, in one instance or another, turned out to be more important than the rest.

With the birth of nationwide radio newscasts as a counterforce to the press, writing for newspapers had to become sharper. Moreover, after World War II, when network television burst upon the land and later assumed full color, it also became the first purveyor of news to the nation. And that, too, made a difference in the way news was written in the United States and elsewhere.

When a major story breaks today, therefore, we may expect with good reason that the news bulletins will be spread over our radio, television, and cable sets first (and often included in wire service reports in our news centers as well). Next, if the news is still developing, as is often the case, the broadcast media and cable—in whole or in part—will manage somehow to maintain a running account for as long as is necessary.

The newspapers, which still circulate at the rate of about 64 to

65 million copies daily in this country, remain of great importance to us because many of them are able to provide a detailed, coherent account of the events that may very likely have come to us in bits and pieces from their electronic competition. And the beginning journalist, who may be dazzled by the glamor of television news, might keep in mind that the nightly news programs of the three networks in the mid-1980s had a combined rating of about two-thirds the audience of the daily press.

3

There's News in Names

THE MOST INTERESTING PART of the day's news frequently is about people—and especially people close to home. That
is why newcomers to journalism are always told, "Names make
news." And very often some of these names are featured both in
newspapers and on the mighty tube over great events.

Perhaps it is illogical, even wrongheaded, for journalists to remain
so involved with personalities. But there is no discernible limit to
public interest in marriages and divorces, births and deaths, arrivals
and departures, prize awards, and all the other personal events that
matter so much to all of us as individuals.

It is scarcely a surprise, then, that a newcomer's initial duties for
the press or the electronic media deal with people more often than
not.

Writing about People

Writers who develop stories about people for the news media can't
afford to fall into a dull routine. It is necessary for them to maintain
an easy balance between the objectivity of the reporter and the art
of the storyteller. There is little point in making such a news account
sound like the stencil for a paid advertisement to be inserted in a
column of vital statistics in a country weekly. But it is an even greater
mistake to give way to girlish enthusiasm in emoting about a bride

("pretty little Mamie Pfeiffer looked like a queen") or her erstwhile boy friend ("good old Sam Whistler was every inch a movie hero as the handsome groom") in describing a marriage.

What saves many an account of this kind from disaster is the sharp eye of the reporter-writer who tries to look for the small but interesting details that make this event different from so many others like it. Adjectives won't be of much use in handling such an assignment. And the use of vigorous verbs in the active voice may add to a writer's troubles.

The best approach usually is the simplest—to let the story tell itself without trying to add artificial interest through overwriting.

A Story about an Engagement

There is no formula that will produce news about interesting personalities. Nor has anybody been able to develop a forecasting system to determine how, where, and exactly when such news will become known. Sometimes a tipster will telephone a newspaper or a radio or television station. Or perhaps a reporter, covering another assignment, will pick up a rumor and verify it. Now and then, especially in the case of obituaries, a hospital or a funeral home may originate the news. And in the case of people of prominence, a formal announcement may be made.

This is how Mack Roberts becomes involved in such an assignment during his first week on the job at the *Central City Leader:*

Sally Ward, the reporter at the next desk who specializes in science and medicine, has been busy for some time pawing through mounds of clippings from the morgue. Now and then, she pauses, scribbles a few notes on a sheet of copy paper, and puts a clipping aside for future reference. Having nothing better to do, Roberts asks, "Something important going on?"

Sally responds, "Don't know how important it is, but Mayor Reardon is announcing his daughter's engagement in a few minutes. The city desk got the tip from City Hall."

Roberts is mildly interested. "Ann Reardon, huh? She was in a couple of my classes at State U. Nice kid."

Sally continues with her examination of the clippings. "Did you know her well?"

"No, but I used to see her at parties sometimes. Who's she marrying?"

Sally doesn't answer him directly. "Mardee Fenwick at City Hall says she understands it's a sociologist named Darcy Evans at State U, but we can't be sure. I tried to get him on the phone but his office doesn't answer."

That interests Roberts even more. "Good guy, Evans, had him in a basic sociology course in my sophomore year. But lord, he's a lot older than Ann. Must be fifty anyway."

"Professor Evans is fifty-two," Sally says, consulting a clipping. "His wife divorced him three years ago and they have two children. If he's the guy, I'd say Ann Reardon is taking on quite a load for someone only twenty-two years old."

Joe Stoddard, the city editor, approaches them just then. "Okay, Sally, it's Evans all right, and Mardee's got the story, so we'll be able to make a short piece for the edition."

"Maybe Mack here can take notes and I can get a quick start on the story," Sally suggests. "He knew Ann at State U and had a class with Darcy Evans."

"Sure thing," Stoddard agrees, then adds to Roberts, "As soon as you get done taking notes, go see if you can find Ann and Evans and take a photographer along with you."

Mardee Fenwick, the *Leader*'s reporter at City Hall, has a brief statement from Mayor Reardon announcing his daughter's engagement to Professor Evans. Once Roberts passes it along to Sally, she brushes aside her pile of clippings and writes her story:

REARDON

Ann Reardon, Mayor Henry Reardon's 22-year-old daughter, will be married next month to 52-year-old Darcy Evans, a sociology professor at State U.

The mayor made the announcement today at City Hall saying, "Ann and Professor Evans wanted me to announce their engagement and I'm happy to do it. Mrs. Reardon and I are very pleased."

The mayor's daughter, who was graduated from State U last spring with the degree of bachelor of science, is a first-year student at the State U Medical School. Professor Evans, the father of two children, was divorced three years ago.

The mayor said that Ann, the Reardons' only child, met Professor Evans two years ago when she was a student in one of his classes. Asked about the 30-year difference in the ages of the engaged couple, the mayor observed,

"I don't think that's a very serious matter as long as they love each other."

The date for next month's marriage will be announced later.

end

The formal approach to the news, in this case, was a necessity for two reasons: 1) Sally was pressed for time to produce a short account for Page 1 of the *Leader*'s next edition, and 2) all she had to go on was the mayor's brief announcement and the background of the engaged couple as gleaned from the morgue clippings.

It was a case of "make do" and Sally used every fact she had. Under such circumstances, it would have been a mistake to attempt to do a fancy writing job. To put some life in the story, the city editor quite correctly sent Roberts to the State U campus with a photographer to do a clean-up reporting job.

Necessarily, Roberts was up against stiff competition. Needless to say, the story was worth developing and every television and radio station was assigning on it, as well as the opposition morning paper, the *Central City News*. Whoever got to Ann Reardon and Professor Evans first was likely to get the best break on their own account of their romance.

Under the circumstances, Roberts and his photographer, Art Shepard, decided to concentrate on finding Ann. Instead of wandering aimlessly over the university campus, Roberts phoned Ann's mother at home for her classroom schedule and learned that she was in Linden Hall at the medical school at that hour.

We pick up Roberts and Shepard, waiting in the photographer's car outside Linden Hall, for classes to break on the hour. Naturally, it's a gamble that Ann will be going about her regular routine at a time when her engagement is being announced. But that's the way Roberts has chosen to handle the story and, as things turn out, he guesses correctly. He leaves the car as he sees Ann outside Linden Hall and, fortunately for him, she stops as she recognizes him.

She is pleasant, outgoing, and quite willing to talk about her forthcoming marriage. In fact, she is so pleased because the *Leader*'s reporter is an acquaintance, however casual, that she arranges on the spot for a meeting with Professor Evans, a joint interview, and pictures.

That is what is known to the trade as reporter's luck—you either have it or you don't—and Roberts is smart enough not to question his good fortune. Before long, he has cleaned up his end of the story, turned in his account to Sally, and sent the photographer back to the office posthaste with pictures for the *Leader*'s final edition of the day.

Roberts is, for the moment at least, ahead of the competition. The *Leader*'s final story, done under a joint by-line, begins as follows (with Sally doing the writing while Roberts is on his way back to the office):

SUB REARDON

By Sally Ward and Mack Roberts

Professor Darcy Evans didn't think much of Ann Reardon, the mayor's daughter, when she was in his sociology class two years ago. "I nearly flunked her," he says.

However, the professor admitted today that he'd changed his mind about Ann and she didn't think he was such a bad guy, either. They are to be married next month.

"And I want a great big wedding," Ann added.

The formal announcement of the couple's engagement was made by Mayor Reardon at City Hall, but Ann and her fiancé were anything but formal at the State U campus when they told about their romance.

Neither seemed concerned about a 30-year difference in their ages— Ann is 22 and Professor Evans is 52. They agreed with the mayor, who remarked at City Hall:

"I don't think that's a very serious matter as long as they love each other."

Ann also wasn't worried in the slightest because her fiancé was divorced three years ago and is the father of two children. "I hope we can have children of our own," she said.

But about that sociology class in which they met two years ago, Professor Evans admitted that he didn't think the small, blond, blue-eyed Ann was much of a student. "It looked to me halfway through the course that I might have to flunk her but I wound up giving her a C," he confessed.

"And," she added, "that was after we'd started dating so he wasn't doing me any favors."

Ann and Professor Evans were interviewed at the State U campus after her afternoon classes at the medical school, in which she is a first-year student. She intends to continue her studies. . . .

How Personalities Influence the News

The engagement of the mayor's daughter is the type of story that inevitably attracts a wide audience. Locally, in a place like Central City, it is bound to be discussed and followed as avidly as the romance of a distant British crown prince with a beautiful bride. True, such stories do not have the impact on people's lives that are likely to follow the enactment of a new tax program or a sharp drop in the stock market. But to the average reader and viewer a romance is simply more interesting.

The broad range of news about personalities of all types has a general appeal to mass audiences. For example, if a film actress comes home to her family in Central City to have her baby, it is bound to interest most people who have heard of her or seen her in the movies.

The appeal of diverse personalities is almost without limit as a source of news and the stories that result may be handled in any number of ways. A famous architect who arrives in town to plan for the construction of a new skyscraper is bound to attract interest. So is Dr. Hans Bergin, the local Nobel Prize winner, when he departs for Oslo to receive his award and when he returns from his triumph. The twice-divorced woman artist who marries a millionaire local banker also will be in demand among the news media in Central City, as will the departing president of the State University upon his retirement at age seventy.

People need not command great wealth or influence or lay claim to fame for their accomplishments to be marked out as news figures. Nor do age or beauty or outstanding accomplishment alone make people sought after by television and the press. Even the oldest and the humblest of people may, through sheer force of circumstances, attract the attention of a mass audience without the slightest intention of doing so.

An Old Lady Counts Her Blessings

This is the story of an old lady in modest circumstances that drew a sympathetic response from many people in Central City. It didn't seem like much when the first notice came in to the *Central City Leader*.

An assistant city editor, seeing Roberts reading a newspaper at his desk, said to him: "Take this call on three and see what it amounts to."

Roberts was glad of a break in the monotony. He had been sitting around for hours waiting for an assignment, but the day seemed dull and the news was sparse. Not even the weather was freakish enough to arouse comment. Nor did the caller to whom Roberts talked by telephone appear to have anything worth a story. It was just a clerk in the advertising department who had taken an ad from a funeral home giving the date for services for a ninety-six-year-old woman who had been found dead that morning.

Roberts made notes on the particulars, decided that he might do a short obituary if the city desk wanted it but was prudent enough to telephone the old lady's home to check on the correctness of the address, the names of survivors, and other details. What he learned from the old lady's unmarried daughter, her only survivor, speedily made him change his mind about the routine nature of the story.

He batted out the following for the next edition of the *Leader* on his VDT:

ALDRICH—OBIT

Emily Aldrich, who was 96 years old last month, arose earlier than usual yesterday morning.

She asked her unmarried daughter, Jane, 68, with whom she has lived for 11 years at 1615 Fillmore Lane, "Would you mind pressing my best black dress some time today, Janie?"

Miss Aldrich said, "Glad to, Mother. Are you going somewhere?"

Mrs. Aldrich replied quietly, "I shall die some time tonight and I'd like to be buried in my best black dress."

"Maybe I'd better call a doctor if you don't feel well, Mother," her daughter said.

"There's no need." Mrs. Aldrich repeated calmly, "I know that I shall die some time tonight."

This morning, when Miss Aldrich entered her mother's bedroom to call her for breakfast, she found the older woman dead in bed. Recalling their conversation yesterday, the daughter said, "She looked so well and acted so normally that I didn't believe her."

Mrs. Aldrich, a daughter of Wilmot Stacy, one of the earliest residents of Central City, was married at 21 to a local hardware merchant, Wayne Aldrich, who died 11 years ago. They had four children, of whom only Jane Aldrich survives.

Services for Mrs. Aldrich will be at 8:00 p.m. tomorrow at the Wolsey Funeral Home, 1811 Forest Avenue. Her daughter said she would be buried in her best black dress, as she had wished, at Riverview Cemetery.

end

Roberts dropped his story on the city desk without comment and returned to his desk. Nobody said anything to him about it, but it appeared with his by-line in the *Leader*'s last edition below the fold on Page 1. That was his accolade.

The piece owes its effectiveness to the writer's decision not to do a formal obit because the story is so unusual. By letting it tell itself chronologically, and without histrionics, Roberts was able to convey the emotional impact of Jane Aldrich's experience.

It isn't often such work can be done. But then, it isn't often that an elderly woman in seeming good health accurately predicts the time of her death.

The Handling of Obituaries

The Aldrich obit, of course, is not typical of the way obits are generally handled in the press. What has to be included in such reports are the usual—name, age, time, and place of death, home address, business or profession, cause of death if obtainable, survivors, and whatever facts there are about the subject's life.

It generally comes out something like this:

WELLS—OBIT

Dr. David Hadley Wells, 81, a physician in Central City for more than 50 years, died today in Midland Hospital after a long illness.

Dr. Wells, a magna cum laude graduate of the State University and its medical school, was twice the president of the Central City Medical Society.

He was a general practitioner who resolutely refused to be identified as a specialist although he was frequently consulted by his associates on diseases affecting the aging process such as Alzheimer's disease.

"I want people to come to me to be treated no matter what they think is wrong with them," he often said, "and I never want them to worry if they can't pay me. Their good health comes first."

Dr. Wells is survived by his son, Dr. David Hadley Wells, Jr., who practiced with him in an office attached to his home at 442 Main Street. The elder Dr. Wells's wife, Sarah, died three years ago.

Funeral services will be held tomorrow night from the First Presbyterian Church, Sixth and Forest avenues. Burial will be in the Cemetery of the Pines.

end

There is no attempt here at anything more than the basic information that friends and patients of Dr. Wells would want to know. The obit is told carefully, simply, and with an economy of words. It is in the pattern of concise journalism.

4

News Preparation

THE AMERICAN PUBLIC IS an impatient taskmaster. It expects news upon the instant. And it tolerates no excuses. Therefore, the mission of today's journalists is to provide meaningful background for the news almost as quickly as it occurs. And although the public for the most part neither cares nor understands how this seeming miracle is to be accomplished, it is done routinely almost every day in our newspapers, news magazines, and news agencies, by radio broadcasters, and over both national and local television.

This is why there are instant biographies in print, on film, and transmitted over the airwaves whenever a new president is elected or a great athlete dies, when a famous actress marries for the fourth time or a new chief justice is appointed to the U.S. Supreme Court. It also accounts for the immediate appraisals that appear in the news media whenever there is important new legislation or a decided change in irksome old practices.

Anticipating the News

What happens, in brief, is that journalists must anticipate the news whenever possible as well as arrange to cover it as it breaks.

It is taken for granted, for example, that biographical material will be prepared well in advance of an election to high office—the presidency, the Congress, a governorship, and sometimes a mayoral contest in one of our larger cities.

The print and electronic media, of course, have different requirements for that kind of operation. Newspapers and newsmagazines need biographies of the winners that are well-illustrated, readable, and up-to-the-minute. Radio requires something more concise, but adapted for easy listening. And as for television, both over the air and cable, the picture story of a dominant news figure of the day is all-important.

Newcomers to journalism often assume that a calculated risk is taken on the outcome of elections, to cite one event for which it is journalistic routine to prepare. It's not necessarily so. No matter how great the odds may be in favor of one candidate or another for high office, I've never heard of any major news organization taking a freakish gamble on the outcome.

No, generally, advance biographies plus illustrations are prepared for each major party candidate and slugged, HOLD FOR RELEASE. Then they are filed in newspaper morgues, film libraries, or some other appropriate place by every large news organization. For smaller operations, which numerically constitute the bulk of American journalism, a similar service is provided by the Associated Press and other wire agencies covering everything except network and super-station kinescopes.

This kind of preparation takes days of research, writing, and editing. Moreover, as a political campaign progresses, changes become necessary in the best of advances and they must be made so that the material is kept up-to-date. And when a victor finally is declared once the polls close, or a vanquished candidate concedes defeat, the advance stuff for the winner moves at once for public consumption.

Aside from political campaigns, it is never simple to decide on advance preparations for any event in which more than one person is likely to be featured. It would be extremely risky, for example, to pick the star of a baseball World Series before the first game is played, or, for that matter, a college football Heisman Trophy winner before the season opens, a Wimbledon tennis champion, a Stanley Cup hockey star, or the winning jockey at the Kentucky Derby before the race is run. And yet, there has to be a limit on the number of advances that can be prepared.

For prominent individuals, whose biographies are under almost constant revision, the work and the possibilities for use are both more predictable. The record must be kept up-to-date when they take new jobs or are fired from old ones, when they win or lose law suits, when they marry, have children, or die or otherwise figure in the news.

At almost any time, it may suit the convenience of a newspaper, newsmagazine, wire service, or electronic agency to use the prepared material. But even then, it can't be thrown away; instead, it has to be restored to the morgue or film library and worked over again whenever it becomes necessary.

Who does the original stuff and the updating? Almost anybody who has the time and the ability, except, of course, for television with its special requirements. On newspapers, in lazy late afternoons for P.M.'s or the early morning hours that are known as the dogwatch for A.M.'s, news desks may assign any one of a number of staff people who are sitting around to write or rewrite or update material that is being held for release. Nor is it done entirely out of newspaper clippings, magazine articles, books, or previous radio or television scripts.

Sometimes, an enterprising and energetic reporter will arrange— with the consent of whoever made the assignment—to interview the subject of a profile, whether or not that profile is outdated, to produce material obtained firsthand. Quite naturally, such procedure is to be preferred over continuous rewrites, but it does take time to produce and advances have a low priority in most newsrooms.

Advances are also prepared, whenever possible, for use with the final passage and executive approval of important legislation at the federal or state level. This could be a sweeping new tax reform, a building code governing rental properties, or new regulations for public utility rate increases, among others. Large corporation mergers, the closing of a familiar enterprise, or the opening of a big new one, and similar developments that can be planned for in advance, all lend themselves to such treatment.

Whether it is done or not depends almost entirely on the requirements of the news organization and the advantage or disadvantage involved in trying to get up news and pictures or television footage before the event. After all, not everybody is enthusiastic about advances and few writers welcome what is almost universally regarded in the business as an unrewarding chore.

Preparing for a Major Newsbreak

Mack Roberts, being the newest reporter on the *Central City Leader*, learns what it means to fix up an advance for a big news story during his first month on the paper. As a recent graduate of the State U and the editor of its newspaper, the *State Daily*, he is a natural to work on the story of the selection of a new president for the institution. And, since the university is an important part of Central City, the identity of the new president becomes a major newsbreak for the *Leader*.

A search committee of university trustees and faculty members has been at work for some months since the resignation of the previous president, Dr. Davidson Craig, took effect. It already has been widely reported that the leading candidates for the post are Dean Minor Stanley of the State U Law School and Dr. Winston Parham, the university's provost or number 3 man and formerly the dean of its School of International Affairs. Now there are insistent rumors on campus that the university trustees are very close to a decision, which causes Joe Stoddard, the city editor, to take a look at his stock biographies of Dean Stanley and Dr. Parham.

Stoddard calls Roberts to the city desk and hands him both advances. "Look these over and see if either of them need revision," he says.

The new staffer isn't quite sure what he is supposed to do. "You want me to check them for accuracy?"

"Accuracy, completeness, anything we ought to have in either biography that we don't now have, just in case one or the other man is made the next president of State U."

Now Roberts understands.

When he returns to his desk and reads the piece about Dean Stanley, he calls the university public relations director and checks it for accuracy and completeness. The P.R. man understands what Roberts and the *Leader* need, suggests a factual insert to cover one new career development, but sees no need to change anything else.

The advance for Dr. Parham, however, produces quite a different reaction. After more than a half hour on the telephone with the P.R. director, Roberts has so much new material that he decides Parham's advance ought to be completely rewritten. However, since he was asked only to check both stories to determine if revisions were needed, he returns to the city desk for instructions.

Stoddard listens to the young reporter's findings without comment, then suggests, "Your guy at the university is trying to tell us something."

"I'm not sure," Roberts says, catching the city editor's meaning. "I suppose it could be Parham, but he's much older than the law school dean and a lot of us have thought that the search committee would want a younger man."

"Maybe so," Stoddard replies, "but it's just my guess that you'd better do what your P.R. man says at the university: give us a decent advance on Parham."

"There's not much of the old story I can pick up," Roberts reminds him. "It'll have to be a new story entirely."

"Suits me," the city editor says. "And something tells me you'd better start now and stay here until you finish, even if it means going into overtime. Maybe I'm cockeyed, but I still think your guy is trying to tell us something."

Roberts gets up, but stops short before returning to his desk. "What do I do with the story when I finish? Leave it over for you?"

"I'm a hunch player and I'm staying here," his boss says. "Let me have it a take at a time because I'm having it set in type just in case we need it in a hurry. And," he adds, "be sure to slug it PARHAM, WITH STATE U, Hold for Release."

Roberts, still convinced that the law school dean is a better bet, doesn't argue but does as he is told. After going over his notes, he starts his advance as if it were a breaking news story and the choice of a new president for State U already had been made:

PARHAM—HOLD FOR RELEASE WITH STATE U STORY

Dr. Winston Parham, eighth president of the State University, brings almost 30 years of experience as a diplomat, university faculty member, and administrator to his new post. He is 50.

As the provost of the university during the past three years, he has exerted considerable influence on its policies and programs since the resignation of President Davidson Craig.

During the preceding 25 years, he had compiled a distinguished record capped by his appointment as the United States roving ambassador to the United Nations. He resigned that post when he returned to the university to become dean of its School of International Affairs.

Dr. Parham is married to the former Eleanor Hopkins, a fellow student while both were taking advanced degrees in the School of International Affairs. They have three children: Maude, 20, a junior at the university; Martin, 18, a freshman; and William, 16, who is still in high school in Central City.

Born in 1938 in Central City, the only child of Professor and Mrs. Jeremy Parham (his father taught in the law school), Dr. Parham attended primary and secondary schools here, then took his A.B. at the state university when he was 22, his M.A. in international affairs two years later and his Ph.D. when he was 27. He rose through faculty ranks from assistant to full professor of international affairs in seven years.

Then, after five years as a professor, he attracted wide attention with a scholarly examination of American diplomacy during the Vietnam War. As a result, he was invited to join the State Department and accepted. He eventually became deputy chief of mission for the United States delegation to the UN and a roving ambassador thereafter. . . .

Stoddard, at the city desk, lets the story run. But just as Roberts appears to be winding up, the city editor calls back: "You don't have a single quote in the story so far. Call Parham and ask him what he thinks the responsibilities of the next president of State University are going to be."

Roberts is dubious. He still has the fixed idea that the law school dean, being younger, is likely to get the top job. However, he is hungry, it's getting late, and the city editor is very demanding. Quite unexpectedly, the call to Dr. Parham's home yields results. The provost is very talkative, so much so that Roberts has trouble shutting him off.

In consequence, Roberts writes the following:

INSERT PARHAM—FOLOS 3RD PGH

In discussing the responsibility of the next president before his appointment became known, Dr. Parham said,

"Whoever leads this university from now on is going to have to take account of the dominant position of the United States in world affairs and the absolute need for a closer study of governmental policies and programs.

"That goes not only for the School of International Relations but every other part of the university as well. If we do not do so, we are isolating ourselves from reality."

END INSERT STATE U—PIKUP 4TH PGH

The chairman of the university trustees, Wilson Hartley, a lawyer, announces Dr. Parham's appointment as the next president at 11:00 A.M. the next day. Dick Hylton, the top man in the *Leader*'s rewrite battery, handles the story for the noon edition while Roberts is sent to the university administration building to cover a Parham news conference.

But before he goes, Stoddard calls him to the city desk. "You didn't expect Parham's appointment, did you?"

The young reporter admits, "Frankly, no. But then most people at the university didn't, either."

"Except for your P.R. guy," the city editor reminds him. Then, he is sent off with the admonition: "Never take anything for granted in the news business. You'll get fooled every time."

It is good advice. Whichever way the appointment might have gone, the *Leader* was well protected with usable background material and pictures. That, after all, is the reason for such elaborate backup preparations and hold-for-release material.

An Advance on a Drug Bust

While the story of Dr. Parham's appointment is developing at State U, the city desk receives a tip from its Police Headquarters reporter that a multimillion-dollar drug bust is taking place off campus. The police public information office has told reporters to stand by for an announcement of a large seizure of cocaine with a number of arrests.

Because the story may break very close to an edition deadline, Sally Ward is pressed into service to do a background story on a hold-for-release basis to go with the news when it is announced. As the paper's specialist on science and medicine, she is well able to do such a piece quickly without much risk of exaggeration. She begins her story as follows:

HABIT—SIDEBAR WITH DRUG, HOLD FOR RELEASE

Fear of increasing student involvement with habit-forming drugs is believed to have motivated today's drug bust near the State U campus.

It follows a number of police raids at other college campuses and nearby areas in which large amounts of cocaine were seized and a number of alleged vendors were arrested.

Dean Warren Deventer of the State U Medical School, when informed of the local raid, said, "I'm not surprised. For the protection of our students, the more habit-forming drugs the police can take off the streets, the better. Here in the Medical School, we welcome their help."

Specialists familiar with addictive drugs say that the cocaine derivative, known as crack, is the most dangerous as well as the most expensive new illegal form of narcotics that is being openly peddled in Central City. Exactly how much crack was included in today's seizure did not become immediately known, but it has been the prime target of police raids at other campuses.

Cocaine in all its forms attacks the central nervous system of users. It provides temporary stimulation to humans, but also creates hallucinations. It causes weight loss, upsets the nervous system and attacks physical well-being, physicians say. Prolonged use, they warn, can cause damage to the mind because of the psychological factors in cocaine addiction.

Cocaine, an alkaloid drug produced from the leaves of the coca shrub, is smuggled into the United States from various South American countries. To curb the influx, American armed forces were used in 1986 in Colombia but without marked effect. . . .

With the announcement of the drug bust at Police Headquarters, which included twenty-six arrests and seizure of cocaine estimated to be worth $9 to $10 million, Sally's story was released and used with the news of the raid. Like Roberts's background piece on the new president of State U, it could not have made the edition unless it had been done as an advance.

Mainly because of the electronic competition, these and other methods of cutting down on the time lag in the news due to the publication routine are being used by many newspapers as well as newsmagazines and wire services. But it should be stressed that such advances as those described here, among others, do not involve guesswork. What is required is better reporting and much more writing under pressure.

The development of more advanced methods of newspaper production undoubtedly will cut down on the time differential between electronic news and news in print, but the two never can be equal either in speed or content. For most newsbreaks, the electronic media are bound to be ahead; for the most complete reports, however, the amount of space immediately available to newspapers and newsmagazines cannot be duplicated by most of the electronic media within the present time allocations for individual news reports.

For an informed public in a democratic society, both continue to be needed.

5

Of People, Places, and Things

WHEN RALPH MCGILL WAS EDITOR of the *Atlanta Constitution*, he campaigned day and night for racial integration. To try to silence him, his enemies put bullets through his windows and his mailbox. But McGill wouldn't keep quiet.

In his hoarse voice, the editor counseled his associates on the newspaper, "Hang on! Hang on!" What happened? McGill himself became an issue, mainly among people who couldn't understand his position on racial integration.

The Uses of Human Interest

A mass public often is led for one reason or another to consider a complex subject in human terms. That is one of the reasons for the existence of what is called "human interest journalism," for lack of a more precise term, because it deals mainly with people, places, and things.

Of course, the basis of human interest reporting and writing is considerably broader than that. In its simplest form, it may also deal with the problems of a singer of pop music who has kicked the drug habit or a terrorist who has been converted to a more peaceful life.

At the other end of the spectrum of journalism that we call human interest, however, are people such as Bishop Desmond Tutu whose very name is a symbol of the cause he espouses, opposition to apartheid in South Africa. It is for this reason that Americans such as Ralph McGill and Martin Luther King, Jr. also have made such a strong impression on their times and are remembered years after their deaths.

It is by no means a perfect solution for a democratic society to deal with complex issues on the basis of the people who support or oppose them. But who ever said that democracy, as an ideal, had anything to do with perfection? Or that journalists were capable of resolving public doubts about complicated policies with instant explanations of what was involved?

No, we journalists do the best we can. And like Ralph McGill, many a journalist still says to himself in times of doubt and crisis, "Hang on! Hang on!"

A mass public reads, hears, and views the news of controversial Supreme Court decisions in terms of the conservatism of Chief Justice Rehnquist or the liberalism of Associate Justice Marshall. And as for the vast changes in the tax reform legislation of the late 1980s, that is all too often linked to two of the most influential senators who developed it, Bob Packwood, the Oregon Republican, and Bill Bradley, the New Jersey Democrat, or their counterpart in the House, Representative Dan Rostenkowski, the Illinois Democrat.

But at the same time, balancing these important matters with lighter and more attractive fare, we also may read, hear, or see an account of a pretty nurse who saved an elderly hospital patient from choking to death, a watchful collie whose agitated barking alerted his sleeping family to a basement fire and saved their lives, or a hard-working student who has earned his way through medical school by shining the shoes of his teachers and fellow students.

It's all human interest and it's all a part of the news of this or another day.

The things that people do and say and the places that interest them also are a part of the panorama of journalism. Like the personalities, issues, and causes that are more dominant in the news, such lighter subjects fall mainly into the feature category except when there is demonstrable urgency about presenting them to a broad public. That could be caused by an earthquake, a drought, or some other development that makes timing important.

From Broadway in New York City to the Hawaiian Islands and from Yellowstone National Park to Paradise Valley more than halfway up towering Mount Rainier, places have a special fascination for people and are frequently described, photographed, or shown on television.

That goes, as well, for the troubles of a prominent politician's family about which there is more gossip than news, the slip of the tongue made by an American president who has something uncomplimentary to say about newspeople, and the gallant attempt of a television star with a drinking problem to make a comeback. Many people make up a mass public in this country—as in others—and it is a part of the duty of journalists to cover the news that affects or interests them.

Developing a Human Interest Story

Features dealing with subjects of interest to large numbers of people originate from numerous sources. Like hard news, some crop up in wire service reports or public relations releases. Others may come in as tips from readers, viewers, or staff people. Now and then an editor may have an original notion that produces a feature. And sometimes, a piece in another newspaper or a radio or television squib may suggest something that a reporter may enlarge upon with luck and good management.

At the *Leader*, it is a press release from the Central City and Western Railroad that gives Mack Roberts his first chance at a human interest feature. An assistant city editor offers him the handout as he reports for work at 8:00 A.M. and says, "See if there's a story in this and let us know if you need a photographer."

Even for a P.R. blurb, Roberts fears that the release isn't very promising. It announces the retirement of the engineer and stoker of the rail line's last steam locomotive, "Old 999," with its designation as a museum piece. The engineer, Brian MacIlreavy, and the stoker, Mike McManus, both are seventy years old and have been railroad employees for their entire working careers.

Roberts shoves the sheet in his pocket, then tries to be funny about it. "Want this for Page 1 for the next edition?"

The deskman ignores the wisecrack. "Give me a call once you get to the railroad yard and let's see how it shapes up. On second thought, you might drop by the studio and take a photographer with you."

It is after 9:00 A.M. when Roberts and his photographer, Dave Jeans, arrive at the C.C.W. yard in Jeans's car. A television crew from KTLT-TV already is at work taking long shots of Old 999 wheezing and puffing around the railroad yard. So are a few still photographers whom Jeans identifies as part of the opposition from the morning paper and the state bureaus of the wire services.

"Don't see why they bother," Roberts grumbles, still unable to work up any enthusiasm for the story.

Jeans doesn't pay much attention to him, but grabs his camera and a few extra rolls of film. "Didn't you ever play with railroad trains when you were a kid?" Then, he's off to join the group working around Old 999 and Roberts is left to his own devices. With great reluctance, he follows his photographer.

By the time he catches up with Jeans, Old 999 has clanked to a halt on a siding, let loose a plume of steam, and emitted a deafening whistle. MacIlreavy, the engineer, has clambered from the cab and now stands encircled by newspeople and cameras—a small, elflike Scot with a beaming red face, snow-white hair, and a burr as thick as porridge on a winter's morn. His sidekick, McManus, looks on from the engine's cab and occasionally offers information and advice.

"I was at the throttle of this old-timer when she was put into service almost fifty years ago," MacIlreavy is saying as Roberts approaches, "and that one up there," he points a negligent finger at McManus, "he was my stoker. Took her clear through from Central City to San Francisco, we did, and in record time for a passenger train in those days." He smiles and shakes his head. "O' course, it was nothing like the time airplanes are able to do it in today."

Upon which McManus snorts from the cab above him. "Sure, an' the trains still can get through with more freight than anything that flies." For the benefit of all concerned, he explains, "Old Scotty and me, we lost the passenger business right after World War II, but we hauled freight in 999 until last year."

MacIlreavy adds, "They used her in the yards since last year, mainly for switching, 'cause they knew we was both retirin' this year and they let us play out the string."

Gradually, it dawns upon Roberts that there is a species of romance between these two elderly men and their engine. They speak of her with great affection as the "Queen of the Road" in her time. It is the Scot who finally gives him the cue for the story: "How many fellas d'you think have stayed on the same job, doin' the same thing, without even a small accident or even a scratch, for almost half a century?"

When Roberts calls the city desk after the interview is over and the two old railroaders have gone back to work on Old 999, he says, "I might have a little story for the noon edition and Jeans has some pretty good pictures."

"Hope your story is better'n that," the assistant city editor says. "The *Independent News* has just filed six hundred words about a couple of old guys who are in love with a steam engine."

At last Roberts understands that this is a story about a different age, different people, and an era when steam propulsion still was an important force in the land. Because of his youth, it is difficult for him to visualize Old 999 as the "Queen of the Road" in an age when a man has walked on the moon, space platforms are taken for granted, and "Star Wars" are a possibility. But he tries once he reaches the office and starts his story on his VDT:

RAIL

The era of steam ended today for two 70-year-old railroaders as they dead-headed their Iron Horse, the last in the Midwest, to a siding north of town.

To Brian MacIlreavy, her engineer, and Mike McManus, her stoker, she was "Old 999, the Queen of the Road" because they'd run her back and forth across the land for almost 50 years without an accident—or even a scratch on her sooty frame.

With the ancient engine's designation as a museum piece by her owners, the Central City and Western Railroad, both the engineer and the stoker also retired. But they took their romantic feeling for the steam age with them. As MacIlreavy said,

"I was at the throttle of this old-timer when she was put in service almost 50 years ago and that one," meaning McManus, "was my stoker. Took her clear through from Central City to San Francisco, we did, in record time for a passenger train in those days. . . . How many fellas d'you think have stayed on the same job, doin' the same thing without even a small accident or a scratch for almost half a century?"

McManus boasted about his service, too, saying that "Old 999" remained as a freight engine until last year and since has been used as a switching engine in the CCW yards. As for "Old 999," her only comment on being retired from service was a deafening blast of her whistle and a contemptuous snort of steam for the modern age. . . .

The young man's story plus a picture layout made the noon edition, which both pleased and surprised him. It is never easy for a reporter in the atomic age to imagine that the land ever was very different than it is today. But older generations are a part of the news business, too. As long as they and their memories are still around, all our yesterdays cannot easily be packed away into the history books and quite casually forgotten.

The Uses of Human Interest

It would be a grievous error to consider that journalists use the device of human interest merely to divert or to entertain. It also serves an important function—reaching a large public with intelligence that is likely, in one way or another, to be of benefit to society.

Mack Roberts's next assignment at State U the following week illustrates the point. Professor Fritz Aumuller, a psychiatrist at the medical school, has just received a $200,000 foundation grant for research in Alzheimer's disease, but the university's press release is singularly uninformative on what Alzheimer's is and how the grantee intends to proceed. The announcement has received wide coverage, however, including a story in the *Leader*'s first edition.

But Joe Stoddard, the city editor, tells the young man in making the assignment, "As I understand it, Alzheimer's is a disease affecting the aging process and there are a lot of old people around. So let's have something from Dr. Aumuller himself on what he plans to do—and don't fall for any phony tales about the discovery of a fountain of youth. That died with Ponce de León."

This time, Roberts stops off at the morgue, the paper's library, and reads the scanty material there on Dr. Aumuller's background, Alzheimer's disease, and the donor of the grant, the Mayflower Foundation. He has learned the hard way that it is always wise to prepare for a complicated story if there is time.

The interview at Dr. Aumuller's home turns out well mainly because the professor's second wife, Marguerite, who is considerably younger than he is, explains his passionate interest in doing something to stop the ravages of Alzheimer's disease. Like most scientists, and the reporter learns that his subject is both a physician and a psychiatrist, the professor is impatient with what he considers to be stupid questions posed by laymen. Moreover, he speaks with such a marked German accent that he is difficult to understand.

But, having learned something from his experience with the Old 999 story, Roberts persists, continues his questioning, and, with Mrs. Aumuller's help, comes back to the office with a story. This is how he begins his piece for a later edition:

SUB AUMULLER

Professor Fritz Aumuller has seen both his parents and his first wife fall victim to a disease that causes premature aging and death.

Even though he is a psychiatrist and physician on the faculty of the State U Medical School, he did not know how to treat them, he admitted today.

"But now," he said, "I have the means to develop the knowledge that may help many other older people who are suffering from the same ailment and don't even know it."

Professor Aumuller referred to a $200,000 grant he has just received from the Mayflower Foundation for research into Alzheimer's disease, a usually fatal ailment that attacks the mind, often renders its victims as helpless as babies, and eventually causes death.

"I knew Alzheimer," he said during an interview at his home on
the State U campus. "We worked together in the same laboratory and
I know some of the ideas he had for treating the illness that bears
his name. I'll test them, I'll test some notions of my own and, hopefully,
something will come of my work."
    Professor Aumuller, who is 61, and his second wife, Marguerite,
36, both were excited by news of the grant and made plans to begin
his research as soon as possible. He will continue to meet his classes
for the remainder of this academic year. . . .

Once the city editor reads Roberts's story, he does not hesitate
to kill the earlier hard news account with the usual bang-bang
straight news lead:

    Professor Fritz Aumuller, a member of the faculty of the State U
    Medical School, has received a $200,000 grant from the Mayflower
    Foundation to conduct research into Alzheimer's disease, Dean Roscoe
    Turner of the Medical School announced today. . . .

This thirty-eight-word opening sentence conforms with journalistic tradition but it means very little to a public that has had few
experiences with Alzheimer's disease. Roberts's twenty-three-word
opening sentence gets the reader into the story directly by telling
what the disease is and explaining why Aumuller is so deeply interested in it. The announcement of the grant, therefore, becomes
meaningful as the story develops the reason for it.
    Thus, the devices of human interest add to public comprehension
of what could be an important development in the lives of many
older people. However, it should be noted that the city editor's
warning against falsely raising hopes of a miracle cure has made
the writer take care to avoid predicting success for the new research.
It is something that must be done in handling any news of science
and medicine about possible advances in the fight against disease.

When the Impossible Dream Is Shattered

Inevitably, human beings so often let false hope sway them that
they expect far more than they are likely to receive—and that affects
the telling of the news, too. This kind of thing is usually the result
of boosterism, a plague that is by no means confined to Rotarians
and other civic enthusiasts. Among the youth of the land, it frequently leads to great expectations for rather ordinary sports teams
and performers at every level, both amateur and professional. And,

of course, when the time of reckoning comes and the hometown favorites are crushed, everybody looks around for someone to blame—and the luckless victim more often than not becomes the local newspaper or newscaster or both.

This is precisely what is happening in Central City in the late fall. The local pro football team, the Tigers, has managed to stay in contention for the league play-offs until the leaders, the Fort Worth Texans, come to town. All the local media whip up popular enthusiasm. Every seat in the State U Stadium is sold out for the game days in advance. The fans expect two titans to rock the earth in their battle for supremacy, to judge by what is being written and said. And that makes for trouble.

Sally Ward, a specialist in a field that doesn't include pro football, is drawn into the situation by accident because she is a friend of Liz Drayton, the wife of Paul Drayton, once an All-America halfback at State U but now in his last year as a pro with the Tigers. It has been a bad season for Paul who, at thirty-eight, has been reduced to serving as a backup place-kicker for a newer and younger player.

In consequence, the Draytons—husband and wife and two teen-age children—tend to look on the game with greater realism than others in town. For that reason, Liz asks Sally to go to the game with her: "I want Paul to go out like a champion," his wife says, "but I'm afraid they won't even let him play and he's going to feel hurt and I'm going to need moral support when it's all over."

Sally agrees to go with Liz and the children.

For the first quarter, the Tigers hold the Texans scoreless and twice come close to scoring field goals themselves, but their young place-kicker misses some easy chances. Paul Drayton is still warming the bench in the second quarter when the Texans score twice and lead at halftime, 14 to 0. However, from then on, the Texans slam shut the gates of mercy and, with less than two minutes to go, lead by 42 to 0. Liz cries in anger and chagrin.

Among the sixty thousand fans at the stadium, there is glum silence even when the Tigers are able to cross mid-field. Many are leaving or on the point of leaving when the home team is thrown back to the 45-yard line with fourth down coming up, probably its last chance at a score. Then, as the fans watch in disbelief, Paul Drayton is sent on the field to attempt a field goal.

Sally hears a man exclaiming behind her, "The coach is crazy. He's got a kid place-kicker who couldn't score from 20 yards and now he's asking this old guy to kick a 65-yard field goal!"

Sally, not knowing football, doesn't understand. Liz and the children explain to her that, with the ball on the Texans' 45-yard line, Paul must stand 10 yards back on his own 45-yard line, 55 yards from the opposition goal line, and the goalposts are 10 yards beyond that. The kick, therefore, must travel 65 yards in the air.

It seems hopeless. Someone near them recalls that back in 1970, in a game between the Detroit Lions and New Orleans Saints, Tom Dempsey kicked one for 63 yards—a freakish record if there ever was one. And yet, Drayton prepares as seriously as if it were a routine point after touchdown. The Texans are laughing at him but he pays no attention.

The team line up. The ball is snapped. The holder sets it in place. And just as the Texans come charging in upon him, Drayton swings his right leg in a mighty effort and the ball clears the outstretched hands of the foremost Texan. It sails lazily high above the stadium in the crisp autumn air and descends just above the goalposts.

The people in the stadium watch in stunned silence until the referee, after a moment's hesitation, raises both hands to indicate a field goal has been scored. Then—bedlam. And when the game ends a scant minute later, the place is in such a frenzy that it is almost like the beginning of a victory celebration instead of a 42-to-3 defeat for the home team.

Sally Ward may not know football but she recognizes a unique human interest story when she sees one. She leaves her friend Liz Drayton, who is crying for sheer relief and happiness, and makes her way to the stadium press box, finds a typewriter, and shouts to the *Leader*'s sports editor that she's filing a city-side story. This is it:

DRAYTON

Paul Drayton put on his orange and black football uniform for the last time today before the Tigers–Texans game at the Stadium but he wasn't sure he'd play.

The 38-year-old All-America from State U had been used this season only as a place-kicker, and sparingly at that. Still, his wife, Liz, and his two teen-age children, Ella and Bobby, were in the stands hoping for him.

As Liz said, "I want him to go out as a champion."

It didn't look like he'd get the opportunity. In the first quarter, when there was a chance twice for a place-kicker, Mickey Holborn, 23, and one year out of college, got the call for the Tigers and missed each time.

Drayton had to warm the bench until the score was 42–0 in favor of the Texans and all hope of a victory for the Tigers had vanished.

They not only were beaten. They seemed headed for disgrace after all the foolish predictions of victory this past week.

Liz Drayton was crying. The kids were glum. All about them, people either were silent or getting ready to move out for home.

And then, incredibly, Coach Johnny Evans of the Tigers sent Drayton into the game to attempt a field goal with the ball on the Texans' 45-yard line. It was to be a 65-yard attempt, something that set the Texans to laughing.

But not Drayton. With less than a minute to go, the ball was snapped and set down before him. He kicked it hard and true, then stood back. The 60,000 fans in the Stadium watched in sheer amazement as the ball sailed over the goalposts and the referee signaled a score.

It was a record kick, exceeding by 2 yards a 63-yard field goal by Tom Dempsey in 1970.

As the fans began cheering, Drayton came charging off the field, both fists waving in triumph over his head. And as he did so, the gun went off to signal that the final score was 42–3, which should have been a disgraceful defeat.

But for Liz Drayton and the kids, as for the hometown crowd, it was a victory in a way. They had seen Paul Drayton, the old All American, end his career as a champion should.

end

Why did Sally Ward bother to file for a late Saturday edition when she knew that the cream of the *Leader*'s sports staff was covering the game? The story appealed to her and she wanted to write it, no matter how many others did. And so she filed late Saturday, too late for the final edition because of the volume of sports copy that had a higher priority.

But for Sunday's paper, with a change of the word "today" in the lead for "yesterday," Sally's story was on Page 1 under a picture of the record kicker as he made his last great effort. It showed that editors, too, have heart . . . but that's a different kind of human interest story.

6

Problems for Interviewers

NO MAJOR PROBLEMS have interfered thus far with the handling of interviews we have studied in connection with the writing of basic news. That, however, doesn't mean that the process is without complications.

A Question of Credibility

The greatest problem with most formal one-on-one interviews, especially for beginners, is the credibility of the subject. Consider the following:

It may serve the purpose of a fundamentalist leader of a religious cult to announce with a straight face that he has diverted a hurricane from his city and state through some strange occult process. But how is the statement to be handled in an interview that reaches many good citizens who may have their doubts about it?

Then, too, a veteran actress with a failing memory may recall only one previous marriage when she goes to the altar to take another husband. However, what does the writer do when the clips in the morgue show that the lady actually has had four previous husbands?

And what can be done about a motorist who has been jailed upon conviction of drunk driving for a third time, but still loudly insists in an interview before entering his cell that he never, never, never has had anything stronger than ginger ale?

Confronted with such problems in credibility as these, the average newcomer to journalism usually has to fight back an initial impulse to omit any troublesome matter. That might work once, but it really isn't a very good policy.

Most experienced journalists see nothing wrong with using extravagant claims, such as the one about diverting a hurricane, and letting the reader, listener, or viewer judge how correct it is likely to be.

As for the lady with multiple marriages, the procedure here is by all means to remind her of the record that shows she has had four previous marriages, not one as claimed, and use her response as well as that of her latest husband if he is willing to express an opinion.

The same routine is advisable in the case of the driver who insists he has been wrongfully convicted three times of driving while under the influence.

Experienced reporters know how to check public records quickly either in person or by telephone when necessary. Newcomers, too, soon find out that care must be taken with extravagant statements involving possible libel. A good rule to follow is: *When in doubt, leave out until you check it. Then, ask for a response to the record as soon as you can.*

It often saves a lot of trouble. But as for ducking a problem in interviewing, it seldom works. Furthermore, it is risky to poke fun at something an interviewee says that strains credibility. A child, for example, may not know any better. However, somebody who is known to make outrageous statements expects to provoke a less-than-polite response.

Of Time and the Storyteller

Such complications, usually unexpected, underline the need for a sufficient amount of time for a formal interview. Usually, such arrangements have to be made beforehand. Interviewees, when placed in an uncomfortable situation, have an unpleasant habit of suddenly remembering they must be elsewhere.

For television, that kind of runout isn't easy to do. Most people are flattered to be seen on the tube to begin with. But they are also extremely wary of not looking their best. As a rule, therefore, a skilled interviewer can take care of an incipient rebellion when it arises by soothing the restless subject.

In print, however, the position is quite different. Knowing that a certain amount of time must elapse before an interview plus picture can appear in a newspaper or magazine, a subject may attempt argument, threat, and refusal to continue in order to control what is to be written. Firmness is always advisable in such instances. As for the usual warning that a complaint will be made to either the editor, the publisher, or both, that must be endured. To give in to that kind of nonsense is unthinkable.

There are other difficulties that must be handled in some interviews, one of the slipperiest being the long-distance anecdote. Some subjects are so given to yarning that they try to answer difficult questions by detouring and telling a tall story. It takes tact to steer the interview back on course.

When time is limited, as is often the case at a disaster scene, the questions must be sharp, brief, and to the point—what happened?, how did it happen?, and why did it happen? The main idea is to get responses.

The same precaution applies to the telephone interview, a necessity in the coverage of a disaster or similar newsbreak in a remote area. Every young journalist, I am sure, has heard police reporters at headquarters acting as if they were cops when they are working the phones for information on such stories. Also, reporters covering the courts are frequently tempted to give people on the other end of a phone line the impression that they are either a D.A. or someone connected with the prosecutor's office. Veteran reporters contend, for the most part, that this is a legitimate device for assembling information under deadline pressure as long as they don't actually lie about their identity. However, if a libel suit arises out of what could be an honest error in the quest for news, it wouldn't impress a jury if a reporter had to admit he concealed his identity. No, the *only way* a journalist ought to act in the pursuance of the news is to proceed with full identification at all times, with credentials if necessary.

As for note taking during an interview, not many writers or writing reporters scribble on wads of copy paper nowadays as an interviewee is talking. It never was a good way of preserving an apt remark or an important quote.

The recording devices available to newspeople today seldom bother an interviewee; once they are turned on, they usually are forgotten as the interview proceeds. But that doesn't mean everything in the record may be used without risk. Any experienced writer knows that an offhand remark that may be critical of someone without justification could eventually become the basis of a lawsuit. In addition, some cautious interviewees regret having said something during the course of an interview and ask to have it omitted. Whether the request is granted depends entirely on the interviewer, the news organization, and the circumstances under which the remark was made.

To sum up, while interviewing is a basic method for the development of news and features, the problems connected with the operation should not be underestimated. Nor should a writer ever take anything for granted in conducting an interview. Any questionable statement still is subject to a careful check before it is used.

Don'ts in Writing about Interviews

The simplest and most direct form for the publication of important interviews is to use complete questions and answers. This is generally preceded by a brief italic introduction explaining who has been interviewed and why, the time and place of the interview, and the reason for the prominence given to it. Omissions, if any, are limited to quotes that may violate good taste or invite a lawsuit.

Relatively few interviews, however, can be treated at such length because most newspapers don't have unlimited space. And there isn't unlimited time on television. The media therefore usually use question-and-answer excerpts or a news account of the most important parts of the interview. What is used and omitted then becomes a matter of editorial judgment for both the writer and the editor in charge.

For lesser news or feature interviews (there is a difference between them), the problems common to much writing for journalism and mass communications apply. Many a writer, sitting at a VDT or a typewriter after an interview, has second thoughts. All manner of brilliant ideas may occur to a journalist under such circumstances, but it is seldom that anything can be done to expand the material. The rule, crudely and ungrammatically expressed, probably was first given in the gaslight era of American journalism when all printed material had to be set by hand, one letter at a time, and a single edition for twenty-four hours was all that could be published. As handed down through the years when I first heard it on a New York City newspaper early in this century, it was: *Go with what you've got.*

Every generation of journalist in America since has become familiar with that. It settles a lot of arguments and disposes of grandiose ideas on deadline. If it does not help the print journalist rival the immediacy and brilliance of television, it can and does serve

to maintain the competitive position of the press for this era of electronic progress.

Necessarily, the style in which each interview is written depends
very largely on its content. If it is a newsy interview, providing
fresh information on a current event of importance, almost automatically it will be handled as hard news—that is, a short summary
lead followed by a direct quote as documentation. After that, each
major point follows in the descending order of importance given to
it with a quote to illustrate that part of the interview. Such detail
as the time and place of the interview, the background of the interviewee, and a brief personal description are worked in where
they fit. Most important of all, the whole thing must be handled
quickly on an edition deadline.

For a feature interview, the approach is quite different. The principal rule to be followed for such a story is to begin with what is
likely to be of the greatest public interest and elaborate on this and
other relevant points with quotes in a more leisurely way than the
hard news approach. That doesn't mean space can be wasted. However, the writer's own style in this kind of a feature can make it or
break it.

As for the use of quotes in both types of stories based on interviews, it is a mistake for a writer to string them out and assume that
readers will try to guess at the meaning of some of the remarks.
The writer's job in part is to explain how and why some things were
said. And if a quote is used in whole or in part as a lead for either
a news or a feature interview, then the very next sentence must
identify the speaker, the time and place of the interview, and the
substance of what was discussed.

In interviews with children or older people, it is a great temptation
among inexperienced writers to try to show how clever they are as
writers. This kind of thing never goes over well either with editors
or the public and ought not to be attempted. Not that all writing
has to be sobersides. Far from it. But most humor in writing, experience has shown, should be reserved for specialists in the art.
Not many since the time of Mark Twain have rivaled him as a hu-
morist who was also a practicing journalist.

Writing about a Hard News Interview

It is misleading to go into a one-on-one interview with someone in
public life and expect to come out with a pat news story or interview.
The reporter who does so not only courts disappointment but even-

tually the mistrust of his superiors. However, editors can make the same mistake and often do in a tight spot.

Consider what happened to Sally Ward and Mack Roberts of the *Central City Leader* when they were assigned to interview the governor of the state, Edward B. Farrow, during one of his brief excursions from the state capital to Central City.

As Joe Stoddard, the city editor of the *Leader*, explained it to the two reporters: "Farrow's making a speech here tonight at the Civic Auditorium to try to further his presidential ambitions. I have the advance text, but it doesn't go much beyond what he's been saying all along—that he's available if his party wants him. Still, even that will be on TV tonight and in our morning competitor, the *Central City News,* tomorrow morning. So we'll look pretty bad merely to be repeating the same stuff for the first edition tomorrow afternoon. See if you can get something better out of him, will you?"

At the interview with the governor at the Riverview Hotel, however, very little happens. He knocks down one possibility after another for a good story. As for a current atomic controversy, he simply brushes that aside by saying that he isn't ready to talk about it.

The interview, by common consent, is soon over. It looks like the *Leader* will have to repeat the morning paper story about the governor's speech at the Civic Auditorium because the reporters have turned up nothing new. The governor accompanies them to the door, chattering about his return trip to the state capital the next day.

"No rest for the weary," he says cheerfully. "I'll be up late tonight, past my usual bedtime, and I'll have to leave the hotel by six tomorrow morning to get back to the office."

When Roberts asks, "Why so early?" the governor responds, "Because it takes five hours for that two hundred fifty-mile drive and my wife refuses to fly. And as soon as I can, I'll raise that fifty-five-mile-an-hour speed limit to sixty-five."

Sally Ward scents a story. "How can you do it?"

The governor says, "I think the legislature will go along with me, as long as the federal government permits us to regulate traffic on our own roads. You see, there never was any good reason for that fifty-five-mile-an-hour limit." The governor warms up to his subject, continuing, "It isn't speed that kills. Drunk driving is our biggest problem and the next is getting people to wear seat belts."

"But wouldn't the insurance rates go up if you boosted the speed limit?" Roberts asks.

The governor's response is blunt: "I'm not so sure. The state will have something to say about that."

Sally, like every good reporter with a story, wants to get out before the subject changes his mind. Drawing young Roberts with her, she backs out the door, then says to him, "Hope you can remember all those good quotes. I didn't take a note."

Roberts points to his tape recorder. "I forgot to shut it off and it's still running. No problem. We have every word."

That's how it turns out. The story runs in the first edition of the *Leader* next day under a joint by-line, in recognition of Roberts's initiative, even though Sally writes the story. This in part is the way it's done, with recognition of the governor's Civic Auditorium address downplayed:

FARROW

By Sally Ward and Mack Roberts

Governor Farrow says he'll raise the state's highway speed limit to 65 miles an hour as soon as possible.

In an interview with the *Leader* before his Civic Auditorium speech last night, the governor said, "There never was any good reason for that 55-mile-an-hour speed limit. It isn't speed that kills. Drunk driving is our biggest problem and the next is getting people to wear seat belts."

When the governor was asked whether an increased speed limit would bring about higher insurance rates for cars, he replied, "I'm not so sure. The state will have something to say about that."

Governor Farrow left no doubt about his opposition to the current speed limit during the interview in his suite at the Riverview Hotel, where he was preparing for last night's speech. More than 15,000 persons at the Civic Auditorium heard him demand a change in the federal taxing structure, an issue in his campaign for the presidency.

Important though the presidency is to the governor, it didn't detract from his willingness to discuss his opposition to the current state speed limit. He conceded that no change could come about without the prior consent of the federal government and the approval of the legislature.

What touched off the governor's ire was the 250-mile drive back to the state capital beginning at 6:00 this morning, which he said now takes him five hours. "And," he added, "my wife refuses to fly. . . ."

The remainder of the story then digests the governor's speech, but not at length. Since it was broadcast and also heavily played in the opposition morning paper, there's nothing new in it for the readers of the *Leader*. Instead, they have a better news story—and one in which every motorist will be interested.

As for the technique of trying to get something new to top a widely used news story that breaks at night, that is standard practice for both the print and electronic media but reporters can't always find a handle. When it does happen, as it did in this case, the process is called "freshening up" an old story.

Writing a Feature Story Interview

Mack Roberts was the first to admit, in talking things over later with Sally and Joe Stoddard, that the notion of using the speed-limit angle to "freshen up" news of the governor's visit was entirely accidental.

A few days later, evidently as a reward for his work on the interview with the governor, Roberts was given what is known in the trade an an "overnight" assignment—that is, he was sent out in the afternoon to do an interview about the homecoming of a famous Central City character, Edna Lane, better known as "Shady" because of her success in using that nickname as a blues singer on television and in records.

The problem was almost the same as that involving the governor, only the nature of the news wasn't political this time. It was purely show business, which is part of the journalistic scene, too. "Shady" Lane was giving her first hometown concert in ten years that night at the Bijou Theater on Main Street, Central City, for the benefit of the Shriners' annual drive for crippled children.

Once again, the event would be broadcast. Moreover, if the singer had anything to say to her hometown fans, it would be heard over the airwaves or it would be in the morning paper. To make an impression, Roberts would have to dream up an original angle or stumble across something new as he did in talking to the governor about the speed limit.

The young man had this advantage: he had never before talked with Edna Lane, knew very little about her and her background, and couldn't find much in the morgue clip file that wasn't pure hype. So when he showed up in her suite at the Riverview Hotel, he was eager for first impressions. He didn't get many. The place was jammed with people—her handlers, the Shriners' publicity crew, and television people with their equipment.

It took Roberts awhile to get to Shady Lane and introduce himself, but that didn't help much. The singer nodded, smiled, patted his hand soothingly, and said she'd be with him in just a tiny minute—then rushed off to embrace an elderly man who had just entered. Roberts didn't know what to do; accordingly, he did nothing but decided to stand by and await developments.

Presently, the old man whom the singer had embraced took up a position nearby; for lack of anything better to do, Roberts struck up a conversation with him. He turned out to be an eighty-one-year-old physician, Guy Hallowell, who had treated the singer as a child and had known her and her family intimately.

At first, Roberts was bored by the old man's reminiscences about the hardships of the Lane family and their difficult life on the outskirts of town, the adventures of Edna's two sisters and three brothers (she was the youngest child) and the illnesses for which Dr. Hallowell had treated them without asking for a fee. But soon, despite himself, Roberts realized that he was being given a quite different view of a rich and popular television idol. He prodded Dr. Hallowell for details, particularly about the singer's beginnings, and came up with something completely unexpected.

"Do you know," the old man mused, looking at the handsome blonde in a gold dress who was the center of all attention, "there was a time when Edna couldn't sing a note?"

By this time, Roberts didn't have to force himself to listen. "What was it, a cold?"

"Oh, much worse," was the casual response. "Up to the time she was 12 years old, she was very hard of hearing. If she sang at all, it was off-key."

That was the beginning of the story Roberts had hoped for, something original, something different, about a popular personality. As the old physician related how he had recommended an operation and then paid for it because the family couldn't do so, the reporter saw a quite different personality emerge—a little girl who was determined to make her way with a newfound voice.

Once Roberts had the facts straight, he waited patiently until the room emptied out and he had a chance to talk to the singer alone.

That was only ninety minutes before the curtain was to go up at the Bijou Theater and Shady Lane was understandably rushed. Even worse, she had completely forgotten about Roberts and had to be filled in once again on who he was and why he was there. But miracle of miracles, old Dr. Hallowell helped and the singer clung to him as she verified all that he had said and expressed her gratitude to him.

Roberts had his story. But he had sense enough, even though he was a beginning reporter, to know that the piece itself wouldn't amount to much unless he had a picture of the physician and his one-time patient as a necessary illustration.

Dr. Hallowell was willing. And since everybody else had cleared out except the singer's maid, who was waiting with the costume for the evening, Shady Lane didn't mind one more picture, provided the photographer showed up in a hurry. A telephone call to the night desk did it and Roberts soon had his picture and was on the way back to the newsroom with the photographer. This was how the story began in next day's *Leader:*

LANE

By Mack Roberts

To most of Central City, she may be "Shady" Lane, television's queen of the blues, who thrilled a capacity homecoming audience at the Bijou last night.

But to Dr. Guy Hallowell, an 81-year-old general practitioner from the south side of town, she is still "Little Edna," who couldn't sing a note until she was 12 years old because she was hard of hearing.

The singer and the elderly doctor were reunited just before the concert when they embraced in the star's suite at the Riverview Hotel. "I owe Doc everything!" Miss Lane exclaimed. "He convinced my folks that I needed an operation, then he paid for it because my parents couldn't."

"Shucks, it was nothing," Dr. Hallowell said, seeming embarrassed at his sudden prominence. "I did what any doctor would have done under the circumstances who cared anything at all about the well-being of his patients."

That was why, if there were curious ones at the Bijou last night, they saw a tall, white-haired man sitting alone in a box and applauding as Miss Lane sang the blues once again in her hometown, this time for a national television audience as well. . . .

There followed, in crisp detail and in quotes, Hallowell's story of how Shady Lane and her family had lived in Central City while she was growing up, how she had started her singing career following her operation and how she had fought through to national fame. Nor was that all. The singer herself had supplied fascinating detail about how difficult it was for her at first to listen to the sound of her own voice, how much trouble she had had in learning to modulate it, and how grateful she still was to Dr. Hallowell for his generosity and his thoughtfulness.

The picture of the two, arm in arm on Page 1, helped Roberts's story. But the accolade came from his neighbor, Sally Ward. "Hey, kid, you've made it." Coming from a pro, that meant more to him than anything else.

Luck as a Factor in Interviewing

The interviews cited here with Governor Farrow and Shady Lane depend mainly on reporter's luck. That often is the case. Sometimes, beginners can make things happen merely because they aren't afraid to ask dumb questions. And professionals, on their part, may have been through so many interviews that they don't have either the interest or the patience to pursue just one more small opening to a story.

In any event, the one technique that *doesn't* work when all else fails is the Mr. District Attorney approach—the loud voice, the accusing tone, the cold stare, the suspicious attitude. Too many reporters fail simply by making themselves obnoxious through the use of such methods. It's not that reporters should try to be all sweetness and light; that isn't the point. It's simply that news doesn't develop automatically. Sometimes, it may elude even the best of journalists if they have no luck.

7

Writing about Speeches

OLD-FASHIONED ORATORY, florid in style and extemporaneous in manner, was fashionable for much of the last century.

Few public figures of consequence bothered to scrawl the text in longhand, as Abraham Lincoln did before speaking at Gettysburg to memorialize that epic battle. The idea of publicizing speeches hadn't taken root. And the notion of handing out advance texts, marked for release at a certain time, hadn't yet occurred to anybody of influence.

All that is changed today.

The Story of an Atomic Speech

Early in this century, the view that speeches should contain news instead of being based mainly on rhetoric and philosophy gained wide currency. In consequence, it occurred to a number of public figures that journalists, being familiar with the patterns of news, might do very well if they were asked to provide speeches that contained news. Thus, the modern ghostwriter was born.

It would be a grievous error, however, to assume that such obliging phantoms were confined to the poorly paid reporters of the time. Bernard M. Baruch, a financier and a sometime statesman around mid-century, paid Herbert Bayard Swope, a former editor of the *New York World,* to write speeches for him.

Some of Swope's most celebrated lines, as delivered by Baruch in his role as the United States delegate before the United Nations Atomic Energy Commission in New York City, were:

My fellow members of the United Nations Atomic Energy Commission and my fellow citizens of the world:

We are here to make a choice between the quick and the dead.

That is our business.

Behind the black portent of the new atomic age lies a hope, which, seized upon with faith, can work our salvation. If we fail, then we have damned every man to be the slave of fear. Let us not deceive ourselves: we must elect world peace or world destruction. . . .

There was news aplenty in the speech and it wasn't coyly thrust into the last two or three paragraphs, as is usually the case with government-approved addresses. Basing himself mainly on the Acheson-Lilienthal report that had been widely circulated previously, Baruch called for all existing atomic weapons and all new ones to be turned over to an international body, which would have the right to inspect and control atomic development everywhere on earth.

Since the United States alone had the bomb in that first post–World War II year of 1946, this was considered a generous offer by most Americans regardless of political affiliation. But the Russians saw that it would preclude the development of atomic explosives of their own, turned down the so-called Baruch plan, and in 1949 announced that they had achieved a Soviet-style atomic bomb. With that, the nuclear race was on and so it continues in our own time.

That is the story of one important speech. It illustrates the thesis of what may be expected at the very top level of public policy making when speeches are designed primarily to contain news.

Necessarily, such addresses may be committed to paper by one person but they actually are the work of many minds that formulate a government policy. Much the same procedure shapes addresses of public figures who are charged with responsibility for developing the policies of large private undertakings. The news that is contained in speeches of this character, therefore, cannot be considered the mere whim of a press agent whose main objective is to publicize a client. It is serious business and has to be handled with due consideration.

The Routine for Speeches and Other Public Papers

There is a set routine for the preparation, submission, and circulation of advance copies of speeches and other public papers (announcements, reports, studies of various kinds, et cetera). On the part of the person, government agency, company, or other originating source, the understanding is that the material is accurate but subject to checking, elaboration, condensation, or rewording if necessary. As far as the media are concerned, there is no obligation to use such submissions in whole or in part, much less to pay for any of it.

Instead of seeking free publicity through public relations methods, the sponsors of speeches always have the alternative of buying advertising space in newspapers or magazines or arranging for commercials in the electronic media to circulate their messages. But few do, the theory being that the handouts constitute news and should be judged accordingly.

Would that it were always true!

In any event, the writer who handles an advance of a speech or another public paper on instructions from an editor or news director has the responsibility of verifying its authenticity. As a matter of practice, it is true that handouts from government sources or private commercial, industrial, or social agencies are usually accepted at face value. But every once in awhile, someone tries to play tricks with a phony handout of one kind or another. It never hurts to make a phone call for a routine check, something beginners are well advised to do.

A handout for a speech, for example, is distinctively marked with instructions for use, if it is professionally prepared, together with the name, address, and phone number of the originating source. If the press release consists of the full text of a speech that is to be delivered at some later time, the instructions could be phrased somewhat as follows:

ADVANCE TEXT OF SPEECH BY MAYOR REARDON AT THE
CIVIC AUDITORIUM FOR USE AT ANY TIME AFTER 2:00 P.M.
ON WEDNESDAY, OCT. 1.

If the originating agency, office, or person has something to submit that is of less importance but still believes it necessary to set a release time, the instructions may be phrased merely: "For Release, Wednesday, Oct. 1," which means that the material may be used for morning newspapers of that date or news programs at a time period that is in competition with morning newspapers. If the release is to be held for afternoon or evening use, it will be slugged, "For Release, Wednesday P.M., Oct. 1."

Any questions about this or other matters should be taken up promptly with the issuing source if the handout is intended for use in any form. This is particularly necessary for anything that is issued during a political campaign that might affect the fortunes of a major candidate. Regardless of the lofty attitude most professionals in journalism may adopt toward the use of handouts, it is a serious matter for all concerned to break a press release by using it ahead of schedule or otherwise failing to live up to the firm if unwritten understanding governing its use.

In rewriting a handout, whether it is in the form of a full text or a shorter hard news account, both the originating agency or person and the user cover themselves through documentation either in the lead or the body of the story. If the rewrite has to do with Mayor Reardon's speech at the Civic Auditorium, for example, the opening of the story might be handled like this for the morning paper:

> Mayor Reardon pledged his support last night to the presidential candidacy of Governor Farrow, calling him "the leader we need in an emergency."
>
> In a speech prepared for delivery at a Republican party rally at the Civic Auditorium, the mayor said:

The part of the documentation that shows the story was written from an advance text is the phrase, "in a speech prepared for delivery. . . ." To put it in the first paragraph would be cumbersome, so it is generally used in the story as high as possible and immediately followed by a quote that documents the lead.

What happens if the advance text is changed, or if the speech for some reason is not delivered as scheduled? The newspaper or electronic news program takes note of all corrections as soon as possible, even though the advance text may already have been circulated or broadcast, very often both. That is a part of the risk and inconvenience of using an advance instead of waiting for a speech to be delivered. However, changes in an advance text in themselves sometimes create a better news story than was originally expected.

Let us assume, for example, that Mayor Reardon for reasons best known to himself toned down his advance endorsement of the governor's presidential candidacy and changed it to a lukewarm acknowledgment when the speech was delivered. That would call for a new lead, obviously, and the morning paper might play the re-written account this way:

NEW LEAD REARDON

Mayor Reardon gave what many believed to be lukewarm support last night to the presidential candidacy of Governor Farrow.

In addressing a Republican party rally at the Civic Auditorium, the mayor omitted a description of the governor as "the leader we need in an emergency," a phrase included in an advance text of the speech. Other parts of the advance text praising the governor's record similarly were either toned down or omitted.

The two men have been at odds recently over the governor's refusal to permit the damaged South River atomic plant of the Central City Light and Power Company to reopen. . . .

It is perfectly true, of course, that the public neither knows nor cares very much about the niceties of journalistic procedures and that journalists themselves are too often guilty of overstressing such matters. But when an advance text is radically changed by a public figure upon actual delivery of a speech, the fact cannot be ignored. However, it then becomes necessary for the newspaper or electronic source to explain the background in the course of the news account. That becomes mandatory whether the average reader or viewer cares or not.

Who decides when to stress changes between an advance text and the actual delivery of a speech? In theory, it is the responsible top executive of the print or broadcast medium. But in practice, what it comes down to is the opinion of the local reporter or writer who is handling the story, sometimes both acting in concert. The editor or program director has the authority to kill a new lead or other changes that might seem too drastic under the circumstances, but that seldom happens.

The people on the firing line make most of the decisions on how the news should be handled, which is why beginners seldom are put in such tough spots. When it does happen, as was the case when Bob Woodward and Carl Bernstein broke the Watergate exposé for the *Washington Post,* a lot can ride on the outcome. Had the two young reporters been wrong, it could have badly hurt the newspaper. But as matters turned out, Richard Nixon had to announce his res-ignation as president of the United States, a speech for which there was no advance.

Similarly, when an advance is carried by a wire service or syn-dicate and changes have to be made upon actual delivery of a speech, the local paper or station does have the right to refuse to carry both the original report and the changes that are made in it. But that doesn't happen if the advance is important. Moreover, once the advance has been used locally and major changes have to be made in it, the wire editors for both local newspapers and the electronic media generally make the decisions on what should be done.

Editors and program directors may have the ultimate authority but they are seldom in a position to exercise it. When they have objections, it is usually too late to do anything of substance about them. The news awaits no one's convenience.

Handling a Controversial Speech

Just as advances on important speeches must be checked against actual delivery, raising the possibility of changes in the final account of the address, the advance itself may be used in a form not quite to the liking of the issuing agency.

This is especially true of an advance on a controversial speech where charges of inefficiency, misconduct, or actual criminal behavior may be made. As a matter of basic fairness, those who are attacked—whether as individuals, public officeholders, or corporate executives—should be given a right to reply without waiting for the actual delivery of a speech.

Sally Ward has to handle one such advance because she is more familiar than any other staff writer on the *Leader* with an atomic power mishap that caused a power outage in Central City and the opposing positions of the governor and mayor on reopening a damaged atomic power plant. Mack Roberts, still her neighbor, works the telephone for comment for her story.

This is the situation:

In his campaign to force the reopening of the South River atomic plant of the Central City Light and Power Company, Mayor Reardon decides to address the city council on the matter and issues an advance text of his speech at City Hall. Under state law, however, it is the governor and the legislature who have the final right to authorize reopening of the plant and neither has moved to date. Nor has the Federal Nuclear Regulatory Commission completed its inquiry into the reasons for the shutdown of the plant that created a twenty-eight-hour power outage in Central City. Non-atomic power has long since been restored and has proved adequate for the needs of the community. Yet the company, having invested $2 billion in

the South River atomic plant, is insisting on putting it back in operation but without tangible result.

The problem Sally finds with the use of the mayor's advance is
that he is making charges against the governor and his public service
commissioner, Charles J. McDowell, of "foot dragging" and "inefficiency" in failing to reopen the South River plant. Moreover, the
mayor's advance also criticizes the Federal Nuclear Regulatory
Commission. He quotes President Leonard Kenyon of the power
company as saying that the FNRC "are just a bunch of amateurs
and don't know their business."

Considering that the governor is campaigning for the Republican
presidential nomination, the story has national implications. But an
advance of this kind, if used factually as issued, would be incomplete
without responses from those accused. And that is what Mack Roberts is working on.

Feeling just a bit uncertain as to how to handle so politically sensitive a story, Sally has gone to the city desk to consult her editor,
Joe Stoddard. He listens to the various news points as she describes
them, nods, and tells her: "Let's play it straight and use any response
Roberts gets, advance or no advance. No matter what editorial position the paper takes, it ought not to affect the telling of the news."

That may sound insufferably righteous, but it also is the only sensible position a journalist can take in a public controversy that breaks
in the news columns. Actually, Sally has little choice in the matter
because the advance can be used only in the last edition of the
paper that afternoon. By the time the mayor addresses the city
council at 5:00 P.M., as scheduled, it will be too late to make the
text of what he actually says for that day. And by next day, it will
be old stuff.

Here is how Sally handles the advance, plus the material Roberts
is able to get by phone:

ATOM

Mayor Reardon late today accused Governor Farrow and his public
service commissioner, Charles J. McDowell, of "foot dragging" and
"inefficiency" in failing to authorize reopening of the South River
atomic power plant.

In a speech prepared for delivery before the city council, the mayor
supported a certification of the safety of the South River plant made
by President Leonard Kenyon of the Central City Light and Power
Co., owner of the plant. The mayor said:

"It is unreasonable of the governor and Commissioner McDowell
to oppose the reopening of the South River plant, a $2 billion facility

which would be of enormous benefit to this city. We already have certification that the plant is safe in a sworn report made by President Leonard Kenyon of Central City Light and Power Co.

"This certification has been made to the Federal Nuclear Regulatory Commission, which hasn't acted on it because they're just a bunch of amateurs and don't know their business. The governor has the votes in the Legislature to authorize reopening South River but the only reason he hasn't asked the legislators to act is that he thinks it'll help his presidential campaign to be against atomic power.

"I'm sorry to say that the governor and McDowell are guilty at the very least of foot dragging and inefficiency in failing to act."

Informed of the mayor's charges, the governor responded at the state capital, "Reardon, as usual, is talking through his hat. He wouldn't know South River from first base." Commissioner McDowell had no comment. And in Washington, a spokesman for the FNRC took the same position.

While the city council has no authority to order reopening of the South River plant, the mayor is apparently using a proposed council petition to the governor to try to force affirmative state action. For Central Light and Power, President Kenyon applauded the mayor's remarks saying, "Sure, we have proved we can get along without South River since the accident some weeks ago, but why waste a $2 billion facility? We're ready to go. . . ."

This story illustrates the major problem of those who must write quickly about today's news as it is developing: modern living is complicated and it can't be summed up as simply as A B C, which is what many average readers expect when they buy a newspaper. As for such news on television, many an average viewer switches to a sitcom program or some other form of entertainment as quickly as possible rather than try to understand the complications of a developing news story.

The recipe of television news, as used in the network roundup reports weekday evenings, is no solution. Merely to pretend that the news in every instance can be told in a sentence or two is to be completely unrealistic.

The uses of atomic energy and the consequences for its misuse cannot be made that simple; at the very least, when there is an atomic mishap, television finds it necessary to do a mini-documentary, but shows of that kind take time to produce and cannot be put on the air at once.

Very often, even the added space that a daily newspaper can devote to the problem isn't sufficient to clarify a developing story for the concerned citizen. He may often know the beginning and perhaps the middle, but not the end. That is why weekly newsmagazines still sell millions of copies in this country.

There may be some comfort for the journalist in all this, but not much. Herbert Bayard Swope, who won a Pulitzer Prize for his work as a reporter early in this century, said it best: "I do not know a recipe for success in this business or any other, but I can give you a guaranteed recipe for failure: try to please everybody."

In gathering and handling much of the news that shows how we live today, it is folly to oversimplify and thereby carry on the absurd pretense that all news must be entertaining. For certain kinds of feature and magazine copy, that is possible. But when it comes to dealing with the serious problems of the day, the mission of the journalist is to provide accurate information for the public as quickly as possible.

8
___

Writing about News Conferences

MOST NEWS CONFERENCES must seem to the American public to be exercises in futility. They lack harmony, frequently become noisy and even discourteous, and are likely to be conducted in an atmosphere of utter confusion. And yet, at base, they are the very essence of democracy in action.

What Every Journalist Knows

The news conference operation lends itself to no discernible pattern, no organization that may be even remotely efficient. To a neophyte, it seldom makes much sense, for it is enormously time-consuming without having any stated objective. Nor can anybody expect that there will be a sudden illumination through the device of question-and-answer journalism, a pat answer to any of the perplexing problems of modern living.

The unhappy truth is that news conferences are more likely to compound difficulties rather than resolve them. Following an opening statement by the source, which is frequently self-serving, the subject matter becomes diffuse more often than not. One reporter may ask a question relating to politics, another to social science, still another to personal matters, and there is no connection between them.

Why?

There are any number of reasons. An editor or a news director, knowing that a news conference is scheduled with a familiar news source, may instruct a reporter to ask certain questions. Or the reporters themselves may have their own ideas about what questions are important. Then, too, something the host says may touch off an entirely different line of questioning.

In such a free-for-all, anything may be said and almost anything may happen in consequence. Even to predict that news will emerge from a news conference is distinctly hazardous. If the host is convinced of the hostility of the questioners, the reporters may emerge from the session empty-handed. In short, a totally wasted half hour or so, the length of the average news conference.

The Problem for Writers

What can a writer make out of such a melange? Despite the efforts of generations of journalists, politicians, educators, and social scientists, there is no handy set of blueprints for a writer to follow. Most stories about news conferences are shaped by a hard news pattern of organization, but even that isn't an inviolate rule. For what if the host is a fashion designer who has just taken his fourth or maybe fifth bride? Or perhaps the center of attention may be a movie starlet who was arrested in a drug bust and contends she is innocent.

To hang a hard news tag on every news conference in advance makes no sense. The story has to be judged on the basis of the event itself.

That being so, it follows that stories about news conferences, like most general news, depend for their effectiveness on the judgment and skill of those who write about them. It is not always true that an experienced writer will do better with a news conference round-up than someone who is relatively new at this kind of professional performance. An eager newcomer is likely to arouse public interest in a situation that doesn't appeal to a jaded professional, something that happens over and over again in journalism.

Of course, it always helps any writer if the focus of the story is a person of some prominence or, at the very least, someone who is easily identified to a mass public. If the president of the United States calls a news conference, it means something; if Joe Doakes announces he wants to meet the press, it doesn't. If a millionaire convicted of tax evasion holds a breast-beating news conference on his way to prison, it attracts attention; if an honest wage earner pays his taxes without a murmur, it doesn't.

This may be unfair, but every writer—not journalists alone—often deals in human values that are discriminatory. If everything were peaceful in the Union of South Africa, for example, there would be precious little news to report from that sorely tried land and its embattled peoples.

This tendency to exploit conflict as a journalistic standard of values is the basis of much of the mistrust of news conferences by high-level participants. More than one American president in recent years has put off news conferences at the White House as often as possible or tried instead to communicate with the public through methods less likely to involve controversy. During the unfolding Iran affair, for example, President Reagan did not hold a White House news conference for almost four months. The holders of lower public offices, too, have sought to detach themselves from the reportorial pressure cooker.

All this constitutes a part of the problem for writers. However, it doesn't help any of them to pretend that the average news conference is bland when everybody connected with journalism knows it can't be. Nor can a writer pump up a news conference with an important news personality if nothing of consequence is said or done. It doesn't work. The very fact that news conferences can be trying on the principals makes it all the more difficult to produce a fair and unbiased written account that is both understandable and interesting to a mass public.

What television does in such situations is to take the easy way out—show a reporter asking a question and a news source answering it, then giving a two- or three-sentence summation of the entire event. For the press, that isn't good enough. If newspapers are to go on being published daily, they must continue to use adequate written accounts of significant news conferences. And writers must continue to be found and trained to do the work well.

Holding a News Conference

Setting up a news conference is simple enough for nearly all participants, but there is never any guarantee that it will make the wire services, the evening news on the tube, or the daily newspapers. The ranks of public relations people are full of disappointed flacks who hoped to score a publicity triumph for a client by calling in the reporters. Sheer press agentry turns off working journalists faster than anything else because it is so blatant. It is not, therefore, a factor worth considering here as a part of the total problem confronting writers who deal with news conference material.

For a controversial subject, let us go back to the problem raised by the closing of the South River atomic power plant of the Central City Light and Power Company and Mayor Reardon's attempt to force its reopening. In the last chapter, Sally Ward noted in her final edition story for the *Central City Leader* that Governor Farrow had replied briefly to the mayor's charges of "foot dragging" and "inefficiency." But with the delivery of the mayor's speech at the Civic Auditorium and the wide publicity it has received in both the press and electronic media, the governor decides to make a more extended retort.

Thus, the night desk at the *Leader*'s newsroom receives a note from Independent News that Governor Farrow will hold a news conference at 10:30 A.M. the next day on the state's position regarding the whole question of atomic power. The *Leader*'s capital correspondent normally would handle such a news conference; however, having little background on atomic power, he is the first to suggest assigning Sally Ward, as the paper's science expert, either to do the main story or an interpretive sidebar (a separate story) explaining the background of any proposal the governor sees fit to make.

The *Leader*'s news executives, after conferring by phone with Loren Wilton, the capital correspondent, decide it would be better to overstaff the governor's news conference than to understaff it. As a result, Joe Stoddard, the city editor, calls Sally Ward at home to tell her to head for the capital. As an afterthought, the city editor also sends the young reporter, Mack Roberts, with her because he seems to have made an impression on the governor. Who knows? Roberts, the city editor decides, isn't going to be inconvenient to have around; if he's lucky, he may come up again with something the others don't have.

It is scarcely a surprise, therefore, that so many reporters show up from around the state next morning that the governor's press people shift the news conference from the executive office to the larger press room of the state legislature. There, shortly before 11:00 A.M., Governor Farrow briefly welcomes the newspeople as follows as the still photographers and television cameras zero in on him:

"Thank you for responding so quickly to my news conference announcement, ladies and gentlemen. To get right to the point, I have already said all I am going to say in response to Mayor Reardon of Central City, but I believe I owe the citizens of this state a much wider explanation of our position on the South River atomic power plant. So let's go directly to questions."

Bob Timmons of Independent News, the senior reporter at the state capital, is on his feet at once: "Governor, do you intend to ask the legislature to reopen the South River plant in the immediate future?"

The governor, standing at a lectern in the legislative newsroom with the still and television cameras still focused on him, is ready with a response, which he reads from a sheet before him:

"I cannot authorize the reopening of the Central City Light and Power's South River plant unless the company submits a realistic plan for the evacuation of all people in the immediate vicinity in case of another such atomic emergency. What I have received from the company to date is unrealistic in the extreme.

"Our Public Service Commission, after a thorough inquiry, believes that we narrowly escaped an atomic disaster when the South River plant was forced to close recently. Taken together with a similar incident at Three Mile Island in Pennsylvania some years ago, that constitutes a warning for all of us.

"At Chernobyl in the Soviet Union, we now know that, in addition to the immediate casualties caused by atomic malfunctions there, deadly radiation has spread for an incalculable distance around and is likely to cause damage for years to come. We cannot let that happen here."

Timmons follows up with another question: "Does the company know of your decision and has there been a reply?"

The governor nodded. "The company says it will submit a broader plan for emergency evacuation and we'll take a hard look at it. If we think it'll work, the plant reopens. If not, it stays closed."

John Carbone of the *Central City News* asks, "What have you to say to people who think you're being tough about South River only because you're running for president?"

The governor's reply: "Nuts." He recognizes Sally Ward, who asks: "Is there a scientific basis for your decision based on the intensity of radiation and the distance over which it was detected?"

Farrow's response: "Yes, I'll have the PSC's scientific report for you in about two hours. I can tell you right now that there was enough radiation in the immediate area to scare any sensible person. I'm not going to be responsible for another such ordeal."

The questions now come at the governor from all parts of the press room, some dealing with his position on the South River plant, others with different matters. A sampling:

Q.   A recent national poll shows you're not doing very well in your campaign for the Republican presidential nomination. Any comment?

A.   It's too early to count me out. I think I have a good chance for the nomination and for the presidency.

Q.   At what point will you withdraw if the polls show little change?

A.   I'm in this fight to the finish.

Q.   How are you and Mayor Reardon getting along?

A.   Henry's excitable but he's a good guy. I think he'll see eventually that I'm right about South River.

Q.   Is there any progress in your campaign for a sixty-five-mile-an-hour speed limit in this state?

A.   That depends entirely on the legislature.

Q.   Do you have any plans to go to Washington?

A.   Not until I'm elected to take over the White House.

This is the way the news conference goes for forty minutes before Timmons, as the senior correspondent, calls a halt by saying, "Thank you, Governor." Whereupon everybody except the governor makes a rush for the nearest door to begin writing and filing.

For Loren Wilton, the regular capital correspondent of the *Leader*, and Sally Ward, the decision on who writes what is simple: Sally is to do the atom story, for which she was sent to the capital, and Wilton will handle everything else. All Roberts has to do is transcribe his tape of the Q & A, which he is now doing as quickly as possible.

Here's the way Sally begins her story datelined Midland, the state capital:

ATOM

Midland—Governor Farrow said today that he wanted a "more realistic" plan for the evacuation of the South River area in the event of another atomic mishap.

Unless he gets it, he warned at a news conference today, "I cannot authorize the reopening of the Central City Light and Power's South River plant."

He called a plan he had received from the company "unrealistic in the extreme," and added that a new program would be submitted, saying, "If we think it'll work, the (South River) plant reopens. If not, it stays closed."

Calling attention to massive damage that had been caused at a Soviet atomic power plant at Chernobyl, he declared, "We cannot let that happen here." . . .

The remainder of Sally's story summed up the rest of the South River quotes and the detailed report of the Public Service Commission inquiry upon which the governor had based his decision. While she was writing her account, Wilton was filing his own story, which began:

POLS

Midland—Governor Farrow promised a "fight to the finish" today for the Republican presidential nomination although he is lagging in the polls.

During a wide-ranging news conference, he said, "It's too early to count me out. I think I have a good chance for the nomination and for the presidency."

His "fight to the finish" vow came in answer to a question about when he might withdraw if the polls show little change.

In response to a question about his relations with Mayor Reardon of Central City, who wants South River reopened and gave only a lukewarm endorsement of the governor's presidential campaign, Farrow said, "Henry's excitable but he's a good guy. I think eventually he'll see that I'm right about South River." . . .

The remainder of Wilton's story summed up other newsworthy parts of the conference. Sometimes, in a situation like this, a newspaper will use one story as a lead and the second as a sidebar. This could have been done in the accounts of the governor's news conference by inserting the following about his South River decision directly after the third paragraph of the POLS story:

The governor also made known his decision to refuse to authorize reopening of the Central City Light and Power's South River plant, closed recently by an atomic malfunction, until the company provides him with a "realistic" evacuation plan for the surrounding populace.

But it was the governor's presidential campaign that made national news.

The details of the South River decision, of course, would remain as written by Sally Ward in the second story.

For the electronic media, such planning isn't necessary because television uses the relevant quotes of the news conference after a lead-in sentence by an anchor person, and radio may do the same or fall back on a roundup by the broadcast wire of Independent News. In any event, the governor's handling of the news illustrates dramatically how news conferences make news. Most capable politicians from the president to small-town mayors are equally adept.

9
The Wire Services

THE MARKET FOR NEWS is worldwide. The principal vendors are called news agencies, or wire services, which distribute accounts of all significant regional, national, and international events to their members or clients. In effect, through the use of teleprinters linked by phone lines, this means that there exists what amounts to a minute-by-minute news exchange among all the principal countries on earth and some of the smaller ones as well.

Where the Sky's the Limit

These wholesalers of journalism come in three different varieties: privately owned news cooperatives, privately owned companies that charge fees to clients, and government-owned and -operated services. Outside the United States, some of the privately owned cooperatives and companies are often greatly influenced by their governments without actually being a government service.

In the United States, the dominant service is the Associated Press (AP), a news cooperative servicing both print and electronic members who support it with fees. Its chief rival is *United Press International* (UPI), which depends mainly on the sale of its service to clients and has frequently been in financial trouble. The major news syndicates, which also sell their service, are additional competitors, the largest and most influential being the *New York Times* and the

Los Angeles Times–Washington Post combines. On occasion, the major networks also can originate important aspects of the news in this country, which adds to the prestige of CBS, NBC, and ABC News.

Among foreign wire services, the traditional rival of the American giants for more than a hundred years has been Reuters, the British agency, which once was rated with the Crown and the Union Jack as a symbol of empire. It is a different kind of a cooperative than the Associated Press, being jointly owned by the British press and a domestic news organization known as the Press Association. Other Reuters agreements cover the press in Canada, India, Australia, New Zealand, South Africa, and various countries outside the Commonwealth.

Because of its ties to the Commonwealth and its closeness to the British government, although it is not a formal part of government, Reuters is both an authoritative and economic competitor of the American wholesalers. The British agency sells its service, in the United States, as does UPI. Other national agencies—Agence France Presse, the Deutsche Press Agentur, and Japan's Kyodo service among them—all have a certain amount of importance in varying degree.

Beyond these and their smaller rivals come the government-owned and -operated services that do not pretend to tell the news in the objective manner typical of the American wire services. The most important are Tass, the official service of the Soviet Union, and its closely linked radio and television equivalents. Another governmental voice of major importance is the New China News Agency, the voice of the Communist regime in Peking. Throughout the third world in Asia and Africa, particularly, it is also the fashion for dictators to address both their subjects and the world through government agencies. It is true, as well, among a number of Latin American nations, especially Cuba.

It is necessary in the United States, quite often, to pay close attention to news that originates in major regional dailies other than such national news organizations as the *New York Times, Wall Street Journal, Washington Post, Los Angeles Times,* and *Chicago Tribune.* Among the influential regionals are papers of the stature of the *St. Louis Post-Dispatch, Milwaukee Journal, Boston Globe, Philadelphia Inquirer,* and *Miami Herald* among others and major newspaper groups of the strength of the Gannett, Knight-Ridder, and Newhouse organizations.

Abroad, the global network is rounded out by such authoritative news organizations as the government-owned British Broadcasting Company and newspapers such as *The Times* of London, *Le Monde* of Paris, *Izvestia* and *Pravda* in Moscow, *Asahi Shimbun* in Tokyo, and their equivalents in other principal world capitals.

Taken as a whole, this far-reaching network covers the flow of events between Main Street, USA, and the ends of the earth. In consequence, for an informed public the sky's the limit when it comes to searching out the news of the day.

Writing for a Wire Service

The writer who handles copy for a wire service proceeds in much the same way as someone doing a local story for a local newspaper except that the work must be more concise. However, it is identified and organized differently. To expedite news of importance, there is also a system for the quick distribution of breaking news through the use of a bulletin service. And in news organizations like the Associated Press, there are different services for the print and electronic media, each tailored to the special needs of a diverse membership or clientele.

To illustrate how wire services work, let us assume that a government source has tipped major newspapers and agencies in south Florida that an announcement of a drug bust may be expected from Key West. This tip is handled confidentially within each news organization so that reporters, camera crews, and various specialists can set up plans for coverage at Key West.

The arrangement there is that all hands will agree not to break the story until a news conference concludes at a government office in Key West some hours hence. In all such deals, even if the participating news organizations agree to act in good faith, there is always a possibility that some local reporter not a party to the arrangement will stumble across the story at the scene of the action, where contraband has been seized and arrests made.

This operation, however, goes off as scheduled. The reporters outside the news conference hold open telephone lines to their news desks. Once the news conference is over, their colleagues surge in a confused mass toward the open phone lines and begin dictating. Here is the way the news comes through on the teleprinters of a wire service, the Independent News (IN)*:

*The simulated material and source are used here, as elsewhere in this work, for instructional purposes.

BULLETIN

Key West, Fl. (IN)—A shipload of cocaine with an estimated value of $8 million has been seized by the Coast Guard off the Florida coast, the Federal Bureau of Investigation announced today.

xxx

DRUG

Key West, Fl. (IN)—In a night-long chase off the Florida coast in which shots were fired, the Coast Guard early today captured a small vessel bearing cocaine with an estimated value of $8 million.

The seizure was announced here shortly after noon today by the Federal Bureau of Investigation.

-more-

1ST ADD DRUG X X X BUREAU OF INVESTIGATION.

Frank Farley, an FBI press officer, said the ship bearing the contraband, identified as the *Palomar*, a 6,000-ton freighter of Cuban registry, had been impounded and that its captain and crew of 26 men were under arrest on smuggling charges.

"This is one of the largest drug busts ever made," Farley said. "We have identified the source of the cocaine as Colombian but we haven't yet been able to trace the connection between Colombia and Cuba."

-more-

2ND ADD DRUG X X X COLOMBIA AND CUBA.

Captain George Serrano of the U.S. Coast Guard cutter *Intrepid* told of the gun chase in darkness during which the *Palomar* was captured and brought here under armed escort.

"We were on regular patrol within American waters off the Florida coast when we spotted the *Palomar* and decided to stop her and search her," Captain Serrano said.

-more-

3RD ADD DRUG X X X CAPTAIN SERRANO SAID.

"However, her skipper evidently decided to try to get away from us. He even ignored two warning shots we fired across the *Palomar*'s bow, so we had to open fire after chasing her for about 10 or 12 miles.

"Otherwise, she would have gotten away from us. In addition to the warnings, we fired six shots in all and I'm pretty sure that the other four hit her somewhere amidships. Anyway, that stopped her and we boarded her and took our prisoners and the cocaine without further resistance."

Captain Serrano refused to say, in response to a question, whether the Coast Guard had had a tip that the *Palomar* was carrying valuable contraband. At current street prices in south Florida, the FBI estimated that the cocaine, when cut and packaged, would have brought many times its stated value as a raw product. . . .

BUST IT BUST IT
BULLETIN

Washington, D.C. (IN)—The Coast Guard shelled and captured a Cuban freighter off the south Florida coast before dawn today, wounding eight members of her crew of 26 and seizing an estimated $8 million in cocaine.

xxx

1ST LD DRUG

Washington, D.C., (IN)—Coast Guard shells early today wounded eight crewmen aboard a Cuban freighter off the south Florida coast before the vessel was captured with an estimated $8 million in cocaine.

-more-

1ST ADD 1ST LD DRUG X X X $8 MILLION IN COCAINE.

A State Department spokesman said the United States would investigate the attempted smuggling operation to determine if there was complicity by foreign governments. The announcement of the drug bust was made earlier by the Federal Bureau of Investigation at Key West, Florida.

END 1ST LD DRUG PIKS UP 3RD GRAF PREVIOUS X X FRANK FARLEY, ETC.

Once the State Department has intervened in a story of this importance and disclosed that Coast Guard shells caused casualties, a development that could involve foreign governments, the focus of the news shifts to Washington. However, that doesn't take the reporters at Key West off the hook. What they now have to determine from the Coast Guard captain is what happened to the eight wounded crewmen, where they were treated, and the seriousness of their condition.

The story, being distributed nationally and abroad, can develop a good many other angles as the news report proceeds. It is obvious that such a wide-spreading occurrence would be far beyond the resources of the average American daily. And that also is true of the average broadcasting and cable station which, had a story like this really happened, would be serviced by the radio news division of the wire services in an account that could immediately be read over the air.

This is how the first bulletin could read for broadcast use when adapted for the radio wire:

> Key West (IN)—A shipload of cocaine with an estimated value of $8 million has been seized by the Coast Guard off south Florida. The FBI has just made the announcement here.

The rest of the story, changed from past tense with sentences shortened wherever possible for easier reading, would follow in order. The two wire service news divisions, print and radio, work separately and separate writers would handle the story. This is how the Washington bulletin could read for broadcast use:

> Washington, D.C. (IN)—The State Department says eight crewmen of a Cuban freighter have been wounded by Coast Guard shells. The news comes minutes after the capture of the vessel and an estimated $8 million cargo of cocaine was announced at Key West, Florida.

An Enterprise News Story

There is another important use for wire service copy among daily newspapers, local broadcasters, and cable stations. Sometimes, even if there isn't an obvious local angle, the agency copy may be rewritten because local editors want to emphasize a different angle. Or, with greater frequency, a local angle may easily be developed from a wire service account of distant events.

In such cases, many local editors become chintzy about giving credit to the wire services for originating the story. But to beginners, sourcing ought to be used in a news account even though most readers and viewers neither know nor fully understand the function of a wire service. It is the one time when it is inadvisable to apply one of the most useful sayings in journalism: *When in doubt, leave out.*

Regardless of the whims of individual editors and news directors, sourcing is mandatory at every level for the news that is developed by responsible organizations.

Here is an illustration of how a short piece on the wire about a seemingly routine item of foreign news might very well become a local story of considerable interest in the United States. Assume that an editor on the early desk of a Long Island newspaper, the *East End Record,* a daily published some eighty miles east of New York City in a farming locale, sees the following item on the Independent News wire:

> Warsaw, Poland (IN)—With the approval of the American embassy here, 80 Polish farm workers were issued passports with six-month visas today and some said they were leaving for jobs in New York as soon as possible.

The editor on the early desk decides that could be a story for the *East End Record,* assigns a reporter to do some telephoning, and hopes for results. True, he has no reason to believe that any of these eighty temporary farm workers from a Communist country are going to be used in solidly Republican Suffolk County, New York, but stranger things have happened. In the latter part of this century, Japanese, Koreans, Chinese from Taiwan, and other Asians have been gainfully employed in American industry because they are willing to work at cheaper rates than Americans. Why not an added influx from a Communist land?

Two hours later, when the editor has just about given up on his shot in the dark at what is known as an enterprise story, the reporter he has assigned drops some copy on his desk. This is how the account begins:

FARM

> Several hundred Polish workers are being employed seasonally on Long Island farms this year.
>
> Jaroslav Rudzinski, secretary of the East End Farm Federation, said the men travel on Polish passports granted by the Communist regime in Warsaw and are given American visas good for six months.
>
> "It's an emergency matter," Rudzinski said. "We found that the Poles are good workers, will do jobs in the potato and cauliflower fields that we can't get Americans to do, and they mind their own business. After six months, they go home."

> The use of the temporary workers from Poland was made known by a wire service, the Independent News, which reported today that 80 Polish farm workers were leaving their native land for jobs in this state. They have Polish passports and six-month American visas issued by the American embassy, the agency said. . . .

This type of assignment, based on wire copy, may be expected at almost any time in any part of the United States. Whether a local angle may be developed, of course, depends entirely on the initiative of the reporter and the patience of the editor who makes the assignment. It sometimes happens that the editor may know of a source through which a local angle can be developed, but no reporter, especially a beginner, ought to count on it. Editors are all too often more occupied with their own work.

Necessarily, a beginning reporter will wonder what happens if a local angle can't be developed on such an assignment. Assume, for example, that the reporter for the *East End Record* didn't have the wit and the luck to telephone Jaroslav Rudzinski, secretary of the East End Farm Federation. Instead, some other official may have resented being awakened and asked about an item that was news to him, a stroke of bad luck that can happen to the best of reporters.

Then, the answer is, "Sorry, boss. No story." Unless such a response is given too many times on a telephone enterprise assignment in a news office, it doesn't do much harm to a beginner's chances. But it doesn't help, either, especially if an opposition broadcasting station comes up with the story the newspaper reporter couldn't get.

These are some of the ways in which wire services develop the news patterns of the day and suggest others that are worth separate inquiry. In our system of news distribution, we could not do without the daily files of agency reports. The independent wholesalers of news are a part of the system and will remain so regardless of the further development of electronic communication. No mere instrument, however ingenious, can ask the right questions of the right people, much less produce an intelligent and well-documented news account.

News of a Disaster

The speed with which news is distributed, in this country as in others where a free press operates, makes it necessary to take particular care with the facts when a disaster is involved. Wire service people are trained never to guess or otherwise speculate on what could have happened or what is likely to happen when a story is developing. It is also vital for a writer who is filing for a wire at the point of origin to give the source of all information as quickly as possible.

To show how such news is handled, consider the following as a scenario for reality:

A small aircraft flutters out of a sunny blue sky above a small midwestern town called Carrin. Like a frightened bird, it veers crazily over a school yard where children are playing at recess in midmorning. Then, suddenly, the plane plunges into the wooden school building with a rending crash that is heard blocks away.

Flames shoot from the doomed structure, ignited by gasoline from the wrecked aircraft. Scores of terrified children in the playground run in every direction, crying for help. Soon, the shrieking sirens of fire engines and police cars are heard in the distance.

Within minutes, firemen are fighting the flames with geysers of water from their hose lines. The police cordon off traffic and try to protect the surviving children and teachers.

Newspeople meanwhile have reached the scene. Broadcasters from two local radio stations are giving eyewitness accounts of what they see and hear. Then come the still photographers and reporters from a local daily, the *Carrin Record*. Not far behind, a big truck from a local TV station lumbers in with a camera crew, reporters, and a news director to put together an on-the-scene newscast.

A stringer (temporary employee) of a wire service, the Independent News, phones the nearest bureau in the state from the newsroom of the *Carrin Record*, where he works, with first word of the disaster. All he knows, from copy he has seen crossing the city desk, is that police say a small plane has plunged into a school building and that is what the first story reports out of the city:

BULLETIN

Carrin (IN)—A small plane crashed into an elementary school building here today with undetermined casualties, police say.

EDS: SLUG PREVIOUS BN PLANE
1ST ADD PLANE X X X police say.

Eyewitnesses said the accident set the Belden Elementary School afire but most children and teachers were at recess at the time.

Police were unable to determine immediately how many people were in the wrecked plane or the flaming building. Firemen said it would be several hours before the blaze could be brought under control.

2ND ADD PLANE X X X **under control.**

Principal D. J. Harrison, who escaped from the building with his secretary, Mrs. Geraldine Mullen, said he heard screams from the second floor just after the crash but flames blocked off the staircase.

"No one could survive in all that hell," he said. He and Mrs. Mullen were unharmed. . . .

Ambulances from nearby hospitals meanwhile have reached the disaster scene but there is nothing for doctors and nurses to do. Until the fire can be brought under control, there is no way the building can be entered. As Fire Chief Harold Dawson says when he reaches the scene and reporters clamor for information, "You guys know more than I do. I just got here. Let me get my bearings first."

The chief goes to work. However, it is after noon when the first bodies are carried from the still-smoking building by weary firemen—three children and a teacher. Asked if there are more casualties, one of the firemen mutters, "How in hell would I know? We found these on the first floor and we haven't even gotten upstairs yet or reached the plane."

It is the first hard news to come from the disaster scene, however, and the wire service goes with it on word from its stringer:

BULLETIN

Carrin (IN)—At least three children and a teacher were killed today when a small plane crashed into a school building here and set it afire.

1ST LEAD PLANE

Carrin (IN)—A small plane crashed into a school here today, setting it afire and killing at least three children and a teacher. Several hundred others escaped harm because they were in the school yard at recess.

1ST ADD 1ST LEAD PLANE X X X **at recess.**

A fireman said the victims' bodies were found on the first floor of the two-story wooden Belden Elementary School. "We haven't even gotten upstairs yet or reached the plane," he said, when asked if there were more deaths.

PIKUP: 4TH PGH PREVIOUS "PRINCIPAL D. J. HARRISON ETC.

The story goes through numerous changes, leads, and inserts for the rest of the day on what is known as the P.M. cycle of the wire report. A cleanup story, sent over the wire for A.M.'s, begins as follows:

> Carrin (IN)—The toll in the Belden School disaster rose to 18 dead and 5 injured last night, ten hours after a small plane crashed into the old wooden building and set it afire.
>
> Firemen working in the smoking ruins carried the bodies of 12 children and 2 teachers from gutted classrooms. The bodies of the 4 other victims were found in the wrecked plane.
>
> The 5 injured persons, all children, survived when they managed to reach an old concrete air raid shelter that had been built in the basement during World War II. They suffered only minor injuries, were treated at the scene, and sent home.
>
> Hundreds of other children and their teachers were in the school yard at recess at the time of the crash, 10:33 a.m. (CST). Fire Chief Harold Dawson said efforts to identify the victims in the wrecked plane and determine the cause of the crash were continuing.
>
> The known casualties were . . .

The Independent News radio wire meanwhile has been carrying similar accounts written for broadcast use. From these accounts and staff material broadcast live from the scene, both the local radio and television stations have been giving the disaster full coverage. The local paper, too, has been on the job all day with a special edition that was put out once the bulk of the casualties had been determined.

Throughout the state and nearby areas, Independent News has been the main source of information. For other parts of the nation, the coverage has been thorough but not as detailed as the spot news accounts. This is the way wire services work, in contrast to the print and broadcast media. There are small differences in procedure (the slugging, for example, and the way PIKUP lines read) but essentially the news is handled in pretty much the same way—straight, unemotional, factual, and thoroughly documented.

10

Stormy Weather

THIS IS THE CENTURY in which we have split the atom, made human flight commonplace, shot missiles thousands of miles, and put a man on the moon. But we have not, alas, yet mastered the science of meteorology sufficiently to forecast the day's weather with reasonable accuracy. Nor are we likely to do so soon. The prudent journalist, therefore, still glances cautiously out the nearest window before making a commitment on weather news for public consumption.

Sources of Weather Reports

The National Weather Service (NWS) is the source of many of the forecasts used by American news media. The NWS and its parent organization, the National Oceanic and Atmospheric Administration of the Department of Commerce, have statistics for all purposes plus daily maps to illustrate weather conditions in detail. However, broadcasters frequently use their own weather experts nationally and locally. And as important a newspaper as the *New York Times,* at the top of its half-page of weather data daily, has used this credit: "Meteorology: Pennsylvania State University."

So there is no unanimity in this country about even the source of our weather reports. Nor is the public any the less skeptical about the accuracy of our published and broadcast forecasts despite the search for broader sources. As far as the average reader and viewer are concerned, things seem not to have changed very much since Mark Twain made his celebrated observation about New England weather: "In the spring, I have counted 136 different kinds of weather inside of twenty-four hours."*

Still, weather reporting can't be laughed at. It remains, as it always has, a staple of the day's news and an almost continual topic of conversation. It can't be shrugged off, shunted aside, overlooked, or buried. And with the growing popularity of weathermen and weatherwomen on television, it isn't likely to be.

Admittedly, when the sky is clear and the sun is bright, there is little chance that the weather will make news for at least a few hours. But let the wind shift and clouds come scurrying over the horizon, then the situation becomes uncertain. That's when the trouble begins and a weasel-worded new forecast is pushed out for the public's edification, "Chance of rain."

It doesn't do any good. I have always thought that it would be much better for the news media to admit that weather forecasting, by every possible standard, is an inexact science and publish or broadcast daily weather data on that basis. Sensible people would be the first to understand and applaud. Under existing conditions, weather news remains an almost continual source of uncertainty and, at critical times, irritation.

The situation, therefore, appears to be without remedy. The journalists who work on any type of weather assignment must do the best they can.

Handling a Weather Forecast

Like it or not, something about the weather must be included in the daily reports of the news media in every form—wire services, newspapers, radio, television, and cable.

The wire services generally carry the detailed National Weather Service outlook for the next twenty-four hours and any long-range forecast that is issued. Most newspapers use a "weather ear," that is, a brief boldface summary of the forecast in the upper corner of Page 1, either on the right or left side, with a reference to the inside page on which complete data may be found. As for most of the broadcast media, the use of weather specialists remains routine, rain or shine.

*At a dinner of the New England Society in New York City, December 22, 1876.

At one time, much earlier in this century, it was thought by some fairly influential newspaper editors to be a service to readers to use a brief news story about the weather on Page 1 as well as a "weather ear." The problem, however, was that writers couldn't think of much that wouldn't duplicate the weather ear on a nice but otherwise uneventful day. The result usually turned out to be two or three vapid paragraphs in a style that was supposed to be cute.

Scant wonder that the notion of a separate "weather short" as well as a weather ear died a lingering but unmourned death.

The general practice for the wire services and most daily newspapers now is to use only if necessary a separate story on the weather in the news columns, aside from the usual statistics and weather map. The separate account would include both forecasts and actual storms that affect a large part of the surrounding area.

Forecasting, however, continues to be emphasized by the broadcast media as a weather news feature in fair weather or foul.

Storm Warnings

Anybody who writes or broadcasts about the weather must be familiar with the basic warnings and storm definitions. The following are used by the National Weather Service in its transmissions over radio and television stations:

Small Craft Advisory—Any potentially hazardous condition over water of two hours' duration or more that may include winds of 18 to 33 knots (20.7 to 38 miles per hour).*

Gale Warning—Winds ranging from 34 to 47 knots (39 to 54 miles an hour) may be expected in the area, usually with rain.

Storm Warning—Winds of 48 knots or more (55 miles an hour or more) may be expected in the area, usually with rain.

Tornado Watch—This is a precaution against the possibility of a tornado striking the area. It is a violent, funnel-shaped column of winds that may touch the ground and reach a velocity of 300 miles an hour, giving off a roaring sound and causing great destruction.

Tornado Warning—A tornado has been sighted in the area. These rotating winds move at a rate of about 30 miles an hour in forward

*One knot is equivalent to 1 nautical mile an hour, or 6,080.27 feet, as contrasted with 5,280 feet in a mile on land.

speed and cut an average path ranging from a few feet to more than a mile in width.

Cyclones—Tornadolike winds that rotate counterclockwise in the northern hemisphere, clockwise in the southern hemisphere. Tornadoes and hurricanes all are of cyclonic origin, and are usually accompanied by torrential rain. They reach velocities of 48 to 63 knots on the average [55 to 71.5 miles an hour].

Hurricane Watch—Like a tornado watch, this is a precaution against the possibility of a hurricane striking the area even though the storm may still be twenty-four hours' distant. A hurricane originates over tropical waters and often develops winds of 64 knots or more (72.5 miles or more). While it moves forward at only about 10 to 15 miles an hour, it is very wide and can be from 500 to 2,000 miles in diameter in the Atlantic and Pacific Ocean areas.

Hurricane Warning—This means to take cover. Hurricanes generally move west to northwest in lower latitudes but when they reach 25 to 30 degrees north latitude (roughly off the Florida or northern Mexican coastlines) they may shift direction to the northeast. Hurricanes are the most destructive of all storms.

Rainstorm—Rainfall is measured in inches. Enough rain to cover an acre to the depth of 1 inch would be considered a 1-inch rainstorm.

Snowstorm—Snowstorms, similarly, are measured in the fall of an inch of snow over 1 acre.

Blizzard—Many weather stories and newscasts incorrectly designate a snowstorm of some length as a blizzard. Actually, a blizzard—in the National Weather Service designation—is a snowfall of three hours or more driven by a wind of 35 miles an hour or more that reduces visibility to less than one-quarter of a mile for the duration of the storm.

By paying close attention to these standard definitions, newswriters can avoid a great deal of confusion both in their own news organization and among the public that reads, views, and listens.

It is the fashion among more sensational dailies to write about the weather with vigorous verbs and horrendous images, particularly during the hurricane season or in the midst of snowy winters. That is likely to make conditions seem much worse than they actually are. The style is deplorable because it lends itself to the urge to overwrite, a weakness among journalists.

Calmness and precision in writing are the qualities that should be cultivated by writers who handle weather news. The worse the storm, the more advisable it is for the news media to practice self-restraint. Flooding in the rainy season and freezing temperatures that so often follow a prolonged snowfall are difficult enough to bear without the added hazard of panicky writing or newscasting. It is always a good idea to let the weather story tell itself instead of piling on the adjectives.

Handling a Local Weather Emergency

In many parts of the United States, there are certain periods of the year when freakish weather may be expected. Among the best known are the vernal and autumnal equinoxes, the time when the sun's center crosses the celestial equator. Old-timers on farm lands often refer to these seasonal changes as a time span that could be marked by "line storms."

Such disturbances on occasion may spread over a very wide area, causing serious flooding and other types of storm damage. Whole cities may be affected. In agricultural parts of the country, in particular, damage in terms of ruined crops may run into millions of dollars.

All this makes for news on a seasonal basis—local if the storm is confined to a particular area; national, if it spreads over an entire region such as the Midwest, South, New England, or the Far West.

Here is how the *Central City Leader* put together a summary of tornado damage when a twister struck an outlying residential area. The story on Page 1 began as follows:

> A tornado ripped a quarter-mile path of ruin through the north side suburb of Clayton today, causing three deaths and injuries to 22 other residents.
>
> Striking with a roar heard for miles around, the twister leveled 18 homes in the residential community. Unofficial damage estimates ran into the millions of dollars.
>
> "We were lucky all of us weren't killed," said 89-year-old Matty Tillman, who lives with his son and daughter-in-law, Mr. and Mrs. Will Tillman, and their three teen-age children. All were home at the time.

> The dead were neighbors of the Tillmans, Mrs. Darlene Jowitt, 36, and her 11-year-old daughter, Daisy, and Mrs. Clara Meriwether, 38, a friend of Mrs. Jowitt.
>
> The injured residents were taken to nearby hospitals as soon as the storm subsided for treatment of their bruises. None were considered seriously hurt, doctors said.
>
> The tornado burst upon the suburb at 3:45 p.m., about 30 minutes after the National Weather Service issued a tornado warning for this area. It lasted about 45 minutes, but caused havoc that stunned many residents. . . .

Such an emergency, as covered by local media, can take up hours of broadcast time and many pages of a newspaper. People who are in or near the area hardest hit will want to know how bad it was and how narrowly they themselves escaped. Others in the city, too, will want the details of what happened and how it happened so that they may make adequate preparations to safeguard themselves and their families when the next violent storm strikes.

It is all very much a part of the news business.

Regional Wire Service Storm Coverage

Unless a storm strikes in or near a major population center where a wire service has a bureau large enough to report, photograph, and write about such an emergency, the agency very often has to make do with local reports. These are put together by staff people of member news organizations, if the agency is a cooperative, or those of clients, if the agency sells its service.

This is particularly true when there is a wide-spreading emergency, such as a snowstorm or a flood. Only a news agency the size of the Associated Press is capable of using its own people to round up most regional accounts of storm casualties and damage. The rest are mainly rewrites of local broadcasts and a scattering of material filed by local newspaper staffers who act as stringers.

Instead of putting out a regional summary under a particular dateline, the common practice among agency people is to issue what is called an "undated lead." It remains a summary in essence, but carries no dateline (hence the name, undated lead). Here is how such a piece would be handled by the Independent News, an agency based in the Midwest, to cover widespread flooding following a series of springtime rainstorms:

BY THE INDEPENDENT NEWS

Flood waters driven by high winds surged through parts of eight midwestern states today amid forecasts of more rain in most parts of the area.

The toll of flood-related deaths since the spring rainy season began a week ago reached 31, according to reports tabulated in governors' offices in the affected states. From the same sources came rising damage estimates that now top $100 million.

One of the governors, Edward B. Farrow, said at his office in Midland:

"We're going to need an emergency appropriation from the federal government to feed our needy and house our homeless. This is a major emergency."

Other governors echoed Farrow's view.

In the eight-state region, more than 3,000 families totaling about 10,000 persons have been evacuated from flooded communities. Many police have been serving double shifts throughout the area to prevent looting.

Flood waters were reported to have reached a depth of six feet in some of the southern-most states. The worst floods were along the Missouri River. Along smaller waterways, dams were washed away, spring crops were inundated, foundations of buildings were undermined, and sandbag barricades were pushed aside.

The National Weather Service issued the forecasts of more rain in many sections of the Midwest. Some regions have now had rain for 21 straight days with no relief in sight, the NWS said. . . .

Snow and freezing cold in the winter and periods of sustained heat in the summer also are usual subjects for weather roundups of this kind at both the local and regional levels. It seldom happens that a weather emergency embraces the entire country, however, although an earthquake or a volcano eruption can create a great deal more national interest than a crisis attributed to the weather.

For the broadcast media, particularly television, the picture story is even more important than the factual details. It is impressive to note how quickly, in a flood story, for example, television camera people can come up with spectacular film showing families coping with the crisis. Very often, it tells the viewer more about the feelings of the victims than the best-reported news stories.

There is one factor in broadcast coverage, however, that verges on unprofessional conduct. That is the very recent tendency of forecasters to apologize to a viewing or listening audience for having to report bad news in the form of an oncoming storm, cold spell, or other unpleasantness. Even unfavorable weather predictions, in a few cases, seem to create such a mood among the electronic experts.

It's a silly business and ought to be dropped. Surely, forecasters and reporters are not responsible for the weather or the damage it causes from time to time. If daily newspapers descended to that kind of nonsense, there would be no end to the apologies that might be called for on the theory that the public doesn't like bad news. Broadcast people, by and large, aren't amateurs and shouldn't act like amateurs. It is part of their job to give the news accurately, thoroughly, and objectively. If apologies are to be made, they should be restricted to errors in professional work—and even that is questionable procedure except when it becomes necessary in the course of a legal action.

We may someday attain perfection in predicting the weather for the next twenty-four hours, let alone the next five days, but that time still seems distant. Meanwhile, as journalists, our job is to cover the news, not to apologize for doing it.

11

Writing in Short Takes

Accidents, parades, shorts, and second-day angles . . .
Fires, bankruptcies, cops and robbers . . .
Strikes, handouts, funerals, and speeches . . .
All these and more are part of the routine of writing specialists in daily journalism. The work is called "rewrite" on newspapers and wire services, a misnomer if ever there was one. Much of it is done under pressure, often on deadline, and it comes across the VDTs on the rewrite bank in short takes.

Usually, that could be as little as a paragraph at a time.

Developing a Story on Rewrite

The principal function of staffers assigned to rewrite is to produce terse, well-written news accounts from notes telephoned by reporters. The information from the field has to be transmitted quickly. The judgments on how it should be handled nearly always must be made by the writer.

There seldom is time for a conference with the city desk on what to lead with, what quotes to use, how long or short the piece should be, and other details. If writers don't know the answers or are afraid to use their own judgment, they won't last long.

Should they make a mistake, they'll hear about it soon enough. And if they do good work, they needn't expect a Pulitzer Prize. Writing of this type is generally a team effort and teams get the credit, if any.

The newcomer to rewrite, therefore, had best forget about the plays and movies that depict editors as clowns, reporters as dolts, and writers as maniacs who shout insults at all concerned. Under such circumstances, it would be impossible to move anything to the wire, let alone get out a newspaper or a newscast.

Certainly, there is a place for entertainment in daily journalism. But handling the news is not a process that can be played for laughs. As a rule, the greater the pressure on writers producing major news accounts, the quieter they are. Through experience, the most adaptable among them have learned how to keep their nerves under control. In few words, they have the confidence that comes mainly from practicing their profession under trying conditions.

Watch someone on rewrite when a lead is returned for rephrasing or a paragraph's meaning is questioned. There is no tension, no anger, no back-and-forth with the editor in charge. The well-trained writer in journalism, often without even a word of comment, understands what is wanted and quickly makes the necessary changes in copy, then picks up the story at the point of interruption.

If there are objections to any particulars of editorial direction, these are handled in a quiet discussion once all copy has cleared for the deadline. Changes still can be made in type for a limited time, one advantage that the print media have over broadcasters, for whom words are written on the wind.

Earlier in this century, when the rewrite bank in most places was exclusively male, it was argued that women on rewrite would give way to hysterics. However, during World War II, women took over that function along with almost everything else having to do with news production in a great many places. And wonder of wonders, there were no hysterics even in a dominant news center like New York City.

No sensible editor worries very much today about having women on the rewrite bank. Some of them adapt to the daily pressure cooker quicker than men, showing coolness and great self-control as they turn out well-written copy in short takes on deadline.

Working Conditions for Writers

The newsroom at the *Central City Leader* is fairly typical in its arrangement of desks for editors, writers, and reporters. It is no old-time rathole with filthy floors, battered desks, and pictures of naked women on the walls—Hollywood's idea of what a newspaper editorial department is like. The place is large, carpeted, and neatly arranged with rows of desks topped by VDTs for reporters over two-thirds of the space. It is light and airy, for few journalists smoke today. And those who do usually are old-timers.

The front third of the newsroom at the *Leader* is for its editors, the "brains department," as the reporters tab them. Directly in front of the reporters' desks is a cluster of larger ones arranged in a square. At one desk facing the reporters is the city editor, Joe Stoddard; across from him, at another desk, is his news assistant. On either side of them, a row of three desks is topped with VDTs, typical of the rewrite bank. Telephones, schedules, local copy, and wire copy are in evidence everywhere, but there seems to be no more excitement—much less noise—than there would be in any other large office. Only the teleprinters in the wire room can be clearly heard.

The principal movement appears to be between the city desk–rewrite bank arrangement and the news desks at the head of the room. There, the managing editor and the news editor preside over the arrangement of the edition and direct the work of the copy desk at one side, where the headlines are written on edited copy. In alcoves and wings are the departmental editors and staffs—features, sports, women's, financial, and the like.

There seems neither rhyme nor reason to the arrangement. And yet, it seems to work without difficulty. The *Leader*, after all, is a successful paper and does well in the afternoon and evening field despite the competition of the electronic media, the weeklies, and the myriad of neighborhood throwaway publications, the so-called free circulation newspapers.

It should not be imagined that there is something for the rewrite bank to do every minute. Between editions, the pace slows noticeably. There is time to get up and stretch, walk around, get coffee or a hamburger in the cafeteria, scan the morning paper opposition, or just sit and talk to a neighbor or stare out the window. But when a reporter calls in with a story and the city desk makes an assignment on the rewrite bank, it's time to go to work.

That is when the headphones go on the writer who is assigned and the note taking begins. Customarily, the writer does not interrupt the reporter but saves all questions until the latter signals that he is finished. Then, quickly, the reporter answers a few questions, the writer composes the story on the VDT, and the city, copy, and news desks do the rest. There is no chitchat, no fooling around. Hour after hour, except for breaks during the working day, this is how the rewrite bank does business. It is all very much in the style of a well-trained group of sprinters practicing quick starts. Only, the writers keep on going.

Starting Out on the Rewrite Bank

Mack Roberts shows up on the rewrite bank at 7:00 one morning after he has been on the paper for about six months. His shift is 7:00 A.M. to 3:00 P.M., since he is a replacement for a regular on that trick who is out sick. (Other shifts, aside from the graveyard trick, midnight to 7:00 A.M., are 8:00 A.M. to 4 P.M. and the bankers' hours, 9:00 A.M. to 5:00 P.M.)

Nobody pays much attention to Mack as he settles down at a VDT facing the city desk and glances through the A.M. paper, the *Central City News*. He is enough of a pro now to have brought his black coffee with him in a plastic container from the cafeteria, as he takes his seat next to Chuck Arnow.

Roberts handles his first piece within a few minutes, a routine auto accident from a reporter at Police Headquarters. It's the usual early morning short which the reporter summarizes: "Got one killed, two hurt in auto crash. Here are the names. . . ." As Roberts takes the notes, he has no doubt about how to handle that one. This is how it comes out of his VDT:

AUTO

A small automobile and a city-owned garbage truck collided early today at Main Street and Sixth Avenue, killing the driver of the car and injuring his two passengers.

The dead man was Vernon Arzibashev, 26, of 1111 Mayhew Drive. The injured were Vicki Greenlaw, 19, of 826 Compton Street, and her older sister, Wilella, 27. Police said they had come from a party at the Grimshaw Hotel on Main Street. The driver of the truck, Vincent Albelli, 46, of 4815 Allenby Avenue, was unhurt. . . .

Without being asked to do so, Arnow has been watching the work in progress and now quietly advises the newcomer, "Okay, you made sure not to blame one or the other in the lead but you'd better add a sentence about the sisters' injuries if they were taken to a hospital."

"I didn't want it to run long," Roberts says. "It's just a short, isn't it?"

"Yes, but it has to be complete," is the response.

Roberts follows the older man's advice.

Now comes a clip from the morning paper, an obit, which is to be rewritten from a half-column to no more than seventy or eighty words—Roberts's second assignment from the city desk. He starts batting out the story on his VDT but feels a slight pressure on his arm. When he stops and turns, he sees Arnow does not approve.

"How d'ya know the *News*'s obit is okay?" Arnow asks, then suggests, "Better call the undertaker and check on the time and place for the funeral to begin with. You'll need that for the story."

Roberts checks the few facts he needs for his short rewrite, then begins with the death of the subject of the obit, a former city treasurer. Once again, there is an interruption and Arnow murmurs, "No, use a second-day angle. He died for the morning paper, so we lead with the next step, the funeral. Always update a clip or overnight wire copy if you can."

Again, Roberts is grateful and this time he writes:

JOSLYN—OBIT

Funeral services for Wilbert E. Joslyn, a former city treasurer, will be held tomorrow at 8:00 P.M. from the Valleau Funeral Home, 2218 Main Street. Mr. Joslyn died last night at All Saints Hospital after a long illness. He was 66.

Mr. Joslyn is survived by Mrs. Amanda Harrow Joslyn, to whom he was married for 41 years, and their son, Wilbert Jr., 38, a member of the Central City police force.

The two shorts go through the city desk without comment, which builds Roberts's confidence. In succession, he handles other small pieces dealing with a two-alarm fire in which no one was hurt, a $420 predawn holdup of a pedestrian, the settlement of a strike of laundry drivers, and a short advance on a speech to be given later in the day by a city councilman. Nothing very sensational, but all of it carefully and thoroughly handled with Arnow looking on in approval.

Organizing a Major Newsbreak on Rewrite

By the time Roberts takes off at noon for his thirty-minute lunch period in the cafeteria, he is reasonably sure that he'll be able to handle anything that comes his way. But the moment he returns, he is pitched into the middle of a developing story that is far beyond anything he has worked on so far at the *Leader*.

Arnow, who has been taking notes over the phone, pauses briefly to warn his young neighbor, "Better get set. The boss wants you to write B copy for me on Willard Getchell."

Roberts doesn't have the faintest idea of who Getchell is and how to prepare B copy. He learns soon enough that Getchell, the president of the Second National Bank in Central City, has been indicted by a federal grand jury on fraud charges and the bank itself has filed a bankruptcy petition.

"Looks like Getchell may have gotten away with eight or nine million bucks before they caught up with him," Arnow says.

But as to the B copy, Roberts still wonders. Arnow explains that the story is still developing, the lead can't be written yet but that the chronology of the alleged crime can be put together and so can Getchell's background.

"It's like writing a story backward," the older man explains. "Your B copy will be a bio of Getchell, who he is, how he got into the banking business, and so on. It would be the very end of the story, so you'd start in a way that would fit with the A copy, which goes on top of it. I'll be writing the A copy mainly about the indictment and the various charges against Getchell. We expect he'll be arrested before the two o'clock edition deadline so that's going to be our lead."

It begins to make sense to Roberts—Lead Bank, A Copy Bank, B Copy Bank is the way the piece will be assembled for the edition. He sends for the Getchell clips and soon begins his part of the assignment:

B COPY BANK

Getchell, a major figure in the financial and social life of Central City, often said in jest that he was "born on the wrong side of the tracks." He liked to recall that he maintained a four-point grade average at State U while working his way through four years there as a Business major by tutoring fellow-students.

Upon his graduation when he was only 21, he joined the Second National Bank as a clerk and quickly rose through the ranks to become, successively, the secretary of the bank corporation, a vice-president and, when he was 46, the bank's president and chief executive officer.

Getchell was known to be a generous contributor to the political campaigns of both Governor Farrow and Mayor Reardon of Central City. The banker was a delegate to three Republican state conventions and was slated this year to be a member of the state's delegation to the Republican National Convention.

His wife, the former Mazie Calder, to whom he was married 21 years ago, brought him social prestige as well. A member of the socially prominent Calder family, Mrs. Getchell maintained a lifelong interest in the cultural life of the city.

During the past two years, the Getchells were credited with having arranged for the week-long schedule of performances here by a touring company of the Metropolitan Opera of New York City. They also were understood to have revived the long-dormant Central City Symphony Orchestra under a new conductor, Rafael Santos Cardena.

The Getchells have two teen-age children, Sophia and Mortimer, and maintain a winter home in Florida and a summer home in Maine in addition to the Getchell mansion on Cordelier Drive here. . . .

While Roberts is putting this background piece together, Arnow is writing the story of the indictment from the notes he has taken over the telephone from a *Leader* reporter. Arnow's story begins like this:

A COPY BANK

The substance of the indictment, as announced at federal court here following the grand jury action, was that Getchell allegedly had withdrawn assets of the bank for his own use over a period of several years.

For this reason, the indictment charged, the Second National Bank was unable to meet its commitments and had to file a petition for bankruptcy. However, federal officials pointed out, the bank is covered by the Federal Deposit and Insurance Corp., so that depositors will not lose any money.

Raymond Foraker, the U.S. attorney for this district, refused to specify the total amount that Getchell is accused of stealing, but other sources said it might be in the range of $8 to $9 million. Asked what the banker is accused of doing with the money, one official threw up his hands and said:

"Lord only knows. He just wanted to play the big shot, one of the witnesses said."

The grand jury began hearing testimony in the case ten days ago upon action by the U.S. Securities and Exchange Commission to inquire into the solvency of the Second National Bank. The SEC's investigation did not become publicly known until after today's indictment was returned. . . .

With the A copy and B copy complete, the city, copy, and news desks were in good shape for the edition no matter what happened. At 1:40 P.M., twenty minutes before the edition deadline, Ken Belden, a reporter for the business section, called the city desk to say that the warrant for Getchell's arrest had been issued but still hadn't been served because a U.S. marshal couldn't locate him.

While Roberts took notes from the reporter by telephone, Arnow began his lead as follows:

LEAD BANK

A warrant for the arrest of Willard Getchell, president and chief executive officer of the Second National Bank, was issued today after he was indicted by a federal grand jury on fraud charges.

The indictment was returned as the bank filed for bankruptcy.

Getchell, 57, could not be immediately located by the U.S. marshal bearing the arrest warrant.

END LEAD BANK PIKUP A COPY, THEN B COPY

There were a few other details in Roberts's notes from Belden that were written into the A copy as inserts, but the suspect remained at large. The news, by that time, had been broadcast and televised, so depositors began forming in long lines outside the bank to try to get their money. The doors of the bank, however, remained closed. And that, too, was written into the A copy.

Just two minutes before deadline, Belden phoned again to say that the U.S. marshal, Alton Digby, had located Getchell at the offices of his lawyer, Thomas R. Jakobsen, served the arrest warrant, and delivered his prisoner to the Federal Building where the banker was expected to be released in bail.

There was just time to make the edition and this is what Arnow wrote:

NEW LEAD BANK [subs for LEAD BANK]

Willard Getchell, president and chief executive officer of the Second National Bank, was arrested today on a federal indictment charging fraud.

The indictment was returned after the bank had filed for bankruptcy and closed its doors.

Getchell, 57, was arrested by Alton Digby, a U.S. marshal, at the offices of the banker's lawyer, Thomas R. Jakobsen, and brought to the Federal Building. It was expected that he would be released after bail had been set and posted.

END NEW LEAD BANK, PIKUP A COPY, THEN B COPY

Roberts, having watched Arnow handle both leads and the A copy plus inserts, was relieved that his own role had been reduced to note taking once he had finished the B copy. And yet, even by watching a professional in action on the rewrite bank, the newcomer had learned at least one valuable lesson. That was the all-important matter of attitude and poise. Despite all the pressure and uncertainty that the bank story had generated, the rewrite man had functioned calmly and his copy had been clean, clear, and swiftly written on his VDT.

This is the way some of the best writing in journalism is done. Beginners can't hope to adapt themselves to it overnight. It does take time, experience, and, above all, self-control.

PART II
WRITING IN THE PUBLIC INTEREST

12

On Guard!

IT ALWAYS COMES AS A SHOCK to beginners in journalism that they face some very nasty types of punishment if they mess up in a tight spot. That spot, more often than not, is called "libel."

The Law Can Be Very Tough

What is libel? A good example is to be wrong about calling somebody a crook in print or to read the same thing from a script on the air—and then to be nasty about it as well. What is the punishment? For your news organization, the costs of libel judgments are rising into the stratosphere these days. Necessarily, those who cause them aren't going to be very popular and may expect to find themselves out in the cold sooner rather than later.

Let's be explicit about this:

As long as you are right and can prove you are right, journalism can be most rewarding—and that is particularly true in the field covered by the public interest. But if you are wrong and have no legal defense, watch out! You could be in big trouble.

Here's why:

Although libel law differs from state to state, all state laws agree that there is no such thing as an innocent mistake. In libel, you can't laugh it off and say, "So sorry, pal. Didn't mean it." So you'd better not be bored about learning what you can and cannot do under the law.

The legal definitions of libel come down to this:

Libel is defamatory writing that is published with malicious intent and causes harm to any person, group, or corporation. That also applies to broadcasters who read from a script or use notes. Oral defamation is called "slander."

In civil libel cases, which are most frequent, it often isn't necessary to prove monetary loss. To make things even tougher for defendants, the courts frequently construe malice as negligence, a bad feeling about the person who is libeled, or, in extreme instances, what the law calls a "reckless disregard of the truth." The latter means, in brief, that you knew better than to write or say what you did.

There is another category of libel, known as criminal libel, a crime against the state, for which punishment could be a fine and a prison term for offenders. But such cases are comparatively rare.

Civil libel is hard enough to handle. The number of lawsuits that are filed increase each year and so do the size of the judgments, which now average about $2 million for every jury that returns a guilty verdict.*

Defenses Against Libel Suits

All this is bound to be frightening to newcomers who had the notion that you could get away with almost anything in journalism if you talked loud and fast, looked hard-boiled, and wore your hat on the back of your head. It so happens that there are legitimate defenses, but playing the tough guy or gal isn't one of them.

Defense no. 1 is *provable* truth. To elaborate, it isn't enough for you to know that you wrote or broadcast the truth. If challenged, you must be able to produce the facts that would convince a jury of the truth as you see it.

Defense no. 2 is *privilege*, a legal term. It means that what you wrote is a *fair and true account* of court proceedings or other public records such as formal government, congressional, legislative, or municipal documents.

These two are considered by lawyers to be *absolute defenses*. However, the reporting and writing involved must be demonstrably fair and show absolutely no trace of malice.

*The estimate of Henry Kaufman, attorney, the Libel Defense Resource Center of New York.

There is a third defense that most authorities believe to be absolute, but relatively few beginners are advised to rely on it. It is *the right of fair comment.* It protects the right to criticize the public actions and procedures of public figures in print or on the air, public figures being politicians, entertainers, sports performers, and others in the public eye. The problem here is that the writer must not stray from purely professional comment on a professional performance to reflect on a person's private life or habits with malicious intent.

It's a very fine line and newcomers to journalism are well advised to leave that kind of writing to editorialists, columnists, commentators, analysts, and others in journalism who know what they can and cannot do without undue risk.

The best policy for a beginner to adopt is to be scrupulously fair in anything that is written for publication or prepared for broadcast. And it always helps to double-check the facts for accuracy, as well as to make sure that accurate copies of public records are being used.

Where there is no absolute defense against the threat of a libel suit, one way to try to avoid going to court is for the news organization to issue a public apology. However, most litigants today go for the big cash awards and aren't deterred by fine words. At any rate, if the apology isn't acceptable, then the next best thing is to fall back on partial defenses against libel.

These are what lawyers call possibilities for reducing the amount that a jury is likely to award to a plaintiff. All too often, these "possibilities" aren't very effective, but they're better than no defense at all.

Some Partial Defenses

Defense lawyers in libel cases are eternally hopeful. Almost immediately, when summoned to consultation, they will ask whether the person who is suing might have consented to read and approve in advance whatever was written or quoted about him from a script. I've never heard of a libel suit being called off for that reason; nevertheless, if it ever happened, it would be a defense.

Then, there's a theory that defamatory material may sometimes be used by a news organization in self-defense but, once again, the odds are against its effectiveness. Another possibility lawyers always pursue is the statute of limitations—that is, whether the plaintiff's suit was filed too long after the alleged libel had been committed.

(In most states, the statute of limitations is two years.) But once again, someone bent on suing is going to be prompt about getting the case before the courts, so the statute of limitations is a very weak reed.

There are a few other partial defenses including:

—The plaintiff is a person of bad character. This one is based on a belief in many newsrooms, still all too prevalent, that a known gangster may be "libelproof." In few words, that he is a person of poor repute. The only trouble with that is the necessity of demonstrating that there is absolutely no good in someone with a criminal record and hoping a jury will believe it.

—The libel occurred during the heat of a political campaign. But any jury will ask the common-sense question when deliberations begin, "Isn't a journalist trained to be impartial in the news columns? Should a journalist be thrown off base by writing during the heat of a political campaign?" As a partial defense, this one seems lamentably weak.

—The identity of the plaintiff was confused with the identity of someone else who happened to be a suspect in a crime and ultimately was arrested. Once again, the trouble here is that journalists should not make such mistakes and juries aren't likely to take such a partial defense very seriously.

—The article or broadcast was carefully qualified as to source and language. This means, for example, that a report of a crime was attributed to the police, that the plaintiff was described as a suspect, an alleged thief, or an accused person and not a criminal and that therefore this showed evidence of fairness. It's always a good try but it seldom reduces the amount of damages if a jury is convinced that a libel has been committed.

What it all comes down to is the vulnerability of news organizations to libel suits in the public atmosphere that exists in these times. A managing editor, Bill Wills of the *Bloomington Pantagraph* in Illinois, expresses the general feeling of journalists:

"Mere mention of calling an attorney makes me see dollar bills flying out the window. The thought of a newsperson interpreting the law makes me shiver even more.

"If we convince newsroom employees to be as sensitive to people we write about as we are to unkind remarks about our products, we will lessen the need for legal intervention."*

Wills had reason for his feelings. Another Illinois newspaper that

*Bulletin of the American Society of Newspaper Editors, September 1985, p. 12.

only had about thirty-thousand daily circulation, the *Alton Telegraph*, is reputed to have rolled up a $600,000 bill for defense costs and still lost a $1.5 million libel suit.*

Changes in the Libel Law

There was great jubilation among journalists in 1964 when the U.S. Supreme Court, under Chief Justice Earl Warren, formulated the liberal *New York Times* Rule, so called, as a landmark decision in the determination of libel. In that case, the high court reversed a lower court decision granting a $500,000 libel judgment to L. B. Sullivan, a police official in Montgomery, Alabama, against the *New York Times*. Sullivan had sued when the *Times* published an advertisement, in which, he charged, a civil rights group had defamed him. However, the high court held, a public official should not recover damages for a "defamatory falsehood" unless he (or she) proves "actual malice, that is, with knowledge that it [the statement] was false or with reckless disregard of whether it was false or not."

Seven years later, in *Rosenbloom* v. *Metromedia*, the high court broadened its finding about public officials in libel cases to include still another category, called "public figures." This was defined as "a private individual [involved] in a public event of general concern." Thus, the high court reversed a $750,000 judgment against Metromedia station WIP because the plaintiff, a nudist magazine distributor, had failed to prove "actual malice."

But from then on, other high court decisions nibbled away at the *New York Times* Rule and its extensions. In 1974, under Chief Justice Warren Burger, the court upheld a $50,000 award for Elmer Gertz, a lawyer, without proof of malice. The suit was against Robert Welch, Inc., publisher of a John Birch Society tract. In that case, the high court said it was enough for a "public figure" to show some degree of "fault," which was construed as negligence.

That was further watered down two years later in *Time Inc.* v. *Mary Alice Firestone*. Mrs. Firestone's $100,000 libel judgment against the magazine was upheld on the ground that she was a "private individual" and not a "public figure" so she, too, had to show only "fault."

The confusion between who could and could not be called a

---

*"The American Lawyer," in *The Cost of Libel*, Steven Brill, editor: Gannett, Center for Media Studies at Columbia University (1986), p. 11.

a libel verdict in favor of Ilya Wolston against *Reader's Digest* on the ground that Wolston was not a "public figure" and merely had to prove "fault," not malice.

Another 1979 case, *Herbert* v. *Lando,* which involved the question of malice, caused the high court to permit examination of a defendant's "state of mind." In effect, that meant reporters' notes, editors' memos, and records of staff meetings all could be examined by a plaintiff who sought to prove malice.

One of the unlooked-for results was a movement, covert at first but increasingly sustained, in which reporters and editors were told to destroy their notes of stories that would involve libel. This had nothing to do with *Herbert* v. *Lando,* which dragged on through the courts for years, but it appeared to cautious news executives to be a protective action that was long overdue.

The situation became so prevalent, in fact, that it figured in a 1985 conference of a committee of the American Society of Newspaper Editors (ASNE) at the College of William and Mary in Williamsburg, Virginia. As a part of what was called "damage control," at least two speakers recommended the destruction of "all nonessential notes, early versions of sensitive news articles, and even unpublished or unused photographic negatives."

Richard M. Schmidt, Jr., a lawyer for the ASNE, further cautioned that it wouldn't do merely to destroy evidence relating to articles that could figure in a libel action. To avoid charges of obstruction of justice in the event of a lawsuit, the lawyer explained, news organizations would have to establish a policy of routinely destroying notes and photos on *all* news.*

Libel Suits Are Big Business

What it all comes down to is that many libel suits turn out to be big business. General William C. Westmoreland, the American commander in the Vietnam War, sued CBS for $120 million over a 1982 documentary alleging that he had conspired to mislead the American public. However, after a five-month trial, the general dropped the case when CBS issued a statement saying that there had been no intention to reflect on his patriotism. Both sides reportedly spent a $6 million total on the case.

Another suit of major importance, that of a former Israeli defense

*James M. Ragsdale in the *Bulletin of the American Society of Newspaper Editors,* September 1985, pp. 23–24.

minister, Ariel Sharon, against Time Inc., also attracted wide attention because of the sums involved. However, in this case as in that of Westmoreland against CBS, the plaintiff did not collect. The jury returned a verdict that Sharon had *not* been libeled because *Time,* while having published an inaccurate story about him, did not do so out of malice. In this case, too, the legal costs to both sides were reputed to be heavy but the outcome did not seem to discourage other plaintiffs from seeking relief through the courts.

The point about both cases—Westmoreland and Sharon—is that they involved juries' interpretations of the Supreme Court's *New York Times* Rule. While the matter has been widely discussed both by lawyers and journalists, the only hint that it also was disturbing to members of the Supreme Court came by indirection from Associate Justice William J. Brennan, Jr., as he began his thirtieth year as a member of the high court.

He disclosed in an interview that two members of the court in 1964, when the *New York Times* Rule was adopted, Justices William O. Douglas and Hugo L. Black, had argued that the decision in the Sullivan case "did not go far enough." However, they were in the minority. Going beyond that case to the First Amendment area in general, Brennan's comment also shed some light on the court's divisions.

"Black's and Douglas's position," he said, "was that when the Constitution directs that Congress shall make 'no law' abridging freedom of speech, that means *no* law, and this was something that neither the Chief [Earl Warren] nor I could accept. In our view, there were limits."*

---

*Justice Brennan's views are in "A Life on the Court," an authorized interview with Jeffrey T. Leeds, the *New York Times Magazine,* October 5, 1986, pp. 75–76.

13

Journalists and Their Sources

THERE IS A PERSISTENT BELIEF among most American journalists that the First Amendment gives them the right to protect their confidential sources. The trouble with the theory is that neither the federal government nor the courts agree with it. As a result, these opposing positions are the basis of what amounts to an unending conflict.

The Journalists' Argument

Daniel Schorr, now with National Public Radio, gave the classic definition of the journalists' position while he was working for CBS in 1976. He had been ordered by a congressional committee to disclose the source of an intelligence report he had used. Initially, he invoked the free speech and free press provisions of the First Amendment, then explained to those who were threatening to hold him in contempt of Congress: "To betray a source would be to betray myself, my career, my life. I cannot do it. To say I refuse to do it is not saying it right. I cannot do it."

Schorr's passionate defense of what he believed to be his rights carried the day. He wasn't forced to betray either his source or himself.

Others, however, haven't been as lucky.

The Supreme Court in 1972 decided, in *Branzburg* v. *Hayes*, that journalists couldn't invoke the First Amendment to justify their refusal to disclose confidential sources. Accordingly, contempt citations were issued against Paul Branzburg of the *Louisville Courier-Journal,* Paul Pappas of Station WTEV, and Earl Caldwell of the *New York Times.*

Four years later, on the basis of the Branzburg decision, the high court refused to free four reporters for the *Fresno (California) Bee* who had served fifteen days in jail rather than disclose a confidential source in a bribery case. The court also failed to act on an appeal by William T. Farr of the *Los Angeles Herald Examiner,* another reporter who was jailed because he would not name a confidential source in a murder case.

The worst punishment was given to Myron Farber of the *New York Times* in 1978. He served forty days in jail and his paper was fined $285,000 when he refused to yield confidential files in another murder case. The governor of New Jersey, in which the incident occurred, pardoned both Farber and his paper but that didn't cancel out the forty days behind bars for the reporter.

Since then, various devices have been tried to resolve the argument between the journalists and the courts, but none settled the issue of confidentiality. The so-called shield laws adopted by a number of states were supposed to protect reporters and their sources, but the statutes were far from perfect. A second method, the drafting of voluntary "press-bar guidelines," was even weaker than the "shield laws," although both still are in operation in some states.

The upshot is that journalists and their news organizations take their chances in any tangle with the law over the disclosure of confidential sources. But both are very far from giving up the fight as a matter of principle.

The Issue of National Security

The right of journalists to protect their confidential sources also has become an issue in alleged breaches of national security. In response to a Reagan administration order in 1986 to the Federal Bureau of Investigation to uncover the source of any published or broadcast material that violates national security, the community of journalists remained defiant.

That, of course, didn't stop the federal government. One of the principal movers in this campaign was William J. Casey, then di-

rector of the Central Intelligence Agency. And one of his main opponents turned out to be the same Daniel Schorr who successfully
defended his right to confidentiality before a congressional committee. In a scathing article, Schorr wrote:

"Britain, with no First Amendment, has an Official Secrets Act,
empowering the Government to ban information on national security
grounds. In the United States, despite the First Amendment, the
Reagan administration in recent months appears to have laid the
foundation for an Unofficial Secrets Act."*

Schorr went on to compare the British "D Notice"—D for Defense—with what he called a "C Notice"—C for Casey. In the British
procedure, a "D Notice" is circulated to the news media by the
Ministry of Defense warning that certain confidential materials must
not be disclosed. What evidently was meant by the "C Notice" was
Director Casey's procedure of telephoning editors and others that
they'd better beware of using certain specific data—known in advance to Casey—because it would constitute a violation of national
security.

One story that Casey was able to pare down was a proposed
Washington Post piece about a secret device that a former National
Security Agency worker was convicted of selling to the Soviet Union.
The version that appeared, finally, omitted a key bit of information.

The government's legal offensive against what it called national
security "leaks" included the use of the Espionage Act of 1947,
under which a conviction was obtained in 1985, and the Communications Intelligence Act of 1950 plus new anti-espionage legislation proposed before Congress.

All that, however, did not deter Seymour M. Hersh, a Pulitzer
Prize–winning reporter who disclosed the My Lai massacre during
the Vietnam War, from publishing a book about another sensitive
matter—the Soviet's destruction of Korean Air Lines flight 007 on
September 1, 1983 with the loss of 269 lives. The Soviet regime
had alleged that the airliner was on a CIA spy mission. However,
President Reagan charged the attack by a Soviet fighter plane was
cold-blooded murder.

During Hersh's research, the Russians tried to influence him, he
said, and Casey called him with a threat of prosecution if he disclosed classified information. "It got me very angry," the reporter
said later. "I guarantee you that we in the press have as good a
sense of what's important and what's good for America as the people
in the CIA."

*"The Administration's Unofficial Secrets Act," by Daniel Schorr, *New York Times*,
August 3, 1986, p. 23. Director Casey died in 1987.

As matters turned out, Hersh concluded in his book that the Korean pilot had really strayed over Soviet territory because he had lost his bearings and that the Russians had miscalculated in destroying the plane.*

The Flap over "Disinformation"

The biggest flap between government and the news media in recent years occurred when the *Washington Post* published a proposal attributed to a national security adviser, Vice Admiral John Poindexter, for a program of "disinformation."

The story was obtained by Bob Woodward who, with Carl Bernstein, broke the Watergate scandal that led to the resignation of President Nixon.

The Poindexter memo was aimed at the Libyan dictator, Muammar el Khadafi, against whom the United States had launched bombing raids on April 15, 1986. As circulated by the State Department on August 6 of that year, the memo suggested creating "real and illusory events" through the news media to try to wage psychological warfare against Khadafi.

One immediate result was the publication of a *Wall Street Journal* report on August 25 that the United States was ready to move again to punish Libya. Other papers and some of the networks fell for the same "disinformation" and later regretted it when they found the threat was a nonevent and "illusory."

With the publication of the Woodward piece, the storm broke. Although President Reagan denied that it was his policy to deceive the news media, the flap continued. The *New York Times* ran an indignant editorial, "Lies Wound America, Not Libya." Commentator John Chancellor reported on NBC-TV that "disinformation" was a term invented by the Russian KGB—*dezinformatsiya*—which had now been picked up by our own government. But the most severe blow, despite President Reagan's denials that anybody in his administration was lying, came with the resignation of Bernard Kalb, the chief State Department spokesman.**

Kalb attributed his act to a "crisis of conscience" and explained,

*Reporter Seymour Hersh Unravels the Tragic Mystery of Flight 007," *People* magazine, October 6, 1986, pp. 57–58.

**The *Washington Post* broke the Poindexter memo October 2, 1986; next day, the President denied anybody in his regime was lying. The *Times*'s editorial was published October 3, 1986; Chancellor's broadcast was on October 4. Kalb resigned October 8. The quotations herewith are from his remarks on network TV—NBC, CBS, and ABC all carried his remarks—and from the *Times* of October 9.

"Around a question of credibility, you face a choice—as an American, as a spokesman, as a journalist—whether to allow oneself to be absorbed in the ranks of silence, whether to vanish into unopposed acquiescence, or to enter a modest dissent. . . . Anything that hurts America's credibility hurts America."

There was an outpouring of comment on Kalb's act, which was widely criticized within the government because it came on the eve of a Reagan-Gorbachev summit meeting in Iceland. However, he also had defenders. William Safire took a strong position in the *New York Times* in his favor and against Secretary of State George Shultz. "Secretary Shultz," Safire wrote, "does not see that his willingness to jettison credibility has become a low point in his stewardship at State. Perhaps the Kalb resignation will awaken him. . . ."*

The Beginners' Role

What does all this trouble about journalists and their sources have to do with beginners in the field?

First of all, to some extent, a course taken by the federal government tends to influence governments at other levels—state, county, and local—in their dealings with the news media. Some governors, mayors, and others in public life also have been known to play games with reporters.

But even more important, beginners cannot assume that they will be spared the devious treatment that becomes the lot of their more experienced professional colleagues on occasion. After all, when Woodward and Bernstein broke the Watergate story, they, too, were mere beginners on the *Washington Post*. Still, they asked for no favors from the federal government and received none.

Remember: Watch Your Language

There is another aspect of the law that can affect journalists if they are careless about their language. That is the statute dealing with obscenity.

In *Miller* v. *California*, a 1973 case, the Supreme Court made these points about the obscenity law:

*Safire's comments were in the *New York Times*, October 9, 1986, p. A-35.

—The use of obscenity cannot be defended under the First Amendment.

—A picture, publication, or broadcast is obscene if it appeals to lustful interests or desires, is without any redeeming social or literary value, and *exceeds community standards* in such matters.

The key part of the decision was the definition of *community standards* as the guide which, the high court ruled, would consist of the opinions of a reasonable member of a community about a picture, newspaper, broadcast, magazine, or book.

Well, the beginner will ask wistfully, what community?

The honorable justices left that to the imagination. For example, it was obvious that the concept of obscenity on Broadway, in New York City, was not intended to be imposed on Chehalis, Washington.

As journalistic practice has developed since *Miller* v. *California,* the news media are extremely sensitive to the use of words generally associated with obscenity or vulgarity. The rule here is: "When in doubt, leave out." However, as most newcomers to journalism are well aware, today's journalistic standards are relatively liberal in the description of sex cases.

The courts, moreover, do not seem to have interfered seriously with the growth of magazines that specialize in lurid treatment of sex nor of films of a similar nature that are intended primarily for home use. The press and the broadcast media, however, are still wary of being explicit about sexual matters.

The exceptions seem to be gross misconduct on the part of elected or appointed public officials. Journalists who disclose that a congressman is supporting his mistress at the public's expense, for example, may expect a commendation rather than punishment if past experience is any guide. And those who reveal alcoholic excesses by public officials, similarly are unlikely to be in trouble with the law.*

Such precedents, however, do not mean that it is open season on officeholders who exceed what is broadly construed as normal conduct. In general, most publications take the position that officials' private lives ought not to figure in the news unless they interfere with their official duties. The Associated Press, for example, asks staffers dealing with sex cases to be sure "that the activity impairs or conflicts with a public official's public responsibility," otherwise not to use the story.

*These precedents occurred during the publicity surrounding the disclosure of congressional sex scandals.

Invasion of Privacy

The courts also have served notice that journalists cannot invade private homes or offices, causing injury to people's feelings or peace of mind; nor can journalists, for that matter, portray people "in a false light through knowing or reckless untruth." If they do, the courts have held, that constitutes an invasion of privacy and is actionable.

A key case was the Supreme Court's 1974 decision in *Cantrell* v. *Cleveland Plain Dealer.* Margaret Mae Cantrell, whose husband had died in an accident, charged that a reporter for the paper had entered her home while she was out, then written a piece that indicated he had interviewed her and found her and her children impoverished. That, the court held, was "malicious." It also portrayed Mrs. Cantrell "in a false light through knowing or reckless untruth," and the paper consequently was ordered to pay her $60,000.

In general, therefore, to quote from a U.S. Appeals Court ruling in another case, "The First Amendment has never been construed to accord newsmen immunity from [civil wrongs] or crimes committed during the course of newsgathering."

To illustrate, two reporters for *Life* magazine cost their publication $1,000 because they tried to show that a suspect was practicing medicine without a license. While they proved their charge because one of them posed as a patient and another carried a hidden camera to take pictures of the "doctor," they lost the case because—so the Appeals Court ruled—they had injured their target's "feelings and peace of mind."

Briefly stated, therefore, in the words of an article co-authored by Associate Justice Louis D. Brandeis of the Supreme Court, privacy means a citizen's "right to be left alone" and it is bound to be upheld in the courts.*

Journalists and Public Relations

There are no laws that apply specifically to contacts between journalists and public relations sources beyond those that cover all citizens. However, there are certain accepted practices on both sides that usually make for a better working relationship.

To begin with, no sensible person is going to be naive about what journalists seek and what public relations people usually offer. The

---

*In an article for the *Harvard Law Review* written with Samuel D. Warren and published in 1890.

difference between them is that journalists want news but most public relations people seek to present their clients' interests in the most favorable light.

Despite that, there is room for a modest amount of agreement.

Most public relations people or firms, for example, usually undertake to provide journalists with access to legitimate news sources if necessary. This is particularly required in dealing with public officials. Also, in the issuance of public documents or private statements, especially those that deal with statistics, public relations sources generally guarantee the accuracy of figures and other factual data.

As for handouts that deal with news events, it is expected that public relations sources will conform to accepted news standards even if a statement is self-serving. For example, if an officeholder formally denies a charge of bribery in a public statement about a developing investigation, it would make no sense to deny as well that an investigation is under way. Even if it is done, it won't be taken seriously.

On the part of journalists dealing with public relations sources, they generally agree to observe the various gradations of materials they are offered: 1) on the record and for direct quotation; 2) on the record, but only for indirect quotation; 3) on the record, but attributable only to a particular office or organization; 4) on background, which means that the statements may be attributed only to an unidentified source; and 5) off the record, which means nothing may be used in any form.

Journalists, on their part, agree to observe an embargo (release time and date) on public relations material unless such an embargo is broken. In that case, the rule is that the material is automatically released at once for everybody.

Otherwise, journalists are expected to use their own standards of accuracy, interest, and timeliness in considering whether to use, or not to use, a public relations announcement. They also decide in what form it will appear.

There is an unspoken—but rigid—understanding between well-intentioned public relations people and journalists that the only consideration between them should be the handling of the news. Meals, trips, and other possible benefits to journalists in connection with a public relations activity are not supposed to influence them. Within my own observation, such things seldom become important enough to cause concern on either side.

Finally, for beginners on a public relations assignment, it should be obvious that people will be trying to sell them something but they do not have to buy.

14

The Crime Story

THE BIGGEST CRIME STORY in America toward the end of this century is the war on illicit drug smugglers. It is an activity in which aircraft, ships, and motor transport are used night and day to penetrate the borders of this country in order to sell billions of dollars in harmful drugs to the public. As our government has repeatedly acknowledged, the threat to society is very real. And the enemy, however silent and elusive, is terribly dangerous.

The Mission of the News Media

Despite the increased activity of the nation's law enforcement agencies at every level, from federal to local, the flow of dope into this country continues in huge waves. From schoolchildren in California to nightclubs in New York City, victims of the drug habit testify to the efficiency of the smuggling mobs.

Even though arrests have increased to a point where jails are overflowing in many parts of the country, no end to the illegal traffic is in sight. Although marijuana and heroin were in greatest supply in the 1970s, the center of attention has now shifted to the even more damaging cocaine and its devastating derivative, crack. As for the suppliers, once centered in Turkey and other parts of the Near and Far East, they now are based mainly in Latin America. And as was the case with the liquor smugglers during the prohibition era of the 1920s, there is evidence in many parts of this nation of complicity between some public officials, including law enforcement agents, and the dope smugglers.

This is the story that is being told daily in America by the news media, both print and electronic, large and small. It has become a TV routine to watch an enterprising reporter making a purchase of drugs from a vendor near a school or to read how a newspaper has traced illegal drug shipments to their source. This kind of publicity will not let our elected officials forget their sworn duties, despite all the difficulties involved. It is both necessary and vital.

As early as 1974, Pulitzer Prizes were being won for this kind of exposé. One of the most striking was a campaign by *Newsday*, the New York newspaper, which assigned a dozen reporters for six months to follow the trail of the smugglers of heroin, then the drug most in demand here, wherever it led them. From Turkey to France and from Mexico to even farther south in Latin America, the investigators traced their quarry at a cost of more than $300,000.

The result was a thirty-two-part series called "The Heroin Trail," which won the 1974 Pulitzer award. It dealt in realities, as the following excerpt illustrates:

> The Istanbul narcotics merchants are big business men. They legitimately own hotels, restaurants, shipping lines, nightclubs, expensive houses, and other property. Most of their holdings are financed by their profits from their narcotics dealings. . . .
>
> The direct market for Turkish morphine base is the Mediterranean coast of France, where a loose group of gang leaders, most of them Corsican, convert the base to heroin.
>
> The French gang leaders, who have a working relationship with the Sicilian Mafia, are called *caids* (pronounced ca-yeeds), an Arab word meaning lesser chieftains. . . .*

Probably due in part to this kind of unfavorable publicity, the Turkish government outlawed the growth of the opium poppy under pressure from the American government. (The opium poppy is the source of opium, morphine, codeine, and heroin.) The dope smugglers, however, didn't halt their operations. Instead, they shifted from Turkey to Mexico.

As *Newsday*'s Bob Greene wrote subsequently:

> The Mexican heroin has been supplemented with heroin smuggled from the Far East. There has been no diminution in the amount of heroin supplied to the United States, but there has been a much higher

*The *Newsday* series ran from February 1 through March 4, 1973. This textual excerpt is from one account published February 4, 1973.

profit for heroin dealers. Heroin grown in Mexico and smuggled into
the States through existing smuggling organizations is far cheaper than
Turkish heroin. . . .*

The drumbeat of publicity increased in the decade of the 1980s
as the United States negotiated with Mexico, Colombia, and other
countries where smugglers had been based to cooperate in crushing
the illicit operation. But progress in the war came slowly and often
at great cost. And meanwhile the news media faithfully performed
their often dangerous duty.

The root of the problem was twofold: 1) the popularity of cocaine
among American users and its availability as an illegal stimulant,
particularly in the concentrated form known as crack, and 2) the
enormous profits attached to the smuggling operation in general.
As the news media were the first to find out, only a part of the
American public was indignant about the epidemic use of the drugs.

Then, too, there was difficulty in getting at the source of supply
and eradicating it. For example, even if the Colombian government
had fully cooperated with the United States in its antismuggling
campaign, it never was easy to locate all the places in the Andes
uplands where the coca shrub, source of cocaine, was grown in huge
quantities. (Coca is not to be confused with the cacao plant, the
source of cocoa.)

For that matter, there was a lot of trouble right here in the western
part of the United States over the domestic cultivation of hemp, the
source of marijuana, as a cash crop. With many small farmers in
trouble, marijuana was considered such an easy source of revenue
that it even went on the ballot in Oregon at one time for legalization.

Under such circumstances as these, the need for careful reporting
and clear writing was manifest. Without it, the government could
scarcely have commanded the kind of support it did manage to
arouse among the public at large. The vivid pictorial dramatics on
television may have been extreme at times, but so was the nature
of the social problem.

The Crime Beat as an Assignment

As an assignment, crime has long since outstripped the narrow
bounds of information supplied to the news media from Police
Headquarters. Nor is the coverage of crime in its broadest aspects

*The quotation from Bob Greene is from a letter to me.

limited to the richest, largest, and most powerful newspapers and newsmagazines and their counterparts in television.

It was a youthful editor, Oscar Griffin, who unearthed one of the worst frauds in this century with a few hundred words in his country newspaper in Reeves County, Texas, the *Pecos Independent*. What Griffin wanted to know back in 1962 was why Reeves County suddently has sprouted fifteen thousand ammonia tanks and what was being done with them. Three years later, it turned out that the tanks were a myth, that about $40 million as a valuation for them had been converted into a $14.5 million mortgage. As a result, a local entrepreneur, Billie Sol Estes, was convicted of fraud and sentenced to fifteen years in prison.*

A large newspaper, the *St. Petersburg Times* in Florida, discovered during an investigation that a new road, the 211-mile Sunshine State Parkway, was costing the taxpayers four times as much as its projected $100 million cost. Among the results were the resignation of the chairman of the Florida Turnpike Authority, a state audit of its financing, and other reforms that provided substantial savings for both the state and its bondholders.**

Among those who have contributed to the crime story in this generation, there have been many who've performed heroic feats. But for sheer devotion to the cause of human rights, no journalist has yet approached the accomplishments of Gene Miller of the *Miami Herald*. Because he devoted a dozen years of his young life to developing new evidence in three separate murder cases, four innocent people were freed from prison after they had been convicted of crimes others had committed.

Miller's major triumph was the liberation of two indigent black men, Freddie Pitts and Wilbert Lee, who had been wrongfully convicted of murder. It took the reporter eight and a half years to convince his editors and the governor of Florida of their innocence, but he persisted. Years afterward, he reported that the four beneficiaries of his own crime story were "well, independent, employed and, most important, lawful." The other two he set free were Mary Katherine Hampton in Louisiana and Airman Joseph Shea in Florida.***

---

*Griffin's first article in the *Pecos Independent* appeared February 12, 1962. It was January 1965 before Estes went to jail.

**The *St. Petersburg Times*'s exposé occurred in 1963. Both papers won Pulitzer Prizes for their exploits.

***See the *Miami Herald* for September 20, 1975 for the freeing of Pitts and Lee. The other two cases occurred in 1966.

Main Sources of the Crime Story

For beginners, the handling of the crime story begins with an in-
doctrination into the methods of law enforcement agencies—the local police, state police, the FBI, and their various adjuncts. It is
necessary to know how these units operate, how and when they
communicate with each other, and to listen to some of their radio
exchanges. This can often be done with the help of friendly officials
at any headquarters unit, preferably a local police operation because
it is the most general and affects all the rest.

It is through such initial steps that a writer learns never to use
loosely such common terms as *arrest* or *confession*. For example,
suspects in a crime often are detained for questioning but that
doesn't mean they either are under arrest or face arrest. Similarly,
someone who is being questioned in connection with a crime may
make certain admissions, but that doesn't necessarily constitute a
confession.

Such points have to be stressed for newcomers because it is li-
belous *per se* (on the face of it) to report wrongfully that someone
has been arrested or has confessed to a crime. The way to be sure
that an arrest has been made is to determine the specific charge in
the case. As for a confession, it is wiser to defer use of that particular
term until it appears on a public record or is announced for the
record by a qualified public official.

It also helps a writer who handles a crime story to be familiar
with the precise legal definitions. These may be readily obtained
from law enforcement officials when needed, especially in cases
involving murder. There is, after all, a difference between charges
of murder in the first degree, murder in the second degree, and
manslaughter. Moreover, robbery (a crime against a person) and
burglary (unlawful entry in a structure to commit a felony or theft)
also are vastly different.

Landmark cases in the area of law enforcement, too, should be a
part of a journalist's knowledge, especially the so-called Miranda
Rule. Most police organizations use that rule by reading what they
call a "Miranda card" to inform defendants of their rights immediately upon being placed under arrest. The case referred to was
that of Ernesto Miranda, an Arizona truck driver, whose conviction
of rape was reversed by the Supreme Court because he had not
been informed by police of his right to remain silent and to obtain
a lawyer.

As for crime statistics, they should be considered within the context of the times. The Federal Department of Justice has reported, for example, that half of all violent crimes committed in this country are not reported to the police. The same survey showed that two-thirds of all personal and household crimes, similarly, are not reported. The statistics were based on interviews with more than 100,000 people in 49,000 homes.

It may well be asked, therefore, what importance can be attached to an annual survey that shows crimes have been reduced in number. In a recent year, as an illustration, the Bureau of Justice's statistics showed almost 35 million crimes were committed, a slight decrease over the previous year.*

Writing a Sensitive Crime Story

Responsible journalists customarily are wary of injecting emotional terms into any crime story. They argue that it only adds to public confusion if the story is at all sensitive. Customarily, therefore, the tendency is to tell the story "straight" both in print and on the air without any emotional attempt at prejudging the issues involved. That, so the journalists' reasoning goes, is for a jury to decide at a properly conducted trial. Most newspapers, except for the sensation-prone that struggle for more readers, insist on such a style, even if it is criticized as wooden, but they tell the story at somewhat greater length than the electronic media.

Having received those instructions, Mack Roberts wrote the following for the *Central City Leader* about a tragic police case he had covered earlier that day:

BABY

Mrs. Kristin Folwell's ten-week-old daughter, Lucinda, was found smothered to death under a blanket in her crib shortly before noon today, the victim of what her mother said was an accident.

However, when police arrived after being summoned by a 70-year-old neighbor, Mrs. Wilella Carsten, Mrs. Folwell was arrested on a charge of manslaughter.

Mrs. Carsten, who discovered the baby's death, charged the mother had been negligent by permitting the baby to slip under the blanket and become entangled in it. The 22-year-old mother collapsed when she was questioned by police at her home, 6216 Deneton Drive.

*The statistics were for 1985, in which the crime rate—that is, of crimes that were reported—was at a thirteen-year low. The Associated Press carried the Justice Department's announcement in its file for October 8, 1986.

Summoned from his office at Tilling & Margrave, architects, at 321
Main Street, where he is employed as a draftsman, Craighton Folwell,
24, at once came to his wife's defense.

"Isn't it bad enough to lose our baby through this unfortunate accident," he asked reporters, "without having this old busybody next
door making these preposterous charges against my wife? She always
comes over here every day, looking for trouble."

Folwell said his wife was in no condition to leave their home to go
through the formality of being booked and fingerprinted. "They'll have
to wait awhile for that," he added. . . .

This is a difficult story to cover and write, particularly for a beginner in journalism. Under the circumstances, Roberts was well
advised to keep it in low key when an older and more experienced
reporter, Cary Blackwood, relieved him so he could return to the
newsroom with the story.

Had it not been for the unusual situation surrounding the baby's
death and the arrest of the mother, the reporter would have called
the office and turned his facts over to the rewrite bank. But in this
case, the city editor and the managing editor were troubled by the
way the story had developed and both wanted to be sure the piece
was handled in low key.

"But make it complete," the city editor, Joe Stoddard, said. "And
remember, never jump to conclusions while a news story is developing as this one is. Just try to be fair to everybody involved."

It was good advice for the writer who handles any crime story,
and particularly a sensitive one. That was what Roberts tried to do.
It was an important part of his training for other news that he soon
would be covering. If he couldn't bring a dope smuggler to justice
or free someone who had been unjustly convicted, he could at least
be fair to people who were caught up in a personal tragedy.

15

In the Cause of Justice

THE COVERAGE OF THE NATION'S COURTS, in theory at least, ought to be a comparatively routine matter of recording testimony and judgments. Every experienced court reporter knows, however, that it isn't so. And newcomers soon discover disquieting circumstances that affect both the judiciary and the citizens who look for the impartial legal protection of their rights. For in these changing times, there are so many political, social, and economic crosscurrents that both law enforcement and judicial patterns of conduct inevitably are affected.

The Sources of Contention

Challenges to the courts are not new in American history. In the long conflict over states' rights versus federal rule, President Andrew Jackson refused to support a Supreme Court decision against the state of Georgia when it sought to expel Cherokee Indians within its borders. And as most bright schoolchildren know, Abraham Lincoln, before entering the White House, attacked the high court's pro-slavery ruling in the Dred Scott case.

In our own time, it remained for an attorney general of the United States, Edwin Meese, to make the most sweeping assault on the Supreme Court and its authority. He declared publicly that the high court's interpretation of constitutional law is not "binding on all persons and parts of government henceforth and forever more."*

What appeared to bother Meese in particular was a Supreme Court ruling of well-nigh thirty years' standing that unanimously upheld a school desegregation decision against the state of Arkansas. This, the attorney general asserted, was "astonishing." He found it "at war with the Constitution, at war with the basic principles of democratic government, at war with the very meaning of the rule of law."

Why the outburst at such a late date, when the principle of racially desegregated schools had been accepted for so long? Legal scholars pointed out that Meese's point of view had its roots in conservative opinion that continued to resist legal precedents supporting such mild social advances as relief for Social Security disability cases and affirmative action in behalf of greater rights for women. It was the attorney general's view that the courts should defer to elected officials in deciding cases involving abortion and affirmative action, to name only two, in all but rare cases.

No less a legal power than the president of the American Bar Association at the time, Eugene C. Thomas, expressed concern that such disregard for the status of law could "shake the foundations of our system." But Meese was unrepentant and seemed unlikely to back down. At the time, a new conservative chief justice of the United States, William H. Rehnquist, had taken over for a session in which the high court was considering cases involving women's rights, free speech, and the separation of church and state.

Assessing the long conservative effort to sway Supreme Court decisions, at least one observer for a major newspaper wrote that the then solicitor general of the United States, Charles Fried, the Justice Department's lawyer in the high court, was "pursuing an activist agenda to change the court's direction in several cases."**

There were other aspects of the American judicial system that also had an effect, to some degree, on the coverage of the courts. Following a nationwide survey for the *Christian Science Monitor*, Howard James wrote that the system was complicated and, to a degree, out of date. He called the case overloads horrendous, even for competent, hard-working judges at every level—county, state, and national. He also observed that there were a few bad judges here and there, petty tyrants who tended to bring discredit on the rest.***

*Speech at Tulane University, reported and criticized in the *New York Times*, October 26, 1986, pp. E-4 and E-24.
**William Freivogel in the *St. Louis Post-Dispatch*, October 5, 1986, p. F-1.
***James's thirteen articles in the *Monitor* won a Pulitzer Prize.

Conflicts Between the Courts and the Press

Another factor that should be taken into account by those who report on the courts is the position of the press itself under the First Amendment. The complications here stem from decisions at the highest judicial level that the rights of a free press must give way to the right of fair trial in any case where they clash. Moreover, it is common knowledge that some judges have resented the aggressiveness of the press in examining cases of judicial error or outright wrongdoing.

As for radio and television, which usually maintain a low profile when such conflicts arise, they can't help being affected by whatever happens to the press.

It follows that beginners who are assigned to court coverage and have some legal background are lucky. Those who haven't had previous legal training ought to be aware minimally of the following decisions that ultimately will affect their work:

1. *Zurcher* v. *Stanford Daily,* 1978. In this case, the Supreme Court gave police the right to raid newsrooms without a warrant to seek evidence of the commission of a crime; what crimes, unspecified.

2. *Smith* v. *Maryland,* 1979. Here, the Supreme Court further empowered the police to force disclosure of the records of journalists' phone calls in connection with alleged criminal acts.

3. *Gannett* v. *DePasquale,* 1979. This was the decision that most upset the press, for the high court here gave judges the right to close pretrial hearings to the press.

4. *Richmond Newspapers* v. *Virginia,* 1980. Although this case did not weaken *Gannett* v. *DePasquale,* it affirmed the right of press and public to attend criminal trials in open court.

Nevertheless, a legal authority, Alan U. Schwartz, warned, "This is a period of dark caution for the press and therefore for the country."

Commenting on the issue of press freedom in a different context, Judge Harold R. Medina of the U.S. Circuit Court of Appeals for the 2nd District wrote years ago: "The prospect in this pretrial period of judges in various criminal courts of high and low degree sitting as petty tyrants, handing down sentences of fine and imprisonment for contempt of court against lawyers, policemen, reporters, and editors, is not attractive. Such an innovation might well cut prejudicial publicity . . . but at what price?"*

The courts have suffered prejudicial publicity over the years, true enough, but not without justification. A part of the record shows the following cases that originated with press inquiries:

—Impeachment of a federal judge in Illinois after an investigation by the *St. Louis Post-Dispatch.*

—Disclosure of corruption in some of New York City's municipal courts by the *New York Evening World,* now defunct.

—Resignation, trial, and imprisonment of Federal Judge Martin T. Manton following charges of fraud in the *New York World-Telegram,* now defunct.

—Allegations of machine politics in connection with the appointment of two federal judges in Nevada, charges that were published in the *Sacramento (California) Bee.*

—For the same reason—allegations of machine politics—confirmation of a candidate for a federal judgeship in Massachusetts failed following a campaign in the *Boston Globe.*

—Resignation of Associate Justice Abe Fortas of the Supreme Court following publication of a critical article in *Life* magazine.

In the removal of Federal Judge Harry E. Claiborne of Nevada as a result of a Senate impeachment trial, the first in fifty years, the government itself took action. The judge already had been convicted of filing false income tax returns and was serving a two-year prison sentence, actions that caused the Senate to hold him responsible for bringing the nation's judiciary into disrepute.**

Writing about Court Actions

In such an atmosphere, it follows that journalists covering the courts are well advised to write about legal actions in general and court trials specifically with great reserve. This is neither the time nor the place for extravagance of language, misplaced humor, or other irritants between bench and bar on the one hand and press and television on the other.

The public is best served by maintaining a style that is factual,

---

*Judge Medina's remarks, as quoted by Philip Kerby in the *Los Angeles Times,* December 3, 1975, were made at the conclusion of a study of free press issues by a judicial committee of which he was chairman.
**The *New York Times,* October 10, 1986, p. 1.

clear, impartial, and informative. The following is an example of how a complicated story involving the public interest could be handled at the outset for the *Central City Leader:*

TRUCK

Five of six defendants pleaded guilty today in federal court to extorting $2 million in bribes from trucking concerns at Central City Airport.

Federal Judge Armin Lazar continued the trial of the sixth defendant, Marchie Veno, after three other members of his family and two business associates changed their pleas from innocent to guilty.

The trial had been under way for two weeks.

What the five admitted was a conspiracy to shake down trucking concerns at the airport under threat of damaging their business. Each could receive up to 20 years in prison under the Federal Racketeer Influenced and Corrupt Organizations Act.

Those who admitted their guilt, in a deal with federal prosecutors, were Gennaro Veno, the 82-year-old patriarch of the alleged crime family, and his oldest sons, Sal, 48, and Vinnie, 45; Max Hamad, 49, a business associate of Gennaro, and Len Guero, 42, Hamad's partner.

Marchie Veno, 39, youngest of Gennaro's sons, maintained he had no knowledge of the alleged plot. . . .

The Organization of the Courts

Our legal system is based on the Constitution of the United States and those of the fifty states and territories.

In the federal courts, there are about 650 judges aside from the 9 justices of the Supreme Court and around 15,000 other court officials and employees. Most federal judges are appointed for life by the president of the United States and work at three main levels— the district courts, the appeals courts, and the Supreme Court.

Each state, territory, and the District of Columbia has at least one federal district court and a clerk's office. Numerically, California has the largest number of such courts, forty-two, and New York is next with thirty-eight. Next come the federal courts of appeals that are set up in eleven circuits and three special areas with the Supreme Court at the apex. There also are special federal courts—a Tax Court and a Court of International Trade.

The judicial system of the fifty states, from which appeals are carried into the federal system, is much larger. However, no two state jurisdictions operate in the same way, although the laws governing their work, in most respects, are similar. In all, there are more than 1,000 state courts with several thousand judges and more than 100,000 employees.

At top level, most state judicial organizations are similar to the federal system although most state judges usually have to stand for election. Each state has one or more appeals courts at the apex of its system. These are followed in descending order of importance by the workhorse courts of original jurisdiction that bear a variety of names—Superior, Supreme, Common Pleas, amd others. These workhorse courts often are located in the various counties of each state. There also are separate county courts in a number of states.

Below that level, the judiciary system branches out into a maze of inferior courts. . These are generally city courts, ranging in importance from police or magistrates' courts, poor people's courts, and courts of justices of the peace to special jurisdictions covering traffic, family matters, juveniles, and others.

The newcomer who is assigned to any court in the land—whether a specific case is involved or not—should telephone to the clerk of the court for whatever information is available once the assignment has been given. Merely to show up unannounced and flash a press card is not a very good idea. People in court clerks' offices usually are harassed, or act that way, and too often give short shrift to people with inquiries, including reporters.

It is an amiable myth that all courts welcome the public. In most places within my experience, even lawyers not familiar to court attachés may be given a hard time. Reporters, in consequence, should show no resentment if they don't receive the red carpet treatment. They should not even expect it.

The reason for advising, even urging, reportorial self-restraint becomes apparent when the work load of the federal district courts alone is considered. In most recent years, these courts—the smallest number in the American system—have handled about 20,000 trials that resulted from the commencement of around 240,000 legal actions. Of these, civil actions accounted for most cases—about 200,000 that were winnowed down to 14,000 trials. The 40,000 criminal cases, however, were far more time-consuming with a majority involving embezzlement and fraud, drug abuse, theft and robbery, forgery and counterfeiting.*

Necessarily, the case load in state, county, and municipal courts is much greater and the extent of both civil and criminal cases is

*See annual reports of the Administrative Office of U.S. Courts for figures for specific years. The figures above are rounded out.

much broader. It follows that the bulk of the news of the courts develops on this level. And it is here, too, that most journalists receive their first lessons in court coverage.

The Routine for Court Actions

There is no common procedure in the coverage of the courts for any jurisdiction, civil or criminal. Federal, state, county, district, and municipal courts vary widely in their routines. What journalists are obliged to do, in most instances, is to examine the legal papers of a newsworthy action before it goes to trial, discuss them with lawyers for both sides and, if possible, with judges and ex-judges not connected with any specific case.

Most civil proceedings today involve automobile damage cases and other suits for damages. Additional civil actions include bankruptcy cases, petitions for injunctions, and suits for divorce or separation. Formerly, all these were divided in general into *suits in equity,* which were brought to compel or bar judicial relief, or *actions at law,* which covered mainly personal and property matters. Such legal distinctions, however, are fading because some states now have abolished the differences in the two classifications and other states are likely to follow.

In either instance, however, the routine has not changed.

Thus, civil actions begin when a complaint is filed and the defense responds with another legal document. Then, pleadings before a judge are in order. The procedures thereafter are roughly as follows in most states:

A venire (panel) is ordered if the case is to be tried before judge and jury and jury selection is the first order of business, with the first juror automatically heading the group. If no jury is to be chosen, the trial begins at once.

In either case, the plaintiff proceeds with an opening statement by a lawyer, then the presentation of witnesses. The defense is permitted to cross-examine each witness. Frequently, there is redirect and recross examination, as well.

Once the plaintiff's case is complete, the defense generally asks for a dismissal. In most instances, the judge denies the motion upon which the defense's case is presented in a manner similar to the plaintiff's.

After that, both sides sum up, the judge instructs the jury on points of law that may be at issue, and the jury then retires. Upon receiving the jury's verdict later, the judge has the option of letting it stand or revising it (if the award is considered excessive in a damage suit, for example).

If there is no jury, the judge often takes the case under advisement and issues a verdict in due course. In either event, jury decision or not, the verdict may be appealed.

Criminal procedure varies somewhat. Generally, it begins with an arrest and the arraignment of a defendant, who is allowed to plead to a charge lodged by the state.

In misdemeanors heard before an inferior court, the case may be disposed of with an immediate hearing. However, when a felony is involved, an inferior court decides only whether there is sufficient evidence to bind over the defendant for action by the grand jury.

If that happens, bail is set for the defendant while awaiting the grand jury's decision. This body, in most states, consists of twenty-three members but may consist of as few as a dozen, who hear evidence against a defendant to determine whether the case is sufficiently strong to proceed to a trial. If the grand jury hands up an indictment, the defendant goes before the court for a plea. Should the plea be innocent, the trial proceeds.

The general trial routine, as outlined for civil cases, is followed as a rule except that criminal defendants under indictment do have the right to a jury trial unless they plead guilty at the outset. If the jury returns a guilty verdict, the judge either pronounces the sentence or remands the prisoner for later sentencing. That depends on the law in that particular jurisdiction.

In any event, the case may be appealed—and generally is.

Plea Bargaining as an Alternative

Because of overloaded courts, harassed prosecutors and weary judges have cut down the number of criminal trials in recent years by adopting a procedure known as plea bargaining. What happens is that prosecution and defense enter into a deal, as in the truck story, to curtail or entirely avoid a trial. The defendant bargains for a lighter sentence than might be expected from judge and jury and generally succeeds. As for the prosecution, that is one less case to take to trial. Both sides, at least in theory, benefit under such arrangements.

However, many concerned citizens have asked whether such deals actually undercut the judicial process. Certainly, the risk is always present and the alertness of an inquiring press isn't always a guarantee that plea bargaining is above suspicion. Still, the deals continue to be made.

Press and public do have the right of inquiry, as is manifest in such legislation as the Federal Freedom of Information Act (FoI) plus the various "Sunshine Laws" and "Open Meetings" statutes that have been created in recent years at all levels of government.

The parent law, the Freedom of Information Act, was approved by Congress and signed by the president in 1966 as a means of making available to inquirers any nonclassified documents pertinent to the government's business. In the first ten years of its existence, the act made possible the production of 125,000 government communications of various kinds to inquiring persons, groups, and organizations. About 25,000 other requests were denied in whole or in part, after which 3,700 appeals were filed, with about 400 finally yielding information. Some of the data obtained from the government under FoI disclosed CIA experiments with drugs to control the human mind, the training of local police in some cities as burglars, and suppressed details about the espionage convictions of Julius and Ethel Rosenberg.*

The various other "Sunshine Laws" and "Open Meetings" statutes also were effective in varying degree. But neither press nor private inquiries, pressed by law or by investigative tactics, have slowed the increasing pressure toward plea bargaining.

It is not something that the framers of our Constitution were able to foresee when that basis of our legal system was adopted in 1789. But they also did not have to grapple with the complexities of modern life, an underworld empire of crime, and a massive drug-smuggling operation in a nation of almost a quarter of a billion people. Life was a lot simpler in the original thirteen states, clinging to the Atlantic seaboard, that had just wrested their liberties from British rule.

Covering the Appeals Process

Journalists often are so engrossed in the crime story of the moment that they sometimes do not pay sufficient attention to the appellate process whenever a jury verdict is announced. It does happen, after years have passed, that a sensational finding of guilty against a

---

Louisville Courier-Journal and Times, January 9, 1977, p. 1; *New York Times,* August 8, 1977, p. 1. The *Quill* magazine, February 1976, p. 6.

prominent defendant is reversed either on retrial or on appeal to
higher courts.

Because a vindication of innocence is seldom as dramatic as the
punishment of the guilty, the reversal does not make as great an
impression on the news media and the public.

In twenty-five years as a working journalist during which I was
assigned to some of the most engrossing trials in America's legal
history, I remember no warning against overplaying a guilty verdict.
The most I can recall, as a means of assuring fairness, is a decision
to use the term *innocent* rather than *not guilty* in leads reporting
that a trial defendant has been freed.

That, of course, was based on the possibility that the word "not"
might be carelessly omitted in the printing process, something that
has happened now and then.

This is not to say that journalists in general, including myself, are
gung ho for the prosecution in cases that attract wide public attention. But in a long trial of any kind, civil or criminal, it is inevitable
that both the public and journalists are going to be influenced one
way or the other by the presentation of the evidence.

Necessarily, it is a part of legal strategy for the contending forces
in the courtroom to produce this kind of impression and journalists
are well aware of it. They should, as an entirely professional matter,
be particularly careful to maintain a posture of fairness in their reporting.

The following account of the reversal of a verdict in a murder
trial, as it would have been prepared by the Independent News
agency and published in the *Central City Leader,* illustrates the
importance of the appeals process:

CRANCH

Midland (IN)—Minor Cranch was acquitted today of murdering his
wife, reversing a guilty verdict of four years ago.

The 68-year-old former mayor of Midland arose in a crowded courtroom here to thank the jurors publicly. "You have given me back my
life," he said.

Cranch had been accused of poisoning his wife, Ethel, in what the
state called a "mercy murder" as she lay unconscious in a local hospital
after an auto accident.

The defense had argued, successfully this time, that the former
mayor would have been unable to induce his wife to swallow a poisoned
pill, as charged by the state, while she was comatose. Medical testimony before Superior Court Judge Denis Deloyer supported Cranch.

In returning a guilty verdict in the case four years ago, a jury then showed that it believed the state's case charging Cranch with a mercy killing. . . .

Such reversals as this are not hypothetical. The acquittal of Claus von Bulow in a Rhode Island courtroom three years after he was found guilty of attempted murder is an illustration of the reality of the appeals process.*

The problem for journalists is that they must tell the news as it happens and they are in no position to forecast the outcome of an appeal. Thus, a finding of guilty in a murder case, for example, is bound to attract more attention than a reversal that may come years later. Yet both accounts are privileged under the libel law. Both accounts are necessary in the telling of the day's news. And both presumably would be professionally handled.

With twenty-twenty hindsight, it is easy to fall back on the philosophic observation of an eminent student of the English language, Yogi Berra, and exclaim, "It ain't over till it's over!" But that doesn't really solve the dilemma for reporters and writers who have to produce interesting accounts of daily events under deadline pressure. About the most that can be expected, in any account of a trial verdict, is to stress the announcement of an appeal without speculating on the outcome.

The maintenance of a proper balance in writing about court actions is every bit as necessary as any check for fairness and accuracy.

*The von Bulow verdict of innocent was pronounced June 10, 1985 and carried nationally by the wire services, networks, and major newspapers three years after he had been found guilty in what the prosecution called the attempted murder of his wife, Martha (Sunny) von Bulow.

16

Writing about Localities

ONE OF THE PRINCIPAL DIFFICULTIES in American journalism today is to cover the many problems of overlapping governments in an efficient and understandable manner. People are usually turned off by complications, having more than enough of them in their daily lives. But there is no way of always telling the local story in simple terms.

For awhile, around the middle of this century, shifts in population suggested that public interest in purely local affairs might be declining. However, the Census Bureau now reports that our metropolitan areas are growing at a faster rate than the areas in the rest of the country. In fact, the bureau's projections indicate that such growth patterns are likely to continue until the middle of the next century.*

The news media, therefore, are obliged to continue to pay the closest attention to the multiple problems of our cities and surrounding areas—housing and public transportation, electric power and water supply, schools and public health, finances and unemployment, among others. The local story, in sum, has become more important than ever before.

*Changing Population Patterns, a report by J. G. Keane, director, U.S. Census Bureau, 1986.

Factors in Local Coverage

It isn't so long ago that many otherwise responsible newspapers proceeded on the theory that news of most American cities could be obtained merely by stationing a reporter at City Hall, another at Police Headquarters, and a third at a principal court building. What the people of our cities were offered then, mainly, was a running political commentary on mayors and elected judges, an occasional scandal, news of taxes and budgets, and a never-ending stream of police and court items.

That wouldn't be enough today to satisfy the more critical readers of a country weekly. Indeed, the better newspapers have expanded their metropolitan staffs to cover suburban areas as well as the heart of our cities. And local television, quick to realize the needs of the populace, does a lot more with local news in its expanded one- and two-hour daily news programs. That is all to the good.

There are complications, however. The principal one is determining how far local interests extend. For example, when a city merges its public schools with those of a surrounding county for administrative purposes, as has happened in Knoxville, Tennessee, this considerably enlarges the education beat.

Furthermore, developing forms of government such as the New York–New Jersey Port Authority and the Tennessee Valley Authority cut across state lines with marked effect on local economies. Such governmental changes as these have a lot more impact on metropolitan areas than do technical advances in local rule, such as substituting a city commission–city manager operation for the more familiar mayor-council form of administration.

Even more important, what the federal government does or does not do can have a decided effect on lower jurisdictions. To illustrate, city dwellers are well aware that cheaper foreign competition in both industry and agriculture can run up our nation's trade deficit. But will federal boycotts that discriminate against foreigners bring an end to such trade conflicts, or will that simply increase unemployment? This is a dilemma for our cities.

The point is beyond argument. Any editor who has to make up a schedule for reporting assignments knows that city, suburban, county, state, and federal functions and their effects on people in the mass cannot be put into separate compartments. Moreover, in many cases, the officials in varying jurisdictions have to work together, as will be seen in the next chapter on budgets and taxes.

Once, in an effort to avoid such complicating factors, it was the fashion of newspapers with a large circulation to try to describe a complex situation in terms of its probable effect on John Smith, the average citizen, or Bill Jones, the average officeholder. Such devices are still used here and there nowadays, but they don't help very much.

Writers on local affairs, for all their ingenuity, have not yet been able to hit upon an easy way to inform the public of the manifold complications of urban living. Nor is it likely that anybody will come up with a formula that will create instant understanding of the position of a mayor who has to decide either to cut city services or raise sales taxes.

It may be possible for television to duck a story about cost runovers in the construction of a new bridge or about poor highway design in favor of an old movie that is entertaining for a mass audience. That is the easy way out. But these are the things that a local newspaper cannot avoid covering, whether or not they are popular. If writers moan that there is too much dull stuff in the paper, and some do, it amounts to a confession of ineptitude.

Handling a Local Problem

Consider the following two leads that were prepared for the same story in the *Central City Leader* about the community's problems with its State Psychiatric Hospital. The first was turned out by a rewrite man, Morry Corrigan, and centered on an interesting personality:

DEROZIER

If you are afraid of working with mental patients, Dr. Felix deRozier won't even talk to you.

"I want people in my hospital who are on the side of mental patients, who don't run away from them," he says.

Dr. deRozier, a tall, good-looking 56-year-old psychiatrist, is the director of the State Psychiatric Hospital in Central City which is looking for more nurses and more space in which to treat an overflow of mental patients.

In an interview today, Dr. deRozier said. . . .

The second lead is written by Sally Ward, the *Leader*'s specialist in science and medicine, who did the original story on which Corrigan operated. In the language of the trade, what Corrigan did was to "jazz it up." But what Sally wanted to do was to explain the city's problems with the State Psychiatric Hospital and hope that in some way the publicity might help relieve a difficult situation. This is how she began:

HOSPITAL

The State Psychiatric Hospital in Central City is overcrowded with mental patients, needs at least 30 additional nurses, and 100 additional beds.

These were the conditions described by most of the current staff, both psychiatrists and nurses, during a week-long study of the 120-year-old institution in a crumbling downtown area of the city.

In response, the director, Dr. Felix deRozier, admitted to over-crowding but argued he couldn't hire some of the nurses who applied because they "actually are afraid of working with mental patients."

He continued, "I want people in my hospital who are on the side of mental patients." . . .

The choice between the two beginnings on the same story presented the editors with a problem of their own. The rewrite man's lead subordinated the hospital's troubles and emphasized a colorful and opinionated character. Sally's story, however, stressed the unappetizing truth, something that many people don't like to read.

When Sally's story was published as she wrote it, the newspaper came down on the side of the public interest rather than glib readability. Her piece was not very comforting; still, it did give the people of the city the facts about a disagreeable situation. That is why newspapers are still published despite the superior entertainment value of television, films, and drinking parties in the nearest saloon.

There is plenty of room for readable stories in any good newspaper or magazine, particularly in sections devoted to entertainment, other cultural affairs, and sports. But somewhere, somehow, and at some length, citizens do have to be informed about the workings of their community. Somebody has to take that task seriously. Otherwise, the democratic ideal can dissolve very quickly into total confusion.

Local Government and Public Relations

The growth of a public relations psychology among city officials is another factor that creates difficulties in getting at the root of local issues. Understandably, a mayor or other city official who is facing reelection wants to put the best possible face on the way local problems are handled. That is also true, naturally, of city managers who are hired on a contract for a specific period.

It follows that the public relations people in government, many of them former journalists, are going to do their best to persuade their erstwhile colleagues that all's well—"and let's have a drink."

That, too, is an easy way out of handling a difficult job. To co-operate with the publicists in local government is a lot simpler than fighting them and their bosses. Reporters who ask too many questions at City Hall are generally viewed with dark suspicion by public relations people.

This is not to say that public relations people in local government thrive on cover-ups and misinformation. Most of them are well aware that such a policy, once it becomes known, will only hurt their own credibility as well as that of the officials whom they serve. What actually happens in practice is that reporters who are intent on breaking a less than flattering story about local government get their information from sources other than public relations.

In short, although an inefficient or untrustworthy officeholder may want to conceal, it is the journalist's mission to reveal. Here is an example of the difference between a news and public relations approach in a wire service story out of Washington about the federal surplus food program, as published in the *Central City Leader*:

FOOD

Washington (IN)—The federal government has given away more than three billion pounds of food in the past three years, mostly cheese and butter, but state and local agencies are critical of the program.

Georgiana Halavy, a social service consultant here who has spot-checked the results at state and local levels, said today:

"Theoretically, everybody should love the food giveaways, but all I've heard so far are complaints that the program is a mess, that nobody can tell when the food is going to arrive, and that a lot of it is spoiled."

A spokesman for the Agriculture Department said, however, "Everything is running smoothly. This is a great program for the needy and everybody agrees on that." . . .

The remainder of the story takes up the conflicting claims, point by point, and matches them so that the reader doesn't really know what or whom to believe. That, too, is a part of an official defense posture, but it doesn't make it any easier for the public to get at the facts. Nor does it benefit the government in the long run.

Actually, the fault is that of the news service and its editors, who are reluctant to take a position against a program that can be of so much benefit to the needy of the land. For if the complaints are groundless, perhaps they should not be circulated. And if they have some merit, the unfavorable publicity could conceivably lead to at least a few necessary reforms. Merely to publish a story that balances "on the one hand" with "on the other hand" does no good at all.

Covering the Counties' Business

Caught between the needs of the localities and those of the states, the county governments in the United States are often put in untenable positions. A part of their business is to try as best they can to safeguard the environment and protect the natural resources of the countryside—water, woodland, and the like. And yet, much of the county funds used in this country go to extend or repair existing highways and thrust new ones into lands that ought to be protected.

Unless there is a scandal in the administration of so contradictory a program, the public seldom hears very much about the work of county governments. But here, too, news can be made that is of importance to the entire region. The following account of an extended plan of environmental protection in the *Central City Leader* illustrates the point:

LAND

The Northward County Legislature approved a controversial program today of buying 6,300 acres of unused, unimproved land in the county for $40 million.

Meeting in special session here, the legislators voted 62–36 to authorize issuance of bonds to finance the purchase of the acreage outside Central City. It is part of a long-range program to protect the environment.

Legislator Hamilton Mardelon, speaking for the opposition, warned that the land purchase program would touch off a runaway rise in the value of real estate in suburbs outside Central City's limits.

"You're just going to encourage a lot of wild speculation in land without protecting a single tree or rabbit or even a babbling brook," he said.

For the majority, Speaker Lenore Rountree gave assurance that the environmental program will work. "There's going to be no real estate speculation in land because of this program," she said. "I have assurance from the governor of that. What we will do will be to preserve some of our precious land now for the use of our children and our children's children." . . .

When the States Make News

The local citizen usually feels the heavy hand of the state only when a state police car flags down a speeder or the legislature votes a tax increase or some other onerous measure. It isn't often that the very real benefits of some state actions for its localities are in the day's news. Essentially, the reason for the imbalance is that most of the benefits, aside from a rare tax cut, are undramatic.

As a veteran legislator once observed, "The only time we get any real notice in the news is when we make people mad."

There is, unhappily, a certain amount of truth in that. Aside from politics and errors of commission and omission among public servants, the daily operations of tens of thousands of state officials across the land do not readily lend themselves to picturesque moments on the tube during evening news programs or headlines in the press. Now and then, there may be pleasantly written feature stories about some colorful aspect of little-known state business, such as the work of experimental farm research teams or medical reports on better public health protection. But more often than not, this is the extent of the news of the day at the state level that tends to be constructive:

BOOKS

Midland (IN)—The State Board of Education today turned down all textbooks proposed for English classes from the second through eighth grades.

"One reason for the trouble we have in maintaining a reasonable degree of public literacy goes right back to our primary school English classes," State Education Commissioner Theron W. Carinder said. "If we had better textbooks, I believe we'd have better results."

On the commissioner's motion, the board unanimously rejected a dozen series of English texts but allowed the publishers to come up with revisions within a year. The action affects an estimated 1 million public school students in the state. . . .

In the Matter of Proportional Representation

There are times in America when a newspaper has to go beyond the presentation of the news to risk its very existence in an unpopular cause. One such issue is proportional representation.

To beginners in journalism, that sounds difficult. What it means is that, in some parts of the country, rural areas are overrepresented in the state legislatures and cities are underrepresented. What happens? The rural areas, naturally, get what they want but the needs of the cities—better education, health, and welfare facilities, for example—come second.

It follows that no politician wants to take on the powerful farm vote in such situations; the cities, having less voting strength, are well-nigh helpless. So it remains for a newspaper to take a big risk and campaign for the principle of equal representation.

That can be expensive in more ways than one. In addition to cutting at the heart of a newspaper's existence through reduced advertising, many readers—particularly young ones—will find such issues dull. Then, too, that kind of work can't be entrusted to a single reporter or even a few. A team has to be created to make a careful inquiry and establish the facts. Only then can an appeal be made to the federal and state courts for legislative reapportionment and a fair division of power between cities and rural areas.

This kind of thing can be handled by a great newspaper with a large staff and impressive financial resources. But very often, it turns out that a smaller paper has to do the job because no other agency, civic group, or political party will. Here is how the *Central City Leader* began one such campaign in the opening article of a series:

VOTE

Voters in most rural districts in this state outnumber those in the cities by as much as 4–1, a six-month survey has disclosed.

The survey was conducted by a team of reporters and researchers from the *Central City Leader*.

In one area alone, Southward County, it was found that 42,369 people reside in one rural area assembly district while a nearby urban assembly district has only 10,485 people. Most other counties show the same imbalance, researchers said.

The *Leader*'s team found that voting patterns in the state were heavily influenced by the dominance of rural districts. At the last legislative election, an analysis showed that only 25 percent of the people in the state chose the majority of the Senate, the upper house of the legislature, while only 16 percent picked a majority of the assembly, the lower house.

Upon being shown the results of the *Leader*'s survey, Mayor Reardon of Central City said, "This must be made the basis for an appeal to the U.S. Supreme Court and to the state courts for a reapportionment, a redrawing of our legislative and congressional district lines. Under the landmark case of *Baker* v. *Carr*, the Supreme Court outlawed this kind of thing. . . ."

The difficulties of reporting team work such as this should not be taken lightly. But if political parties and civic organizations won't undertake it as a rule, and if public officials look the other way more often than not, it remains for a newspaper to do the job in the public interest.

While there are rewards within the profession for such activities*, it should not be assumed that the people of a state, county, or even of a locality will be properly appreciative. Reapportionment may be important as a basic principle of a democratic society, but it isn't as interesting to a mass public as a football game or a television soap opera.

Journalists, however, cannot limit their activities to what is popular and easy to do. The tougher the story, the more worthwhile it is likely to be.

*The Hutchinson News, Kansas, with a circulation of only about 50,000 at the time, fought for reapportionment in its home state before the Supreme Court's Baker v. Carr decision and won a favorable ruling from the state's courts. The News was awarded the Pulitzer Prize gold medal for public service in 1965.

17

All about Money

FEW JOURNALISTS ARE ADEQUATELY PREPARED to explain the complications of government finance to a mass audience. For that reason, at the local level particularly, an institution known as the Budget School has been founded. Not every city or county has one, but where they do exist they are invaluable. Under the terms of an agreement between reporters and city officials, lectures and question-and-answer sessions about a forthcoming budget usually are spread over several days but all information is embargoed (that is, held up) for release until a specified time. In that way, so the theory goes, nobody has to do a rush job and paw helplessly through three hundred or so pages of figures to find out what the news is.

That doesn't mean all government fiscal problems are easily handled, however. No administrative budget ever gets through a legislative body—a municipal council or similar group—without changes. There also is such a thing as a budget veto by a mayor, governor, or higher official at the federal level. Still, "Budget Schools" are a good way of dispelling confusion at the initial stage of reporting.

Handling a Local Financial Story

Writers who handle news about government fiscal plans at any level must always ask first of all, "How much will it cost?" and next, "Who pays for it?" To translate, will the money come out of higher taxes, fees, and other charges or will there be cuts in services, layoffs, and other economies?

Writers have to follow a budget through all steps, from initial submission to legislative changes, conferences to reconcile differences, and finally a news conference with experts following final action. Then hard questions must be asked and clearly understandable answers given.

Some writers believe quite mistakenly that they can brush off stories about government financing by keeping them short and using as few figures as possible. The theory here is that the public neither understands nor cares. The slightest exercise in poll taking, to be described in a subsequent chapter, will demonstrate that the public *does* care. If someone owns a house and the property tax is about to be boosted 15 percent, there's going to be a lot of interest in what was done, how it was done, and why it was done. The same is true of a stiff boost in sales taxes or other levies, not to overlook the public outcry that invariably accompanies a deep cut in social services.

No, budget making is no empty exercise, a game to be played at the Treasury Department of the federal government between budget-making officials or their counterparts down the line to the smallest locality. For if we make certain demands of our government at various levels, we do have to pay for it in one way or another.

It is futile to try to shrug off the whole process by attributing it to inefficient and sometimes grafting public officials or muttering, as uninformed people will, "It's just a lot of politics." The fact is that most public officials do try to perform honestly and efficiently. When politics enters into their financial planning, it is usually in the form of criticism by the members of the opposing political party of the way incumbents are running the government.

Through that necessary kind of give and take, plus the close examination of the final product, the truth is likely, in theory, to emerge. And if the theory turns out to be wrong, then numerous investigations into the possibility of a financial scandal result.

To short-cut this process in any way, particularly in the press accounts, is to short-change the public.

Responsible editors are the first to insist on thorough reporting and clear writing in any account of local government financing. While it may be beyond the scope of all but the most powerful national news organizations to check the annual spending exercises of the federal government, such costs at local, county, and state levels customarily undergo the most careful scrutiny by both the press and public service groups. And that is as it should be.

To illustrate how a story about local finances may be handled, consider the position of Mardee Fenwick, the City Hall reporter for the *Central City Leader,* who has just finished covering the adoption of the city's budget by the municipal council. That process began weeks before at the Budget School. Instead of giving the main facts to someone on rewrite and going off to lunch, Mardee has been told by her city editor, Joe Stoddard, to grab a cab to the office and write the story herself for the next edition.

Stoddard says dryly, "I'd like to make sure this is done right. You know the story. I don't. And I'd rather not take a chance on letting you give it to somebody on rewrite. You're the expert and a 12½ percent increase in the property tax is an important story. Let's give our readers some detailed information, shall we?"

Mardee accepts the assignment, leaves City Hall promptly, and arrives at the office by cab. Actually, she is relieved to be able to write the story herself because it is more complicated than the levying of a property tax increase. A 5 percent sales tax has also been enacted for the first time and 122 city employees have been marked for either early retirement or discharge.

Why all the taxing and economizing?

The city's budget director, Marshall Jadwin, previously had told Mardee and other City Hall reporters at a news conference after the council acted, "We have to comply with the legislature's new budget-balancing law. We have to match income with outgo and begin to pay off our city debt."

"That," the city editor had commented when Mardee gave him a quick summary by telephone, "is one hell of a story. It looks to me like everybody is getting shafted. Did the mayor have anything to say?"

"He blamed the governor for putting through the Penniman-Grob budget-balancing law in the legislature," was Mardee's response.

It was then that the city editor told her to write her own story in the office for the next edition. He knew that he had the day's biggest story to lead the paper.

Writing a Local Budget Story

Mardee, just four years out of college as a business major, had been attracted to journalism almost immediately after receiving her degree. The *Leader* had had the good sense to hire her, give her a chance to absorb training, and stationed her at City Hall to exercise her business skills in the reporting of local government. The idea

was good. Very few reporters, after all, have even a basic acquaintance with business procedure and business insensibly affects much
of municipal government. So Mardee's assignment paid off.

This is how she began her story for the next edition of the *Leader:*

TAX

A new 5 percent city sales tax on everybody, a 12½ percent boost
in property taxes, and a loss of 122 city jobs are included in the new
$45 million balanced budget adopted by the municipal council today.

The budget for the next fiscal year, beginning June 1, is 6 percent
higher than the current one.

In defense of his action in approving the budget, Mayor Reardon
pointed out that the city had no alternative because of the state's
Penniman-Grob budget-balancing law, recently approved by the legislature.

"In addition to the usual costs of running the city, we now have
to begin paying off the city's debt over the next five years," the mayor
said. "Go ask the governor why he put that budget-balancing act
through the legislature."

Marshall Jadwin, the city budget director, echoed the mayor's comment at a news conference saying:

"We have to comply with the legislature's budget-balancing law.
We have to match income with outgo and begin to pay off our city
debt."

At the governor's office, it was said he would have no immediate
comment.

When the news of the 122 job losses through retirements or dis-
charges hit city departments, there was consternation among many
older employees. One grizzled police sergeant, a veteran of 30 years
on the force, demanded:

"What in hell are they trying to do at City Hall? If they cut the
police force much more, they'll be turning the place over to
thieves. . . ."

After summarizing the job losses and the reaction to them, Mardee's story then considered the new city sales tax, which was to come
atop an existing 10 percent state sales tax. There was derogatory
comment, obtained by other reporters in street interviews and by
telephone, on this aspect of the city's new budget as well. Nor did
the writer fail to point out that a revolutionary new federal tax law
drastically affected taxpayer deductions for local and state sales taxes.

As for the property tax increase, that was dealt with last in the
order of major changes. To have given that particular tax boost the
greatest attention, in the city editor's judgment, might well have
opened the newspaper to criticism in view of the widely held real

estate holdings of the publisher. In fact, the publisher, R. J. Cotteman, after hearing a radio news summary of the budget, telephoned the managing editor to be sure that the focus of the story was on the sales tax and the argument over the budget-balancing law.

In any event, the story ran two columns in the next edition with illustrative pie charts to show where the money to run the city was coming from and where it would principally go. It was, as the city editor had anticipated, the big story of the day. He was pleased at the way his young City Hall reporter had handled it, saying, "Good work, Mardee. Now, back to City Hall and keep after the mayor and budget director for an overnight story for tomorrow's first edition and we'll keep trying for comment from the governor." He hesitated, probably out of uncertainty more than anything else, then asked, "Is there any chance for a reconsideration of this budget?"

Mardee shook her head. "I don't see how it could be done. If the mayor had wanted to, he could have withheld his signature on the budget bill to show he didn't like it, and the whole operation of the city government would have had to close down in three days, when the current fiscal year ends. But the mayor didn't do that. He signed the budget bill because there really wasn't anything else he could do. And we'll start paying for it three days from now."

"If nothing else happens," Stoddard told her, "then that's your lead for the overnight. Let people know they're going to pay another 5 percent for everything—and watch the stores put out the word for bargain shoppers. The next three days are really going to be something in this town!"

He was right. It would have been next to impossible to play down a story so fraught with economic and political consequences for the people of an entire midwestern city. Nobody on the *Leader* even suggested it.

Federal Fiscal Problems

The financial problems of localities, important though they are, seldom have the economic impact of the fiscal affairs of the federal government. With a national debt in the neighborhood of $2 trillion and an annual budget deficit that has been hovering around $200 billion in recent years, the economy is bound to be affected sooner or later. As fiscal conservatives have often pointed out, "We will have to pay for this some time."

David A. Stockman, a former federal budget director, described his own position while in office in this manner: "I soon became a veritable incubator of shortcuts, schemes, and devices to overcome the truth now upon us—that the Federal [budget] gap couldn't be closed except by a dictator. The more I flopped and staggered around, however, the more they [his associates] went along. I could have been wearing a sandwich board saying, 'Stop me, I'm dangerous!' Even then they might not have done so."*

It was bound to turn out that way as long as federal spending was unchecked. Presidents, cabinet officials, and budget directors other than Stockman came up with schemes to keep spending and taxing down.

Congress passed the Gramm-Rudman-Hollings law, proposing to wipe out the worst federal deficit within five years, but it was just a dream. Even if the Supreme Court hadn't knocked out one of the new law's key provisions, it never would have worked.

What was involved in Gramm-Rudman-Hollings was the Canute principle—the children's tale about ever-hopeful King Canute who commanded the waves of the ocean to come thus far and no farther. The Congressional version had it that if spending and taxing didn't balance on schedule, automatic spending cuts would take effect, half of them from national defense.

On top of all else, Congress's revolutionary new income tax program was designed to raise more money. One way was to close loopholes through which some wealthy corporations and individuals escaped all payments. Another was to cut numerous deductions and establish two levels of taxes for every taxpayer. To soothe public opposition, millions of low-income people were removed from tax schedules.

Yet, despite an atmosphere of self-congratulation in which the legislation was adopted, the federal debt continued to endanger the solvency of government at every level in the land. Why? In the latter 1980s, the interest on the national debt reached 14 percent of the federal budget. Nor was there any likelihood that it would soon recede by any significant amount. There were other consequences, as well. The value of the dollar fell in foreign markets against leading foreign currencies. And while borrowers frequently had to pay higher interest for bank loans, they often noticed that they received less interest on their deposits.

Here is how news of the federal government's financial problems was translated into terms that had an impact on planning in just one area of major importance to localities, counties, and states:

*David A. Stockman, *The Triumph of Politics* (New York: Harper & Row, 1986).

ROADS

Washington (IN)—Federal highway funds to bolster state road construction are unlikely to increase for "years to come," an informed source said today.

Because of tight federal operating budgets, the source said, the prospect was for a reduction in such funds rather than an increase.

The comment came in response to a proposal for widening the current two-lane Midland Expressway from Central City to Midland to three lanes and extending it northward beyond Midland.

The proposal originated with the State Transportation Department in Midland. . . .

This piece of wire copy, instead of being marked up and used in the *Central City Leader,* was routed to the city desk by the telegraph desk. At the city desk, Joe Stoddard saw possibilities for a better story and assigned Mack Roberts, who then was on the rewrite bank, to call the State Transportation Department at Midland for details.

Roberts wound up talking with the State Transportation commissioner, Durward Leighton, and also obtained a comment from Governor Farrow's office. That gave him a story that appealed mightily to local motorists, who had been complaining for years that the narrow Midland Expressway wasn't suitable for the heavy traffic it was carrying, particularly on weekends.

Here is how Roberts's story began, using the wire service tip as it had been confirmed at the state level:

ROADS

The state's plan for widening and extending the overcrowded Midland Expressway suffered a damaging blow today because of tightening federal budgets.

In a telephone interview from Midland, State Transportation Commissioner Durward Leighton said he had been informed by Washington that he could not count on increased federal funding for "years to come."

"If we are going to widen the Midland Expressway from two lanes to three lanes and extend it beyond Midland as planned," Leighton said, "we'll have to get more money from the state to make up for what we'd expected from the federal government."

At Governor Farrow's office, where the news also had been received, an official who would not permit use of his name said, "That just about kills the Midland Expressway project unless we can get the federal government to reconsider."

The official said Governor Farrow would make a special trip to Washington early next week to see what, if anything, could be done to release emergency funding for the Midland Expressway proposal.

The Central City Automobile Club has complained for years that the Midland Expressway's weekend traffic constitutes a hazard to any motorist who uses it. This is particularly true of the road between Central City and Lake Hartigan, 30 miles north of Central City, during summer weekends.

Commissioner Leighton, in the state budget for this fiscal year, had obtained a preliminary grant of $22 million to make a beginning on widening the expressway between Central City and Lake Hartigan.

"It's beginning to look as if that's all we're going to get," he said. However, he decided not to abandon the total project until the governor makes one more attempt to obtain additional federal funding. . . .

This kind of news frequently originates in Washington and is translated into local information through the methods Roberts used for the *Central City Leader*. It illustrates how a pinch in federal financing can vitally affect the home front.

18
--

News and the Economy

IT IS EASY FOR JOURNALISTS to report the news of the economy in good times. Business prospers, employment is high, most people feel secure enough to plan for the future, and governmental problems are few.

But in any economic downturn, especially if it is severe and prolonged, the news changes dramatically. It is then that our principal economic indicators signal that stormy weather lies directly ahead. Savings in banks are down and interest rates drop, unemployment rises, bankruptcies increase, and governmental policies fluctuate in emergency fashion.

Just about the only constant, as far as public interest goes, is news of the wealthy and famous regardless of the state of the economy. *Fortune* magazine's annual listing of the wealthiest 500 and *Forbes* magazine's similar designation of the richest 400 both are eagerly scanned. And anybody who wins big money in a lottery also becomes news because so many want to know how it was done.

The Human Condition as News

But what of the average hard-working citizen? It has always been difficult to tell that story. During the 1980s, for example, an economist estimated that the real median income of the top 10 percent of the population rose by more than $7,000 while the income of the bottom

153

40 percent fell by more than $200.* But is that news? The answer is
not really pertinent by current standards. Why? Mario Cuomo once
observed while he was governor of New York, "Poverty is not the
kind of story that makes easy headlines or even easy listening."**

Cuomo was painfully correct, of course. And yet, whenever the
economy goes sour and many people are in actual distress, it would
be an irresponsible news organization that chose to ignore such disagreeable facts. The economic indicators quite naturally tell the
story. But are statistics enough? Can mere figures reflect the degree
of human suffering, even desperation, that bad times bring?

Consider, for example, the nation's economic position as the national debt approached a record $2 trillion with budgetary deficits
for a fiscal year being in the range of $150 to $200 billion for most
of the 1980s. By reason in large part of overproduction of oil do-
mestically and a flood of cheap imported oil, the oil-producing states
of the Southwest were going though hard times. And primarily because of a pile-up of domestic wheat that was overpriced on the
international market and couldn't be sold, the Midwest farm belt
also was suffering through a recession.

The consequences may not have been felt all over the country at
once, but there was no mistaking the indicators that pointed to an
economic downturn—falling interest rates, a decline in the value
of the dollar against leading foreign currencies, rising demands in
Congress for the passage of protectionist legislation, and worst of
all, the slow increase in unemployment.

The problem for the news media was twofold under such conditions: 1) Would the continual presentation of bad economic news
make matters worse? 2) And if so, how could the adverse psychological effect be cushioned? Almost certainly, experienced journalists expected that bad news as usual would feed on itself; however, they also knew that there was no way of cushioning the blow.
As always, good times could be celebrated but bad times had to be
borne with fortitude.

Writing about Hard Times on the Farm

The way the farm crisis was handled is a case in point. It was obvious
from the start, when farm prices began falling, that the nation as a
whole could not be indifferent to what was happening. Nor did the

*Prof. D. M. Kotz, University of Massachusetts, *New York Times*, October 19, 1986,
p. F-3.
**Cuomo spoke before the American Newspaper Publishers Association in San
Francisco, April 23, 1986.

journalists fail to do their work. The statistics that told the story of the downturn once again marched across Page 1 and were also reflected on the evening news programs of the networks. And once again, the stories of personal crises dramatized the problem for the rest of America. The televised report of a small farmer being forced off his ancestral land told the story better than anything else on the evening news.

Very soon, as the farm recession developed, the question for journalists became, "What people, what individual families, should be selected to show the condition of the area as a whole?" For writers and television people who were familiar with rural life, the answer came readily. What they did was to go directly to a family farm, a vanishing institution in America, to tell its story in terms of the people who were trying without much hope to preserve it.

The story was one of heartbreak, so it had to be told in muted terms.

Here is how Mack Roberts, who was born and brought up on a midwestern farm, began an account of such an experience for the *Central City Leader:*

FARM

Artie Davisson, who is 46, has worked his 200-acre wheat farm north of Central City for most of his adult life, like three generations of Davissons before him.

Together, they have lived off the land with their families—these Davissons—for more than a century. But now, Artie says, he'll have to give up pretty soon.

"It's either that, or find me a job in the city, unless I want to go bankrupt. And that I'd rather not do," he says.

Artie isn't mad about it. Just depressed, as is his wife, Hope, 44, and their three teen-age children.

He sighs, rubs his hands down the side of his blue jeans, and stares away in the distance at his ripening wheat. "It's a good crop," he murmurs, almost to himself. "In normal times, it would bring me enough to live on, maybe buy my wife a new winter coat and keep the kids in school. But the way things are going . . . " He broke off and shook his head.

What is happening to Artie Davisson is also happening to nearly all of the survivors who still own family farms in this area. High interest rates for farm loans from banks and low interest rates for savings, a worldwide glut of wheat, and rising competition from abroad all have combined to make this a tough year for the Davisson farm and many others.

Some blame the rapacity of small-town banks, but Artie doesn't. "They have got to survive, too," he explains, then continues, "Actually, my bank's been real good about everything, gave me more time to pay and tried to help me out in other ways. It's not to a bank's interest out here to let a farmer go broke."

Again he shakes his head. "But, you see, this is the fourth tough year in a row for me and it looks like I'll have to get off the land this time or go bankrupt. And I hate like hell to go bankrupt."

What makes the difficult choice almost traumatic for Artie is that his father, grandfather, and great-grandfather all were able to make a living by working this same family farm. "And I hate to think," he says, "that I'm not as good a man as they were in their times. But I guess, maybe, with the big corporations buying up farm land, these times are different. . . ."

There is unashamed emotion in this story. It is not because the reader is sprayed with adjectives or besought by the writer to pity the farmer. No, the emotional content arises primarily from the restrained reporting of the circumstances in which the farmer finds himself. Notice, too, that the style differs markedly from the concisely written straight news story, for this is a news feature and it requires an entirely different approach—no bang-bang lead, no quick quote, no fast condensed summary. Feature writing takes space because it deals, in the main, with the human condition.

As to the subject matter, which is bound to be depressing to many readers, it is a reflection of the times. Ordinarily, both mass circulation newspapers and television prefer to feature upbeat news of great successes, beautiful people, and the like. Editors and news directors know from experience that depressing news isn't likely to build either readership or electronic audiences. However, when there is an economic downturn, it sometimes becomes insulting to people down on their luck to have to read, see, and hear exclusively about how well off some people are and how wonderfully fortunate those people have been in all their dealings.

This is why muted accounts of misfortune, such as the Davisson story, appear in the news media of areas of the nation that are going through a difficult period. But the journalistic offerings at such times cannot be completely mournful. There has to be some relief. And sometimes it comes to public attention in this fashion—a Sunday story for the *Leader* developed by Sally Ward:

WHEAT

Millie Ballard was an organic chemistry major at State U 21 years ago when she married Freddie Ballard, her childhood sweetheart, and joined him down on his family farm at Endicott, just north of the Central City line.

But Millie turned out not to be an ordinary farm wife, for today she was awarded $200,000 and a share of future profits for her new chemical treatment to produce a strain of disease-resistant wheat. The Alarset Chemical Company, which closed the deal with Millie and Freddie Ballard, will produce the new chemical under the trade name Milarson.

"It's a made-up name," Millie explained cheerfully during an interview in her big, well-lighted kitchen. "Part of it is the first three letters of my name, but I just had to put in the son because I've always wanted one." She smiled, then went on, "It's not that Freddie and I don't love our three daughters. That we do, very much. But it would have been nice to have a son, too, to work the farm someday."

To Freddie, who was also in the kitchen drinking coffee, that didn't matter so much because Millie's years of part-time chemical research paid off in such handsome fashion. "Look right over there at what used to be our pantry," he said, pointing to a half-open door at one side of the kitchen. "That's where Millie spent all her spare time— made a little chemical laboratory out of it and sometimes she really chased us all out of the house with the awful smells that came out of her test tubes. . . ."

"But that $200,000 doesn't smell too bad, does it?" Millie broke in with a grin.

Freddie clasped both hands above his head, as if he'd been a winning prizefighter. "Hell, I'll suffer through a lot more smells out of that pantry for $200,000, Mil," he said. "I sure would never have made it on the farm. . . ."

Such stories, of course, can't be created out of thin air and such good fortune doesn't occur very often down on the farm. But feature pieces of this kind do help to vary the monotony of bad news that invariably rolls across the country in depressed times. It is the responsibility of editors to make certain that the human condition is not reported on exclusively in shades of black and gray.

Magazines, which aren't tied so closely to the patterns of breaking news, frequently handle such feature presentations better than either the newspapers or television. It is one reason, perhaps, for the survival of magazine-type journalism and the prosperity of most of our leading magazines. By being able to give writers more lead time to develop a story and greater space for pictures, some of them in well-printed color, magazine-type journalism has maintained a strong presence on the American scene.

It isn't an accident, therefore, that stories such as Sally Ward's piece about Millie Ballard turn out to be done in magazine style. Good reading, by whatever name it is called, is still a prime necessity for successful journalism, no matter what the state of the economy may be.

Handling News of Labor Unrest

One of the by-products of times of economic stringency is a certain amount of labor unrest, mainly in industrial areas. Most news organizations have specialists in labor news who are familiar with the ups and downs of contract negotiations, work stoppages, layoffs, forced retirements, and strikes.

To the newcomer to journalism, caught in the middle of such difficult situations, it is sometimes bewildering to get at the real news of what is happening. For as in any negotiation—and labor troubles generally do lead to negotiations for a settlement—neither side is willing to state a position publicly until a settlement is well-nigh certain. If there is any news, then, it may not be authoritative because the information will come mainly through leaks or background interviews (no sources named) of interested parties.

For the newcomer to journalism who is assigned to a labor story the only recourse is to be completely professional—to be fair to all contending parties, to check every claim, to make no assumptions until there is assurance of agreement, and to use moderate language in anything that is written or broadcast. Anything less than this is likely to inflame an already touchy situation.

Overanxiety to be first with a story, too, may prove damaging in a number of ways. And it doesn't necessarily happen to a beginner in journalism. A veteran reporter for the *Central City Leader*, Archie Vanable, picked up a story from a union official that the Central City Telephone Company, long known for its favorable labor relations policies, had decided to abolish more than ten thousand positions within a year as an economy move. Vanable checked with the company's top supervisory people and was given neither a confirmation nor a denial—just a stiff upper lip "no comment." He went into the paper with a story that began:

PHONE

> The Central City Telephone Company intends to eliminate 10,000 jobs within the next year.
>
> Sources familiar with the company's labor policies said that the move was being planned because of tightened economic conditions. Sources at the company would neither confirm nor deny the decision to trim the labor force. . . .

Vanable shouldn't have been so quick to get into the paper with a touchy story. As matters turned out, the *Central City News* next morning came out with the real story, which was quite different:

PHONE

May Withington, who has been a sales representative for the Central City Telephone Company for 28 of her 53 years, plans to take early retirement soon and a new job with a travel agency.

Mrs. Withington is among about 10,000 veteran employees who have been offered a bonus to take early retirement in addition to a generous pension toward which the company and the employee contribute equally.

Cindy Regnery, chief of the company's Labor Relations Department, said, "There's nothing new in this. It has been company policy for many years to offer a bonus for early retirement to any employee who is likely to be eligible for retirement after 30 years. We'd much rather do that than to fire our younger people indiscriminately when it becomes necessary to reduce the work force."

Mrs. Withington agreed. "It's a good deal for us," she said. "We can take the offer or not, as we please, but I think most people are willing to take it. I know I am. I've already been promised a good job at a travel agency. . . ."

True, the bonus for early retirement at the telephone company that was offered to ten thousand employees doesn't make as exciting a story as Vanable's, but what good is an inaccurate story in a difficult labor situation? It only serves to make things worse than they really are. Few labor unions these days are gung ho for violence on the picket line in the spirit of the 1930s. And there aren't many relics of that era in corporate America who are willing to let a difficult labor situation drift into a confrontation without making at least an attempt to be conciliatory. When a strike does occur nowadays, it amounts to a confession of failure on the part of both sides.

Journalists, at any rate, should be careful not to be caught in the middle. Self-restraint is an intrinsic part of professional journalism.

The Role of Public Officials

When all factors in a powerful economy are set on "go," there is very little that public officials have to worry about under all but emergency situations in America. Except in places where there are signs of extreme voter apathy, a majority of elected officials generally feel secure enough to trust their fate to the electorate when the time comes to run for reelection or to retire gracefully from public office.

But if a particular community, state, or region is in the grip of an economic downturn, for whatever reason, then even the least sophisticated public servant knows that a vengeful electorate may seek satisfaction at the polls. It isn't that public officials are held responsible in general for the economy; rather, they are the most visible presences on the political and economic horizon and the public is likely to punish them for uneconomic policies, real or fancied.

Knowing this, any public official who faces reelection in times of recession is likely to take defensive measures to assuage the wrath of the multitudes at the ballot box. It is under these circumstances that Governor Farrow, who has made no secret of his presidential ambitions, comes to Central City to address a conference of public utility executives from various parts of the state.

The possibility for exciting news from a setup of this nature is not very good as Loren Wilton, the *Central City Leader*'s chief state capital correspondent, is the first to acknowledge. When Wilton comes to town with the governor, he tries to tone down the expectations at the *Leader* that the governor will break some thundering news.

"Farrow doesn't have an advance text for this one," Wilton tells the city editor, Joe Stoddard. "His press secretary isn't even sure what he intends to talk about, and my shorthand is lousy if he's really going to talk off the cuff."

Stoddard provides Wilton with a small tape recorder against the possibility that the governor may confound both his staff and the correspondents by making news in his talk to the utility executives. And once Wilton reaches the Great Plains Hotel, where the conference is being held, he's glad to have the tape recorder with him. For Charles McDowell, the state's Public Service Commissioner, sees him in the lobby and tells him: "Better get upstairs to listen to the governor, Loren. He's hot under the collar and I think he's going to rip into the utilities people."

So it turns out. The governor wastes no time getting down to cases with the 250-odd utility executives after being introduced by President Leonard Kenyon of the Central City Light and Power Company. What the state's chief executive is worried about, as he makes clear from the outset, is the disparity between corporate and individual tax rates in the state's taxing structure. Now this may not be a very sexy subject to the average reporter, but Wilton, having a nose for political news, suspects that Farrow is deeply concerned that the downturn will cost him his shot at the presidency.

As the session develops, it is apparent that what the governor is trying to do is to pave the way for a proposal he intends to make to the state legislature to reduce the brackets for individual state income taxes and raise those for corporate profits, the utilities, and all others. Wilton is thankful, as the session continues into an acrimonious question period, that he had the good sense to accept the tape recorder from Stoddard at the *Central City Leader* office.

This is the main part of the story Wilton writes for the last edition of the *Leader:*

FARROW

Governor Farrow said today that he intends to propose higher corporate state tax rates next year and lower rates for individuals.

Speaking before the state's public utility executives at the Great Plains Hotel, the governor also pledged his best efforts to take several million people near the poverty level off the tax rolls altogether.

"If the federal government is able to do this through tax reform," Farrow said, "then we ought to be able to do it at the state level, too."

The governor added that he will call on the legislature to enact tax reform at its next session.

During a question period following his speech, which was extemporaneous, Farrow rebuked President Leonard Kenyon of the Central City Light and Power Company for pressing him publicly to approve the reopening of the company's closed atomic power plant here.

"I'm not going to make any deal with you, publicly or privately," the governor snapped. "When you consider that the plant is safe for operation, you may apply to Commissioner McDowell of the Public Service Commission for a permit and he will handle the matter as he sees fit. I shall not interfere."

Kenyon, after criticizing the governor's tax plan as "unfair to corporate business," had pointed to the state's refusal to let the atomic power plant operate as further evidence of an antibusiness bias on the part of the Farrow administration.

Governor Farrow did not specify exactly what figures he had in mind for the tax proposals he intended to submit to the legislature for its approval, but he frequently mentioned the federal tax reform plan with approval. Just how closely he intends to adhere to the federal tax brackets, however, remained a matter of conjecture.

In his remarks before the utility executives, for which he used handwritten notes scribbled on what appeared to be a sheet of hotel stationery, the governor charged that "too many corporations in this state are either not paying enough taxes or are juggling their financial statements so that they pay no taxes at all." He went on, "I'm going to see that all our corporations pay their fair share of the expense of running this state instead of leaving it to overtaxed individuals to do it for them. Millions of our people at the lower end of the income scale ought not to be paying any state tax at all."

Asked during the question period if he referred specifically to the state's utility companies when he accused corporations of avoiding their fair share of tax payments, the governor grinned and replied, "You can use your imagination on that one. The guilty ones know who they are and so do I. . . ."

The point about the Farrow story is that some of the nation's major economic reforms have occurred during slack periods. Obviously, when times are good, public officeholders are happy to claim credit for a surging economy and seldom propose sweeping changes. However, in an economic downturn, journalists may expect proposals such as the one Governor Farrow made to show that political leaders are aware we do not live in the best of all possible worlds. It always pays to keep a tape recorder handy, in any event, against the possibility that an important speaker may not always put his most newsworthy remarks in a text that is prepared for advance release.

The Position of Corporate News Media

Sometimes, newcomers to journalism ask quite logically whether a publisher or station owner, being corporate representatives themselves, ever dictate the handling and the play of a story that affects corporate financing. I suppose it does happen now and then; in the Great Depression, I recall one publisher who was so upset over President Franklin Roosevelt's New Deal reforms that he ordered all his writers, even those in the news columns, to use "Raw Deal" when they normally would refer to "New Deal." What happened was that any self-respecting reporter wrote about "the Roosevelt administration" and ducked the publisher's order in that way.

Actually, such prejudices in the news columns are rare in American journalism—at least they have been in our time. Interference with the news by a network or chain newspaper executive could not be kept secret, if it happened, and would serve to undermine public credibility in the entire organization. Wise proprietors, being unwilling to take such risks, usually keep hands off the news operation unless they have to cut the size of the staff. Otherwise, in considering any article or newscast, professional media owners generally apply only two tests: "Is it accurate and is it fair?" That is the way it should be.

19
———

Writing about Social Problems

THERE SEEMS TO BE NO LIMIT to the scope of journalistic inquiries into a wide variety of social problems that have
developed in America during the closing years of this century. They
range from discrimination against minorities to the effectiveness of
Social Security, the protection of women in the workplace to damage
to the environment, the treatment of disadvantaged children to the
safety of school bus transportation. And there are many more.

On Handling a Social Inquiry

No model can be provided to fit all such inquiries. However, the
writing in general should conform to basic professional standards
of fairness, accuracy, and objectivity. Sensational treatment of any
social issue should be avoided by all means; as past experience has
shown, scare headlines and emotional appeals on television can only
damage the cause involved.

On reasonably familiar subjects, such as school bus inspections,
concise reporting and writing ought to be the rule. Necessarily, on
subjects that may be unfamiliar to the general public such as toxic
shock syndrome or Alzheimer's disease, more detailed information
is required. Where news-feature treatment is decided upon, in any
event, considerably more time or space should be provided for both

the reporting and the writing. These things can't be done in ten minutes.

Here, for example, is how a series on school bus safety began in the *Central City Leader* after Mack Roberts had been assigned to work on the project following numerous complaints from worried readers:

BUS

Nearly 20 percent of the bus drivers who transport children to and from Central City's inner district primary schools have a record of traffic violations.

Some also have out-of-state licenses that conceal more serious faults.

These are the principal findings of a month-long survey by the *Leader* of the records of the 522 men and women who operate vehicles servicing the city's inner district primary schools.

The study was undertaken in response to numerous complaints from concerned parents both to the office of School Superintendent Harley Klapper and the editor of the *Leader*.

When the results of the inquiry were placed before the superintendent, he promised quick action, saying, "If the situation is as bad as it looks on the basis of these findings, some of these drivers are going to be out of jobs. We can't and won't take chances with the lives of our children."

The violations found on the licenses of 97 of the drivers that were inspected by this reporter included speeding, failure to stop at dangerous crossings, running red lights, and carrying an overload of passengers.

In the cases of those with out-of-state licenses, there was no way of determining immediately what the driver's previous record was in this state. But State License Commissioner Barry Flory pointed out that drivers who are disqualified in one state for any reason generally obtain out-of-state licenses in order to continue working.

"I'm all for a federal licensing system for truck, bus, and taxi drivers," he said. "In that way, we can have a quick check on the people who drive these vehicles on our highways and make sure that they are, in all cases, well qualified and dependable. . . ."

It should be emphasized to newcomers in journalism that the initial article in a series such as this is only the beginning of a writer's work. Each subsequent article must be just as newsworthy, just as carefully researched, if anything at all is to be accomplished. Even after the series ends, much remains to be done. Generally, the writer who originated the series follows the actions and reactions that result from it. Nor are the issues ever quickly settled. In any inquiry as extensive as the one herein illustrated, months may go by before the issues are resolved.

Public Information and the Public Mood

The familiar journalistic technique of matching one side against another doesn't work very well in handling some social issues. Abortion is one of them.

Beginners in journalism are often surprised by the deep emotions that are aroused on occasion by the most elementary discussions, in print or on the air, of a subject such as legalized abortion. People on either side sometimes cannot bear to talk reasonably about the subject and approach hysteria instead. That makes for a very real journalistic problem.

Yet, it will not do to pretend, as some try, that the problem does not exist. In America, there are estimated to be at least a million and a half unwanted pregnancies annually. Nor is there any secure method of birth control for women that can safely be recommended. Both the pill and the intrauterine device have disagreeable features.

However, anti-abortion forces continue their battle despite a 1973 Supreme Court decision (in *Roe* v. *Wade*) that legalized abortion. As late as the 1986 mid-term elections, anti-abortion proposals went before the electorate in Oregon, Massachusetts, and Rhode Island and were defeated by the voters in all three states. But that will not end what amounts to a divisive national debate about the issue.

Under the circumstances, the only recourse for journalists in handling news about abortion is to report concisely and fairly what actions have been taken by either side without attempting to moralize or otherwise comment. If television people decide to put on a special presentation, no doubt experts with varying points of view will be found to discuss the problem. And the same is true for newspapers and magazines that devote space, time, money, as well as qualified people, to ventilate an important social issue.

It is hopeless, however, to expect to avoid discussions of abortion, legal or not. As an example, in a panel review of sexual problems before the American Society of Newspaper Editors, the writer Shere Hite had this to say:

"It is true that there is no very good birth control measure at this time. . . . The problem is, looking at the teen-age pregnancy rate, one constantly hears things like, 'Well, girls should learn to take the birth control pill.' Or, Planned Parenthood had a little button, 'You Can Say No.' But it is always put on the woman that she is the one who is supposed somehow or another to control this. We are the moral whatevers of this world. Actually, I think there should be a big campaign to teach boys. . . ."*

Occasionally, someone comes up with a different idea for handling a social conflict that agitates the public. Jonathan Freedman of the *San Diego Tribune* in California, for example, was assigned to do a story on the spread of the disease called AIDS (Acquired Immune Deficiency Syndrome) and its consequences and decided on a novel approach.

For his research, he visited a public bathhouse to describe the environment in which the disease is sometimes contracted or spread. Then, to emphasize the consequences of the affliction, he spent some time at a nearby hospital to note what had happened to AIDS victims and how they were being treated.

"The way to get to the issue," he said, repeating the familiar litany of the journalist, "is through the human dimension."**

However, not all journalists agree that the reporting of sensitive issues is that simple. Roger Simon of the *Baltimore Sun* put the journalist's position in such matters with unusual candor as follows:

"I do not think we should kid people about what we do. I do not think we should kid new reporters about what we do. Someone wrote that reporters are always selling somebody out. In this profession, a large part of the time we use the stuff of other people's lives to do what we do—to put stories in a newspaper.

"You try to do that with sensitivity and respect for the human beings you are dealing with. But we do use other people's lives. . . . We can tell ourselves that they can choose not to talk to us and they can. But using people at their most vulnerable moments, at their happy moments, at their sad moments, is simply what we do. . . ."

That, naturally, applies also to all media, and especially television, where the human condition is sometimes depicted so vividly and movingly. It is scarcely to be wondered at, therefore, if the most well-intentioned journalists arouse an unsympathetic public reaction now and then in the handling of sensitive social issues. The combination of public tensions and tough-minded journalistic methods for getting a story is, all too often, a highly combustible mixture.

It is one reason for the prevalent public attitude toward journalists after more than three centuries of experience with the breed.

*Ms. Hite is quoted in *Proceedings of the American Society of Newspaper Editors, 1986*, pp. 49–50.
**Freedman's assignment and Simon's comment are in ibid, p. 219.

The Struggle for Equality

Instead of remaining continually in the middle, journalists *are* able to handle reports of progress on some long-term social issues with a degree of confidence. One of them is the advancement of women's rights, surely a cause that has few declared and dedicated opponents at this late date. And yet, the role of women in the American workplace is still not easy, as witness the Supreme Court's 1986 decision in *Meritor Savings Bank* v. *Vinson* that sexual harassment is a form of illegal sex discrimination.

This is no theoretical legal position. The records of the Equal Employment Opportunity Commission (EEOC) bulge with complaints of sexual harassment in the workplace; moreover, hundreds of cases arising from such unpleasant experiences are still awaiting trial in the federal courts. The EEOC, since 1964, has been the chief enforcement body for Title VII of the Civil Rights Act, which made it illegal for employers to discriminate on the basis of sex.* But illegal or not, the practice has continued to be so offensive to women employees that the issue still crops up in all parts of the land.

Here is a carefully written advance account of a suit to be tried in federal court, Central City, as it was prepared by Ethelreda Ridley of the *Central City Leader:*

SANDO

    Melissa Sando, a 26-year-old former secretary in the State License Bureau here, begins suit in Federal Court today for $100,000 damages against the state charging sexual harassment.

    Ms. Sando, in her complaint, alleges that Elbert Rizal, her supervisor while she was employed by the state, offered her a promotion and a $3,000-a-year pay boost but only on condition that she entered into sexual relations with him. When she refused, she said, she was fired.

    Rizal, who is married and has four children, denies the charge. Ms. Sando contends, in her suit, that the state is responsible for Rizal's alleged behavior because he occupies his office by reason of an appointment from Governor Farrow.

    The case will be tried before Federal Judge Cardule and a jury.

    Floyd Manable, attorney for Ms. Sando, said his client brought suit under guidelines issued by the Equal Employment Opportunity Commission in 1980. "Those guidelines," he explained, "specify that sex-

*For a history of this issue, see Tamar Lewin, "A Grueling Struggle for Equality," the *New York Times*, November 9, 1986, pp. F-12–13. In 1987, the Supreme Court went even further toward outlawing sex discrimination in the workplace.

ual harassment consists of unwelcome sexual advances, requests for
sexual favors, and other verbal and physical conduct of a sexual nature
that the Supreme Court has held to be illegal."

Manable cited a Supreme Court decision of June 19, 1986 outlawing
"hostile or abusive work environment" as applied to women who have
been victimized through sexual harassment. . . .

Inquiries into Improved Health

Almost anything having to do with improved health is likely to interest a population with a growing element of older people.

The problem here, for both writers and their audiences, has to
do frequently with translating medical and psychiatric terms into
language that the general public can understand. Sometimes, this
is done by quoting a knowledgeable physician or psychiatrist. Occasionally, a writer who specializes in science and medicine can
do the job without expert help. But when all else fails, then the
reporter has to fall back on the oldest of the devices of journalism,
the personal story.

The danger, in such cases, is that the personal element may be
exaggerated and thereby weaken the validity of the account. But
first-rate journalists know that and take precautions accordingly. As
for beginners, they must looks to sympathetic editors or news directors for assistance.

The personal account, in most instances, stresses information
about better health care, new kinds of treatment for known diseases,
the advantages and disadvantages of new types of medication, and
the recognition of symptoms of relatively rare ailments. However,
the story cannot be told in a vacuum. If the account features the
manner in which a famous person dealt with a crippling illness, so
much the better. If it is the reporter's own story, that usually works
well, too.

But the point is that the story must provide the public with new
information that is useful. The piece cannot be turned into a mere
medical or psychiatric exposition of somebody's pet theories. It will
be too difficult for the public to understand, for one reason; for another, it may even be misunderstood by uninformed people and
thereby cause unintential damage.

To be explicit about the method of writing, Norman Cousins, the
former editor of the *Saturday Review,* used his own experience to
emphasize the importance of laughter to good health. In so doing,
he interested a highly sophisticated audience about an unusual, even
an inspiring, medical experience.

For Nan Robertson of the *New York Times,* the problem was quite different because the subject, by no stretch of the imagination, could be made entertaining. Ms. Robertson had been struggling for years to overcome a dangerous and (at the time) relatively new illness called toxic shock syndrome, which could have been fatal. All she knew about it at first was that it was an infection. But as she noted her symptoms and realized others might contract the illness, she determined to do something about it.

What she did, being both a courageous and public-spirited journalist, was to study her own case thoroughly. Then she wrote a detailed account of what had happened to her and how her illness had been successfully treated. For her work, she was awarded a Pulitzer Prize.

There were several points of difference between the experiences of Norman Cousins, the editor, and Ms. Robertson, the reporter. But in both cases, the results were gratifying to both the writers and their news organizations. And, most important of all, the public was well-served.

Writing about Human Needs

If journalists performed such services earlier in this century for a popular press that was more sensation-minded than it is today, the resultant benefits often came about by accident rather than design. Today, the operations of responsible news organizations are geared to deal more effectively with social problems, especially those that affect the human condition. To show how qualified reporters go about their work now, consider the manner in which Sally Ward, as the *Central City Leader's* specialist in science and medicine, handled the following case:

In her daily contacts at the state university, Sally has learned that a sixty-two-year-old history professor is working with a normal class schedule and even swimming daily despite his five-year treatment for a little-known blood disease. It seems to her like a story, but she knows perfectly well that it will be difficult to obtain the professor's permission to write about him. Academics are notoriously shy about personal publicity having to do with anything but their professional work.

Moreover, without the permission of the subject, Sally realizes that the *Leader's* management won't dream of letting her do a story about the case.

She decides to circle warily about the subject to determine what can be done. First, she learns the name of the physician, a hematologist, who is treating the professor. However, the doctor warns that he will provide details and permit the use of the information only if his patient agrees. It takes awhile to convince the professor that t his story will benefit others who suffer from the same ailment, but eventually he gives in. And finally, Sally is able to begin her story as follows:

BLOOD

Professor Hanford Munn teaches a full class schedule and swims nearly a mile a day although he suffers from a blood disease that has often proved fatal to others. He has taught at State University for 36 years.

Dr. Munn, a specialist in American history, credits his physical condition to a potent drug, prednisone, and the care given him by his physician, Dr. Mark Gilliland. The professor is 62.

Dr. Gilliland, a hematologist, believes that Professor Munn's ability to survive and live a normal life is due primarily to his excellent physical condition and his love of long-distance swimming in the State University pool.

With Professor Munn's permission, the physician described the case this way today:

"Dr. Munn came to me about five years ago, saying he felt tired, and wanted to know what was wrong with him. I determined that he was suffering from hemolytic anemia, an illness in which the red blood corpuscles are destroyed much faster than the body can renew them. We don't know why this happens.

"I prescribed prednisone but warned Dr. Munn that it wasn't a cure-all and had undesirable side effects. As a precaution, I put him on a minimal dosage. To my surprise, his blood condition showed an amazing improvement which I can account for only by Dr. Munn's excellent physical condition and his years of long-distance swimming.

"Even more remarkable, he doesn't seem to suffer any of the drug's familiar side effects, one of them being a decided change in appearance—almost a moon face. . . ."

As will be seen, the intent of the story was to provide information to people in Central City who may be suffering from such an ailment. It was quite the opposite of the sensational approach of a "loony-house exposé" of long ago. The writing was quiet, even reserved, and properly qualified to show that both patient and physician have consented to the publicity.

It was, all in all, a part of the professional approach to journalism that has very largely replaced the razzle-dazzle school from earlier days.

But, as any intelligent beginner will want to know, aren't there unlooked-for problems in this new approach, too? Isn't it possible, in describing treatments for obscure ailments, that perfectly normal elderly people may imagine that they, too, are suffering from debilitating illnesses? Perhaps. But in practice, the results are generally beneficial. The risks, if any, are worth taking, most editors and news directors believe.

Discrimination: A Never-Ending Struggle

Since America is primarily a nation of immigrants, it has always seemed strange to thoughtful citizens that racial and religious discrimination has continued to plague much of our society throughout this century. Nor do American attitudes show any signs of overwhelming change.

There have been so many discriminatory currents and crosscurrents throughout our history that it would be difficult to trace them all. But among the major elements, these have appeared in the news, both at home and abroad, with painful regularity:

In the first great wave of immigration after 1900, Jewish refugees from eastern Europe and Russia settled on Manhattan's lower East Side because they found so many doors elsewhere closed to them. By the time a second wave of Jewish immigration began from Europe in the wake of Hitler's rise to power in Germany, the essential character of the lower East Side had changed so the new refugees found homes elsewhere.

By that time, discrimination in some of our largest cities had spread to embrace the millions of blacks who had come North to find a haven and greater opportunities than they were offered in the rural South. For the majority, their quest was in vain; yet, they remained, for the most part, in the big cities rather than return to the farms.

Now, in the declining years of the century, it is the Hispanics— the often illegal immigrants from Cuba, Haiti, Mexico, and other parts of Latin America—who are experiencing the discriminatory attack. And this despite all the laws and commissions that have been created in this country to punish and wipe out discrimination wherever it exists. A limited amnesty program hasn't helped much.

In the rural areas around Central City, there is a special interest in Hispanics, not because of humanitarian considerations, but rather because they are reported to be willing to handle farm chores for low wages. And the hard-pressed farmers, grasping at even the slightest chance to save themselves, indicate willingness to hire the illegals, even to pay their way to the Midwest. Such ads, as they appear in southern tier newspapers from Florida to Texas, quite naturally come to the attention of the *Central City Leader*.

No matter what the motivation, a sudden flow of Hispanic labor to the Midwest would be a story, if it happens, so the paper assigns its chief political correspondent, Loren Wilton, to investigate and report. What he learns in Florida and Texas, however, is not encouraging. The main thrust of this story in the *Leader* sums up the position as follows:

HISPANICS

Miami—Hispanics who are in Florida illegally aren't likely to improve their lot immediately because of the election of the state's first Hispanic-American governor, Bob Martinez.

In Texas, the location of the other large pool of illegal Hispanic labor, the chances for progress for them are even less promising.

And yet, midwestern farmers who hope to persuade some of the illegals to work in the American heartland aren't getting much of a response to ads in both states promising steady work at good pay—and good pay for the illegals here is a lot less than the going rate for American labor up North.

This, in a nutshell, is the outlook for those hard-pressed farmers in the Central City area who had hoped to benefit from the lower wages the illegals can command. After ten days of interviews with both public officials and illegals here and in Texas, the situation is pretty well summed up by Angelo Hernandez, a husky 45-year-old Mexican who is working on a farm in Texas just across the Rio Grande from his native land:

"I cross over from Mexico to work in Texas many times, and I make good money—better than I make in Mexico. And working in Texas I can go home to see my wife and my seven children. But if I go far from the border, who knows what will happen to me? No, I am safer here. And maybe I get amnesty some time to stay in the United States and bring over my family, too."

That is the story, also, among the illegal Cubans and other Hispanics in Florida. Like the Mexicans in Texas, most of them are satisfied with the farm labor and pay they are getting. Also, they don't worry a great deal about being picked up and deported from either of the southern states, but they aren't so sure what would happen to them elsewhere.

The hope for amnesty is based on current American legislation that averts the possibility of arrest, trial, and punishment plus deportation for aliens who have been living illegally in the United States before 1982. However, federal officials in touch with the situation say there is little chance that the amnesty program will be extended to more recent illegal immigrants.

Vargo Immanuel, an official in the State Labor Office here, expects instead that there soon will be a campaign to round up, fine, and even imprison employers who hire workers without legal authority to remain in this country. Not many employers are taking the threat seriously, however.

But midwestern farmers had better save their money instead of advertising for cheap Hispanic labor around these parts. As one Cuban here said, "We never had it so good. . . . Why do we want to run around looking for trouble?" . . .

Truly, the American news media do not lack for social issues to report on and explain in these concluding years of the twentieth century. These are just a few on which the *Central City Leader* has touched—the safety of schoolchildren, the protection of women in the workplace, the issue of abortion for unwanted pregnancies, discrimination for reasons of race and religion, the safeguarding of public health. All these and more are continuing concerns across the land. And in an open society, there will always be others.

20
Political Writing

THE ART OF POLITICAL WRITING, as it has been conducted on this continent for the better part of three centuries, is the most durable practice in American journalism. At its best, it demonstrates what a free press can accomplish in scrutinizing the acts of government on behalf of a free people. At its worst, some of its practitioners—but never all of them—generate mere propaganda for unscrupulous officeholders and worthless causes. Between these extremes, the principled journalists who handle political assignments daily for all our media must struggle for fair coverage in these divisive times.

The Extent of the Assignment

The reading and viewing public nationally pays most attention to news from the very peak of government, the White House. That is understandable—the presidency is the most dynamic force in our form of government. Moreover, the most experienced and talented political writers of our time are among those who report to the rest of us from that notable vantage point at the peak.

Yet, the political beat—as it exists today—neither begins nor ends at the White House, even in Washington, D.C. In the capital, for example, what happens to this nation may be determined sometimes with even greater effect by the Congress or the Supreme Court, the

174

State or Defense Departments, or others among the myriad divisions and subdivisions of government. All must be covered in one way or another, together with the regular local beats that also make news in the District of Columbia.

That is why it fell to two novices in journalism to break a tremendous exclusive story on June 19, 1972 in the *Washington Post*. With deceptive simplicity, it began:

> One of the five men arrested early Saturday morning (June 17) in an attempt to bug the Democratic National Committee headquarters here is the salaried security coordinator for President Nixon's re-election committee.
>
> The suspect, former CIA employee James W. McCord, Jr., 53, also holds a separate contract to provide security services to the Republican National Committee, GOP National Chairman Bob Dole said yesterday.
>
> Former Attorney General John N. Mitchell, head of the Committee for the Re-election of the President, said yesterday McCord was employed to help install that committee's own security system.
>
> In a statement issued in Los Angeles, Mitchell said McCord and the other four men arrested at Democratic headquarters on Saturday "were not operating either in our behalf or with our consent" in the alleged bugging attempt. . . .

It was the first story by Bob Woodward and Carl Bernstein in their Watergate exposé (the Democratic offices were in the Watergate building complex), which eventually brought down President Nixon.*

Yet, despite the demonstrable importance of the political assignment in Washington, a nation approaching a quarter of a billion people cannot be covered entirely from that eminence. The beat, in consequence, begins in the modest city halls of the smallest towns of the various states and territories. It encompasses the governmental machinery of the larger cities, the counties, the states, and the regional complexes typified by the Tennessee Valley Authority and others.

In the biennial Congressional electoral campaigns and the quadrennial presidential elections, this complex governmental organization takes on national significance. It is then that political writers fan out from the nation's capital, other major cities, and the various state capitals to try to gauge public sentiment. The issue every two

*Nixon resigned August 8, 1974 rather than face impeachment before the Congress after the House Judiciary Committee had charged him with "high crimes and misdemeanors" in attempting to cover up the Watergate break-in with denials of any conspiracy.

years is the control of the Congress, every four years the presidency as well as the Congress.

During this intensive scrutiny of the political process in America, new and forceful political personalities break through now and then. Sometimes, as well, writers are able to pick up leads to major political issues that are developing in various parts of the land. And then, too, local scandals with national implications that influence voters can become a part of the assignment.

The process, therefore, is unending. For while public interest is centered on the national picture, political news also continues to be made locally, regionally, and statewide. It is at this basic level that beginners at political writing mainly learn to hone their skills and test their judgment. Their vehicles are the same as those of their peers—the wire services; the newspapers of national, statewide, and local significance; the newsmagazines; and the electronic media. Somehow, the audience for this outpouring of news, speculation, and comment never seems to lose interest in political activity.

Differences in Style and Content

In the first issue of his *Pennsylvania Gazette* in Philadelphia more than two and a half centuries ago, Benjamin Franklin wrote for the benefit of his subscribers, "To publish a good newspaper is not so easy an undertaking as many people imagine it to be."* What Franklin would write about the complications of putting out the news today can best be left to the imagination. What does merit closer examination, however, is the change that time and circumstances have wrought in both the style and content of the political story in America.

The technique of investigation for political purposes was being used well before the Revolutionary War in the thirty-eight newspapers of the thirteen colonies. For example, the twenty-one-year-old editor of the *Massachusetts Spy* in Boston, Isaiah Thomas, managed to obtain and publish damaging correspondence of the then governor of Massachusetts Bay Colony, Thomas Hutchinson. To Hutchinson, Thomas attributed the statement, "There must be an abridgement of what are called English liberties."

That was picked up and reprinted by other papers in Boston,

*This was the issue of October 2, 1729.

Philadelphia, and New York City with embarrassing consequences for the British government. As if that weren't bad enough, the next exposé in the colonial press charged that a half million pounds of taxable tea was about to be unloaded in America. That set the scene in Boston harbor for the Boston Tea Party on December 16, 1773 when the Sons of Liberty, disguised as Indians, dumped overboard eighteen thousand pounds of tea from the sailing ship *Dartmouth.*

There were more such exploits until the break with the mother country came at Concord and Lexington in the opening battles of the Revolutionary War. Isaiah Thomas, an eyewitness that day, began his account in the *Massachusetts Spy* on May 3, 1775 (the battles had been fought fifteen days previously on April 19) as follows:

> AMERICANS: Forever bear in mind the BATTLE OF LEXING-TON—where British troops, unmolested and unprovoked, wantonly and in a most inhuman manner, fired upon and killed a number of our countrymen, then robbed, ransacked, and burned their houses. . . .

There was no nonsense about objectivity in the patriot press, no precise lead that 60 Minutemen and 260 British fell in the first clash of arms at Lexington. Like all the partisans of the patriot press, Thomas's mission was not merely to report the news but to inflame his readers to resist.

That, too, was the mission of the great political journalist of the revolution, Tom Paine. With the adoption of the Declaration of Independence on July 4, 1776, the British occupation of New York City, and General Washington's hasty retreat through New Jersey with his little army, Paine broke the first of his "Crisis Papers" in the *Pennsylvania Journal* on December 19, 1776, beginning:

> These are the times that try men's souls. The Summer soldier and the sunshine Patriot will, in this crisis, shrink from the service of their country; but he that stands it now, deserves the love and thanks of man and woman. Tyranny, like Hell, is not easily conquered. . . .

That Christmas Eve, when copies of the *Pennsylvania Journal* reached Washington's command along the Delaware River, he ordered Paine's article read to his troops.* Then, at dawn, he led them

---

*The activity of the patriot press is related in greater detail in John Hohenberg, *Free Press/Free People: The Best Cause* (New York: Columbia University Press, 1971), pp. 48–59 passim.

in boats across the Delaware to take both Trenton and New Jersey from the surprised British.

Styles in journalism have changed, although a deeply emotional style still is a vital part of American reportage sometimes both in the press and the electronic media. However, even in the most important political developments, today's news articles are doggedly objective and the arguments and reflections are generally on the editorial page. In the *Washington Post* of August 9, 1974, for example, Carroll Kirkpatrick began his account of President Nixon's resignation as follows:

> Richard Milhous Nixon announced last night that he will resign as the 37th President of the United States at noon today.
> Vice President Gerald R. Ford of Michigan will take the oath of office as President at noon to complete the remaining two and one-half years of Mr. Nixon's term.
> After two years of bitter debate over the Watergate scandals, President Nixon bowed to pressures from the public and leaders of his own party to become the first President in American history to resign. . . .

It is on the editorial page, primarily, that judgments are made of such important matters, nearly always in the name of the newspaper rather than any individual. On television, by contrast, it is currently the fashion to introduce a special commentator to make such remarks but it is seldom, indeed, that either the network or a particular station assumes responsibility for criticism of a high public official.

Among the exceptions to general press practice in separating news and opinion are emergencies when strong reportorial emotions may color the news. But this does not always turn out to be something that induces an unfavorable public reaction. On the contrary, the injection of an overwhelming personal reaction at times of stress can illuminate the news and bring home to the reader the stunning effect of great events.

Such was the story that Merriman Smith wrote for United Press International about the assassination of President John F. Kennedy in 1963:

> Washington, Nov. 23 (UPI)—It was a balmy, sunny afternoon as we motored through downtown Dallas behind President Kennedy yesterday. The procession cleared the center of the business district and turned into a handsome highway that wound through what appeared to be a park.
> I was riding in the so-called White House press "pool" car, a telephone company vehicle equipped with a mobile radio telephone. . . .

Suddenly we heard three loud, almost painfully loud, cracks. The first sounded as if it might have been a large firecracker. But the second and third blast were unmistakable. Gunfire.

Everybody in our car began shouting at the driver to pull up closer to the President's car. But at that moment we saw the big bubble-top and a motorcycle escort roar away at high speed. . . .

They vanished around a curve. When we cleared the same curve, we could see where we were heading—Parkland Hospital. . . . We skidded around a sharp left turn and spilled out of the pool car as it entered the hospital driveway.

I ran to the side of the bubble-top.

The President was face-down on the back seat. Mrs. Kennedy made a cradle of her arms around the President's head and bent over him as if she were whispering to him.

Clint Hill, the Secret Service agent in charge of the detail assigned to Mrs. Kennedy, was leaning over into the rear of the car.

"How badly is he hurt, Clint?" I asked.

"He's dead," Clint replied curtly. . . .*

Regardless of changes in style and content, political writing remains a vital force in shaping American thought. From Tom Paine to Merriman Smith, our political journalists have had something important to say to the American people about great events and they have expressed themselves with clarity and force. So a tradition in journalism continues.

Of Political News and Interpretation

A third phase of political writing, known as interpretation, has developed in our time as a kind of bridge between the factual reporting in the news columns and the commentary on the editorial page.

In many of our larger and more influential newspapers, this is often used as a separate article marked "Analysis" and printed somewhere near the news account. Most smaller newspapers permit their political writers to weave interpretation into their news reports of significant political developments when it is necessary.

In wire services and newsmagazines either treatment is possible. Radio and television use such abbreviated news reports in most of their regularly scheduled news periods that there isn't much time for interpretation; however, special commentators do appear on occasion with brief analyses of important newsbreaks. It is in such special reports, mainly, that the electronic media present a point of view in addition to the news.

*Merriman Smith's article was in the UPI file for November 23, 1963, the day after the assassination of President Kennedy. Reprinted with permission.

As beginning journalists may readily understand from the care with which analysis and commentary are handled in the news columns, not everybody who writes or broadcasts politics is given the privilege of interpreting the news.

Often, if some new and untried commentator may be doing an interpretive piece in print or on the air, the point of view may first be discussed with an editor or a news director. But someone of the stature of James Reston of the *New York Times* or Dan Rather of CBS wouldn't be expected to clear with a superior before doing an analysis; as veteran journalists with prestige all their own, they can command public attention for their point of view.

Here is how interpretation is handled through each method for the *Central City Leader* under the following circumstances:

Joe Stoddard, the city editor, has received a tip from City Hall that Mayor Reardon is about to announce his candidacy for a second four-year term on the Republican ticket. A Democratic candidate for mayor, President Cory Bennington of the municipal council, already has declared himself in the race. Both Bennington and Reardon are veteran campaigners, proven vote getters, and are unopposed in the primary elections of their respective parties.

Still, Stoddard worries because the forthcoming election looks to him like a toss-up. With such an even division among the electorate in Central City, the editor reasons that the story has to be written "right down the middle," as the saying goes, so that it is fair to both candidates and their supporters. For that reason, instead of giving the assignment to someone in the newsroom, the editor summons his top political writer, Loren Wilton, from the state capital to handle the story.

This, then, is the setup: Mardee Fenwick, the regular beat reporter at City Hall, with assistance from two others assigned from the newsroom, will cover the story and phone in to Wilton, who will do the writing. There may be a so-called color sidebar by Mardee later to describe the scene and the atmosphere as the mayor makes known his decision.

This is the way Wilton begins his story, weaving in the necessary interpretation where he believes it necessary without consulting the city desk:

MAYOR

Mayor Henry Reardon announced today that he would run for re-election for a second four-year term.

The 58-year-old mayor, heading the Republican ticket, will be opposed by the Democratic candidate, Municipal Council President Cory Bennington.

Neither candidate will have any opposition in the forthcoming primary election, clearing the way for what most observers believe will be a close contest in November.

"I am running on my record," the mayor said at City Hall in making his announcement. "In my first four years, I have given the people of Central City the beginnings of the reforms I promised to put into effect. Now, I am going to finish the job."

The mayor, beaming and ruddy faced, stood before a battery of microphones and TV and still cameras as he spoke. A small group of City Hall employees applauded him and clustered around him as he concluded.

Witnessing the scene in the mayor's office from the entrance, Council President Bennington merely grinned and waved off reporters when he was asked for comment. "It's the mayor's day," he said. "Let him enjoy it. He's in for a trimming in November."

What the mayor has in his favor in his reelection campaign, his supporters believe, is the generally favorable attitude most civic groups have adopted toward his reform program. However, because of cooling relations with Governor Farrow, who gave him strong support four years ago, the mayor cannot count on much help from that quarter in November.

Just how the voters will assess blame for the new taxes and the elimination of 122 city jobs, made necessary by an "economy budget," remains to be determined and could be the major issue in the campaign, some analysts believe. . . .

As Wilton reached that point in his story, Stoddard, who had been reading copy closely on the city desk, came over to him. "Loren," the editor says, "I think we'd better make a separate story out of the interpretation. To put both in the same story is going to make it awfully long and maybe too complicated for the average reader."

Wilton nods in understanding. "What do you want me to cut?"

Stoddard shows him. "Right here after the sixth paragraph, the quote from Bennington. Eliminate the next two paragraphs and let's have the guts of the mayor's statement as he delivered it and any ad lib comments he made at the end before he went back to work. Never mind the color stuff, Mardee Fenwick's coming in from City Hall to do a feature piece on that. And when you finish the lead, then do the separate analysis. Okay?"

Wilton, as a veteran political writer, nods and follows instructions. He notes that the city editor has left in the third paragraph, a part of which is interpretation that is attributed to unnamed "observers," meaning the writer himself. That is the link with his separate analysis which begins as follows:

ANALYSIS—with MAYOR

By Loren Wilton

The Reardon-Bennington race for mayor, a renewal of a political feud of years' standing, shapes up as a grudge fight that may go right to the wire in November.

What the mayor has in his favor in his reelection campaign, his supporters believe, is the generally favorable attitude of most civic groups toward his reform program. On the whole, civic leaders have rallied behind the mayor's efforts to streamline city government, eliminate waste, and promote greater efficiency in the handling of city business.

Where the mayor may be weak, however, is in his willingness to support the reopening of the South River atomic plant of the Central City Light and Power Company. His attack on the governor for "foot dragging" in keeping the plant closed has cooled relations between them and probably will cost him the governor's vigorous support.

Four years ago, Governor Farrow's campaigning made the difference between victory and defeat for the mayor, as both have since agreed.

But Bennington doesn't have everything his own way either on the Democratic side. Some of his strongest supporters were turned off when he decided to support the mayor's controversial budget package of a new 5 percent sales tax, a 12½ percent boost in property taxes, and the elimination of 122 jobs.

Although Bennington since has blamed both the mayor and the state's Penniman-Grob budget-balancing law for his action, some leading Democrats have expressed fear privately that it could hurt him worse than the mayor. . . .

The technique, as will be seen, is certainly not that of a hard news account. However, it also isn't the straight opinion piece that would go on the editorial page as the declaration of the newspaper. What Wilton is trying to do, by balancing one candidate against the other, is to leave open the *Central City Leader*'s option to support either candidate as the campaign progresses. That declaration, of course, will be on the editorial page.

Under the processes of modern journalism the news columns would remain neutral. And if the race is as close as this one is likely to be, that would seem to be wise. To show partisanship in handling the news quite naturally would turn off supporters of one or the other of the mayoral candidates, who might otherwise stick with the paper until it makes an editorial page declaration of where it stands.

Bias in Modern Journalism

There was a lot of rough-and-tumble scare journalism in the American press during its early history. Because of unprincipled attacks on President Washington as a "despot," an infuriated mob wrecked the print shop where the culprit newspaper, the *Aurora*, was published.

Subsequently, because of his sponsorship of the Alien and Sedition Acts, President Adams also drew such scathing criticism that a number of editors were jailed and one was deported to England. Even after the despised laws expired, President Jefferson was thrown into a feud with some of his press critics.

Nothing even remotely resembling that riotous period has happened in these times, but the press has remained a ready target in American public life.

"Give-'em-Hell" Harry Truman, in campaigning in 1948 for re-election to the presidency, bitterly attacked the press as his major enemy because, he charged, it was controlled by Republican publishers who opposed him. Fewer than forty years later, President Ronald Reagan's far right adherents in the Republican party were just as vehement in their criticism of political writers as liberals who were bound to attack the Reagan administration at all costs.

So there was room to doubt, had the public been so inclined, whether the Republican publishers or the liberal political writers (to take Truman and Reagan people at their word) controlled newspapers—and possibly the rest of the news media as well. The truth, as always, wasn't that simple.

Whether critics of journalism appreciate it or not, the rise of professionalism in journalism has done much in modern times to reduce political bias in the news media. The uncomfortable feeling among both owners and newspeople that the public is increasingly critical of news operations has also played a part in a growing pressure for fairness in the handling of political campaigns.

This may not make life any easier for the political writers of tomorrow, but it is the best that can be done in this turbulent day and age, as witness the argument that developed between ex-Senator Gary Hart and the Miami Herald in his drive for the 1988 Democratic Presidential nomination. When the Herald put five reporters on Hart's trail and found him briefly in the company of a young woman not his wife, he gave up his formal campaign even though he denied any impropriety. His supporters thereby denounced "keyhole" journalism. It was not a glorious moment for journalists.*

---

*Hart withdrew May 8, 1987 in Denver. See Denver Post and other newspapers for May 9, 1987.

21

Polls, Polltakers, and Writers

IT WAS NOT SO LONG AGO, as politicians figure the passage of time, that election forecasts consisted mainly of uneducated guesses by political writers. What the journalists had to do was to listen to the exaggerated estimates of victory by the contending forces, take private counsel with veteran politicians and others, and then put on paper their best judgment of the outcome.

The system was erratic but it usually worked pretty well if there was a wide swing of public sentiment toward one candidate or another. In close races, however, the guessers frequently were wrong. The coming of scientific polltaking since then may have improved the journalists' position, but complete accuracy can scarcely be guaranteed even today for election predictions.

As for polls on a wide variety of other subjects involving public opinion, from television ratings to Soviet-American relations, the only guarantee of their accuracy is the reputation of the sponsoring news organization, if any.

Conducting a Public Opinion Poll

In the era before social science intruded on journalism, many a journalist considered quite mistakenly that public opinion could be tested by talking to almost any group on a street corner about a given subject. It didn't work. A group of downtown middle-class shoppers almost anywhere in America could scarcely be trusted to speak for the much larger sections of poor people in outlying sections of town. Furthermore, a reporter with any sense at all could tell that prosperous business people at a Rotary Club lunch would have one opinion on a subject such as unemployment benefits while workmen on a union picket line outside a strike-bound factory would have quite another.

It was mainly to eliminate such disparities that polltaking organizations developed the concept of a true random sample of public opinion. This is defined roughly as a selection process in which everybody in a given area has an equal chance of being chosen for interviewing.

In telephone polls, which are generally used nowadays because they are easier, quicker, and cheaper to do, it is a relatively simple matter to divide the names in a telephone directory. For example, if there are 150,000 names in the directory and a sample of 1,500 names is desired, that means every hundredth name is to be called. If nobody answers or the person called won't participate, the next name on the list is usually called.

By using Census Bureau maps, telephone directories, and other data, polling organizations develop random samples on a nationwide basis and can come up with a survey overnight if needed. This is often done by the Nielsen organization with its television ratings polls, as well as other samplings that try to determine public reaction to a new tax law, a coming sports event, or an international conference, to name just a few possibilities.

The more expensive process of person-to-person interviews is conducted in much the same way, only in this case the interviews must take place in certain specified spots to make sure that the laws of probability are observed. Each polling organization has its own formula for picking a place and time for such interviews and collating the responses.

Now as to accuracy in polltaking, that is called a "confidence level" in social science jargon. Most polltakers are satisfied with a 95 percent figure.

To put it the way the polltakers do, this is how a Harris Survey described a study of public faith in our institutions:

> This Harris survey was conducted by telephone within the United States between Nov. 9–13 among a cross-section of 1,247 adults nation-wide. Figures for age, sex, race, and education were weighted where necessary to bring them into line with their actual proportions in the population.
>
> In a sample of this size, one can say with 95 percent certainty

that the results are within plus or minus 3 percentage points of what they would be if the entire adult population had been polled.*

To be explicit, Harris and others who work with a sample of this size are willing to accept a deviation of as much as 6 percent ("plus or minus 3 percentage points") to achieve 95 percent accuracy. Using statistical tables to reduce the error factor to plus or minus 2 percent at a 95 percent level, a sample of 2,401 is needed; for plus or minus 1 percent, it would go to a prohibitive 9,605. At the other end of the statistical spectrum, a sample of about 600 would entail an error risk of plus or minus 4 percent, which is a lot, too.

The Record of Polltakers

While informal polltaking by newspapers goes back more than a century, the first major modern venture was undertaken beginning in 1916 by the *Literary Digest* magazine with a postcard poll sent to millions of persons during presidential campaigns. There wasn't too much concern about the *Digest*'s stunt until 1936, when the magazine predicted that Governor Alfred M. Landon of Kansas would overwhelm President Franklin Roosevelt. The result was quite the opposite, with FDR beating back his Republican challenger, forty-six states to two. The *Digest* soon after suspended publication.

At just about the same time, such veteran polltakers as George Gallup and Elmo Roper opened for business and did pretty well with their scientific sampling procedures until the Truman-Dewey presidential campaign of 1948. Gallup was wrong by 5.3 percent, Roper by 8.4 percent and both understated the Democratic vote.

With changes in the system, most major polltakers recovered and went along nicely until another close election occurred, this one being the Carter-Ford presidential election of 1976. Most polling organizations picked Ford, the Republican, to win by 1 percent but Carter triumphed by that figure. Gallup, who had covered himself by saying the vote was too close to call, commented, "The plain fact of the matter is that you have to be lucky."

But luck wasn't a factor in 1980 when Ronald Reagan surprised most of the polltakers with a landslide victory over President Carter.

*Statement included with announcement of polltaking results in "Confidence in Institutions Rises Sharply," the Harris Survey, dated December 17, 1984.

So the risk still exists, as it did before polltaking was introduced to both journalists and the American public on a scientific basis. And any political writer who has to do an election forecast must take it into account.

There is still another drawback to the practice of calling elections of any kind well in advance. The record of Americans for participating in elections in the latter part of this century is not very good to begin with, sinking to as little as 10 to 12 percent of eligible voters in some primary elections. Except in races for the presidency that excite wide public interest, experienced politicians generally expect only about 25 percent of eligible voters to go to the polls for an average city or state election.

But when major polltakers publish and broadcast claims that one side or the other has an overwhelming lead, the usual effect is that a lot more voters stay home. The lower turnout thereby can affect the outcome of a close election and veteran politicians and political writers are well aware of it.

That underscores the trickiness of doing a forecast in print or on the air of the outcome of a particularly close race, or one that polltakers figure to be close, because there is no way of determining in advance how many people actually will cast ballots.

On Writing a Forecast Before Election Day

Loren Wilton, the *Central City Leader*'s chief political writer, has drawn the unenviable assignment of doing a forecast piece on a close mayoral election in Central City.

The current polls show the incumbent, Henry Reardon, has a narrow lead over his Democratic challenger, Cory Bennington, the municipal council president. With the election almost at hand, however, there are rumors out of the state capital that Governor Farrow, who has until then taken no side in the battle, may come to the assistance of his fellow Republican.

That, as Wilton realizes, could change the outcome. For even if Mayor Reardon has outraged local opinion by demanding the reopening of a closed atomic power plant and business in Central City has been hard hit by a Midwest farm crisis, it is difficult to imagine that traditional Republican majorities will melt away or disappear entirely.

Wilton decides to talk things over with Joe Stoddard before starting a crucial piece that will appear in the *Leader*, an afternoon paper, on the day before election. The rival morning paper, the *Central City News,* already has come out strongly for the Democrat, Bennington, arguing, "It's time for a change." The broadcast media, as usual, have taken no position but Bennington, a movie-type personality and a convincing speaker, has been given a lot of free time on local late-night talk shows.

Wilton needs information first of all. "Our paper has taken no editorial position so far," he observes to the city editor. "If the governor comes out strongly for the mayor in the next twenty-four hours, is that going to make a difference? Are we going to back the mayor at the last gasp?"

Stoddard assures him, "I went to a conference with the publisher and the editorial page editor yesterday and we're staying on the fence. Just play it safe and don't take sides."

"I can't pick either guy to win," Wilton says. "It really is too close to call, regardless of what the polls show publicly."

The city editor catches the qualification. "Do you have access to a private poll?"

"The governor's press secretary told me last week that the governor's own private poll showed Bennington was ahead," Wilton explains, "But the information was given to me off the record."

"Is that why the governor may jump in on Reardon's side at the last minute?" Stoddard asks.

Wilton shakes his head. "I doubt it. Ever since the mayor called him down for opposing the opening of the atomic power plant, the governor hasn't been very friendly. And, since he's campaigning for the presidency, he can't afford to be on the losing side in the biggest city in the state."

The city editor gives him the "A-treatment," which in journalism is a genial slap on the back and a cheerful, "Your problem, do the best you can, but I'd at least hint at what the private poll shows."

Wilton struggles for a lead and finally comes up with the following after three tries:

MAYOR

Mayor Reardon and his Democratic challenger, Council President Bennington, are in a neck-and-neck mayoral race with the opening of the polls only 24 hours off.

From all available indications, the long and bitter mayoral campaign is too close to call.

Although three major polling organizations show that the mayor has a 1 to 2 percent lead as he approaches the finish line, at least one private poll by a neutral source gives Bennington the edge by about the same figure.

The problem with accepting such polls at face value, however, is that statistically they allow for a plus or minus error of 3 percent. Social scientists are quick to point out that both the public and private polls show that the candidates' margins are less than that.

Nevertheless, in formal statements issued at their respective headquarters, both Reardon and Bennington claimed victory. Reardon predicted he would win by 100,000 votes while Bennington forecast a much closer win by 10,000 to 15,000.

Actually, if either side is to receive a last-minute boost, observers believe it will have to come from Governor Farrow, who has remained neutral so far in the contest.

If Farrow should give a strong last-minute endorsement to his fellow Republican, Reardon, it might be enough to tip the balance, some observers believe. However, the governor's continued silence might have just the opposite effect.

All efforts to determine the governor's plans so far have yielded nothing but vague speculation that he was considering a plea for the mayor. But at the governor's office, a knowledgeable source said, "Don't bet on it."

The mayor and the governor haven't been on speaking terms since their argument over the proposed reopening of the South River atomic power plant. The governor is known to have resented the mayor's criticism of his position in keeping the plant closed for reasons of public safety. . . .

This is the way the story runs in the paper with little except routine editing changes. It will be noted that the polling information, the basis for the "too close to call" finding, is given up high as documentation for the lead; also, that the narrowness of the margins ascribed to either candidate are shown to be meaningless because they are within the statistical margin of error.

To professionals, however, there is one questionable aspect of Wilton's otherwise carefully written forecast. That is his use of the governor's private poll, supposedly given to him on an off-the-record basis. Even if the political writer has not identified the source, he knows he is likely to be accused by the governor's people of violating a confidence.

His defense, not unknown in such cases, is that he and the governor's press secretary were talking on background (that is, for use but without identifying the source) when the matter of the private poll came up. In the confusion of what was on background and what was off the record, complications political reporters always fear, the poll was used on a nonattributable basis.

Why did the political reporter risk the displeasure of his source

when he really didn't need the private poll for his account? First
of all, he suspected that the information was being "leaked" to him
in such a way that the governor's people could claim innocence.
And then, too, the city editor had suggested using the information
for public knowledge.

In any event, when Wilton reads the preelection-day story next
morning of his rival, Mort Pender, in the *Central City News*, he
feels better about his indiscretion. The *News*'s account goes all out
for the candidate it is supporting. Under a headline predicting a
Bennington victory, the story begins:

> Council President Bennington is favored to defeat Mayor Reardon's
> reelection bid in a close election tomorrow.
>
> In a poll commissioned by the *Central City News* that was completed
> within the last 24 hours, a shift of uncommitted votes to Bennington
> gave him a 6 percent edge over the mayor.
>
> The poll, conducted by Bartram Associates, the firm that forecast
> a Reardon victory four years ago, gave Bennington 52 percent of those
> who participated, Reardon 46 percent, and the remaining 2 percent
> were undecided.
>
> Albert J. Bartram, president of Bartram Associates, said that 1,247
> registered voters participated in the telephone poll, which allows for
> a possible error of plus or minus 3 percent at an accuracy level of
> 95 percent.
>
> "You will note," he explained, "that the 6 percent margin for Ben-
> nington exceeds the allowance for error in substantial fashion."
>
> When the results of the poll were conveyed last night to Governor
> Farrow, a former supporter of the mayor's who has withheld support
> for him thus far in the current campaign, an official who would not
> be identified commented:
>
> "We're not surprised. We have a private poll that also shows Ben-
> nington ahead, but not by as much. It's bound to be very close."
>
> Asked if the governor would make a last-minute declaration for
> Reardon, the official refused a direct response, explaining, "That
> would be speculation and I can't speculate."
>
> However, other sources at the state capital told the *News* that the
> governor had a "very full schedule" today and wasn't likely to change
> it. The break between the mayor and governor occurred over the may-
> or's campaign to reopen the South River atomic power plant which
> the governor had ordered closed.
>
> In analyzing the poll that showed a swing of undecided voters to
> Bennington, Bartram, speaking for his polling firm, said, "We found
> the underlying reason for dissatisfaction with the mayor was fear of
> the reopening of the South River atomic power plant." . . .

It is now apparent to Wilton that the governor's press secretary
really did mean to "leak" the private governor's poll to the news

media—an almost certain sign that the governor was playing an undercover role in favor of Bennington. When subsequent newscasts on local television stations also use the same material, Wilton becomes convinced that this is the case. In a new lead for his forecast next day, he comes as close as he can to implying the governor's role while building up the possibility of a narrow victory for Bennington, depending on the size of the voter turnout.

While this kind of political hanky-panky often occurs on election eve, especially in supposedly close contests, it is not something that beginners at political writing can be expected to handle. It takes a certain amount of apprenticeship to detect these undercover moves and learn to gauge their effectiveness.

Sometimes this backstairs maneuvering to use the media does help a candidate in a close race, but it also can backfire if the opposition becomes aware of what is going on and hollers "Foul!" Then, ninety-nine times out of one hundred, it is those scheming reporters who are blamed, not the politicians who seek to use them and their news organizations.

The one factor that can be testified to with reasonable certainty is that the polling organizations, which have nothing to gain and everything to lose by doctoring a poll, have never been caught at it in any election of significance. They have been wrong, true enough, and probably will be again from time to time. They also will continue to sell their services, but it is difficult to believe that any polltaker of consequence or any political writer will sell out.

That has never been a part of the game in modern times.

22

Writing about Elections

ELECTION NIGHT IS A CHERISHED INSTITUTION in American journalism. Whatever has been said and written during the uproar of a political campaign, the hours immediately after the polls close are dedicated at last to an effort to get at the truth.

Even for the most violently partisan news organizations, the main object, with few exceptions, is to report who won and by what margin. If charges of election fraud are to be made, that comes later. But on election night, no publisher or station owner wants to be put in the position of the *Chicago Tribune* of 1948, which is condemned through journalistic eternity for having elected the wrong man as president.

Beginners at political writing have good reason to remember the picture of a grinning Harry Truman holding aloft the paper with the wrong headline. Mistakes on election night are not easily forgotten.

On Handling Election Night Leads

Despite the development of a computerized society, the counting of votes on election night—even in the largest cities and most technically advanced areas of the land—usually proceeds with appalling sluggishness. Particularly in close elections, the periodic announcement of returns can be exasperatingly slow. It may last through the night and well into the next day.

Writers should remember, in such cases, that the closeness of the race is likely to lead to challenges and demands for a recount that could further prolong the tally. When that happens, the victor on election night is in danger of having his slender triumph reversed. And writers who have assumed that the election finally is over may find themselves embarrassed if they have not reasonably qualified the tentative results.

In highly partisan news organizations, pressures develop occasionally to claim victory for a favored candidate on the basis of an incomplete or even fraudulent count. When that happens, the writer whose name is on the story may be in a tight spot. Unless the evidence is credible, his professional reputation as well as that of his news organization is at stake.

Truth then may become a casualty as well.

Otherwise, when a candidate or a slate of candidates clearly outdistance their foes in the early tallies, it isn't too difficult to write about elections. The main precaution to be taken even in such runaway races is to keep exact figures out of the lead until the count is completed—something that is done in tight contests as a matter of routine.

Here is how a morning paper lead could be written if early returns show one candidate well ahead:

> Governor Meriwether piled up a comfortable early lead last night in his bid for reelection to a third term over his Democratic challenger, Mike Dramon.
>
> With 615 out of 5,780 precincts reporting, the State Board of Elections gave:
>
> Meriwether (R)—821,658
> Dramon (D)—385,281
>
> From the time the first returns were made known after the polls closed at 8:00 P.M., the governor was out in front but did not immediately claim victory. . . .

The reason for this format is apparent. For morning papers and wire services, the tally can be kept current merely by inserting later announcements to replace the figures directly after the lead. The lead itself need not be changed unless the race tightens, the challenger concedes defeat, or the leader claims victory.

For radio and television, where there is no delay of consequence in broadcasting the latest figures, it is sufficient merely to flash the latest figures on the tube and permit a seasoned anchor person to make whatever comments seem appropriate. In that sense, the electronic media cover elections as they would any other contest from sports to legislative voting on major issues.

The one no-no for broadcasters, as it has developed over a long period, is to claim a big lead or outright victory for one candidate before the polls close. That, as mentioned before, discourages late voters from going to the polls and can influence the outcome in an unexpectedly close race. In consequence, especially among networks in national elections, there is a lot of anxious if quiet behind-the-scenes discussion before an anchor person is given the go-ahead to announce a winner in a major contest.

When Elections Are in Doubt

The first clue to a close election occurs when reporters at the scene note that the count, as announced by qualified supervisors, rapidly changes hands. Once again, for the electronic media, that isn't much of a problem because of the rapidity of their communications. But for newspapers, especially when they are dependent on wire service material from distant points, editorial judgment very soon becomes more important than the mechanics of writing.

When there is a statewide election, a newspaper must pay a lot of attention to the way local returns are running as compared with statewide tallies. In a state such as New York, for example, political pundits formerly calculated that a winning Republican candidate had to have a plurality of 600,000 to 700,000 votes upstate to overcome a plurality of Democratic votes that a rival candidate could expect in New York City. Conversely, a Democratic candidate could be behind a Republican rival by no more than that amount of votes upstate in order to win on the basis of Democratic pluralities in New York City.* (A *plurality* is the difference between two candidates in a more numerous field. A *majority* is the difference between two candidates without other opposition.)

In the face of such complications, writers on election night face additional hazards in statewide and national elections. This is where calculators or computers are needed. Here is how the system works:

A statewide figure, issued from the state capital, often lags behind

*The personal popularity of national figures such as President Ronald Reagan on the Republican side and Governor Mario Cuomo on the Democratic side made a difference in the way both politicians and journalists figured such pluralities. The illustration, however, is valid where such divisions exist.

a big city total against which it must be balanced. Moreover, although public interest may center on the top of the slate of each party (a governor, statewide; a president, nationally), the various election boards in numerous precincts must also calculate the votes for other offices.

What it all adds up to is delay after delay—and a lot of busy work on calculators or computers, sometimes both. But when the figures are sparse in one area and large in another, and the total number of voters cannot be known until the tally is completed, little writing can be done with certainty unless the top contest is a runaway.

Thus, wire service accounts of statewide tallies on election night must be blended with the big city totals that a newspaper's own staff produce in greater volume. That means the newspaper's top political writer uses both the wire service material for upstate and the local staff reports for the city to try to come up with a reasonable approximation of the way the election is going.

To illustrate, here is a simulated wire service lead on a statewide election timed around midnight, four hours after the polls have closed in the governorship contest previously referred to:

> Capital City (IN)—Governor Meriwether held a commanding lead last night over his Democratic rival, Mike Dramon, on the basis of a massive upstate Republican plurality.
>
> With 2,401 of 5,780 precincts reporting, the State Board of Elections gave:
>
> Meriwether (R)—2,842,845
> Dramon (D)—989,727
>
> This was a plurality of 1,853,118 for the governor, who is seeking reelection for a third term, with the counting at about the halfway point.
>
> What made that lead all the more impressive was the unexpectedly slender margin that Dramon, a state senator, had in his home base, Metropolitan City, a Democratic stronghold. Of the State Board of Elections's tally for 2,401 precincts, 492 were from Metropolitan City and gave Dramon a lead of only about 250,000. . . .

However, at that hour, the paper's own reporters have the Metropolitan City vote at about the halfway point and a sidebar story for the edition begins:

> State Senator Mike Dramon was running well ahead of Governor Meriwether in Metropolitan City last night, but appeared to face an uphill struggle to overtake the governor's big lead in the rest of the state.
>
> With 1,475 of 2,813 local precincts reporting, the city Board of Elections reported the tally as follows:

Dramon (D)—1,565,842

Meriwether (R)—787,921

The plurality of 777,921 for Dramon at that juncture in the tabulation was not believed to be sufficient to overtake the governor's lead in Republican upstate areas. Although no concession of defeat was forthcoming from Democratic headquarters, the atmosphere was gloomy. . . .

It requires no great feat of mathematics to determine that the governor's upstate midnight lead is almost double that of his Democratic challenger in the city. Barring a last-minute surge of Democratic votes, the governor seems a safe bet for reelection for a third term. But it simply isn't practical to announce a Meriwether victory in advance of either a Republican claim of victory or a Democratic concession of defeat.

Thus, the midnight lead for the paper reads:

> Governor Meriwether seemed to be on his way to reelection for a third term early today as his Democratic challenger, State Senator Mike Dramon, failed to run as well as expected in Metropolitan City.
>
> With the tally at the halfway point in both Metropolitan City and the state as a whole, the governor appeared to have a commanding lead over his rival. On the basis of these partial returns, observers believed that, barring a late surge of Democratic votes from Metropolitan City, the governor could expect to be reelected.
>
> There was, however, no indication as of last midnight that Dramon was ready to concede defeat or that the governor was about to claim victory.
>
> With 2,401 of 5,780 precincts reporting statewide, the Independent News wire service gave this tally from the State Board of Elections:
>
> Meriwether (R)—2,842,845
>
> Dramon (D)—989,727
>
> Of this total, however, only 492 precincts were included from Metropolitan City. Even without that vote, the governor's lead at that stage was in excess of 1,500,000. By contrast, a later count from Metropolitan City showed Dramon's expected Democratic plurality here wasn't even approaching the governor's lead.
>
> With 1,475 of 2,813 local precincts counted, the report from the local Election Board was:
>
> Dramon (D)—1,565,842
>
> Meriwether (R)—787,921
>
> The Democratic plurality for Dramon, 777,921, showed that he was still lagging far behind the overwhelming lead the governor was building upstate. . . .

The point to all this is quite simple as the copy shows: no political writer can hope to win plaudits for style in giving a factual report of election returns as they come in. The best that can be expected is a careful, accurate, and well-qualified statement of what the returns show in the main story and in any sidebars that are written about other developments.

It remains for columnists in newspapers and newsmagazines and anchor persons and commentators on television and radio to try to do the fancy jobs. For beginners, the election night chores are mainly devoted to forwarding the election returns, covering the candidates, and perhaps writing feature pieces about the winners and losers.

Working on a Close Election

In a close election such as the one that is foreshadowed in Central City between Mayor Reardon and his Democratic rival, Municipal Council President Cory Bennington, nothing is left to chance in the advance arrangements by the two daily newspapers. The broadcast media, not having the trained personnel to staff all points, must depend to a very large extent on the wire services, especially the Independent News radio wire.

While the general public is bound to follow television for the first newsbreaks, the political insiders know the clean-up story will have to come from the newspapers. And in case of a recount due to irregularities in a close tally, it is the press that is most likely to be the most influential element in the long run because good investigative reporters seldom get much chance to expose wrongdoing on television.

When Joe Stoddard makes his election night assignments, therefore, he isn't particularly concerned about the television competition. What does worry him is the inside track the *Central City News,* the morning paper, seems to have into the governor's position in the election. In the event of provable fraud or some other irregularity in the counting, what the governor says and does could be crucial.

Knowing that it will be necessary to pull Loren Wilton out of the state capital to write the main election story for the *Leader,* Stoddard picks Chuck Arnow off rewrite as a temporary replacement to cover the governor's office. Next, he knows he will have to assign his City Hall reporter, Mardee Fenwick, to the mayor's headquarters whether the mayor wins or loses.

As for someone to cover Bennington, Stoddard gambles with a novice, Mack Roberts, because the young man has done good work during the campaign and seems to have the happy facility of turning up in the right place at the right time. There is no formula to develop follow the crowd and hope for the best. In any case, Roberts gets the call, an unusual break for a newspaper beginner on election night; on television it would be too risky to put a newcomer in such a tough spot.

But that isn't all the election night duty for the *Leader* by any means. It is possible that the *News,* being the morning paper, may get the complete count in the mayoral race in its final edition along with television and the wire services. But the *Leader's* people will find plenty to do whether the count is completed or not. Three reporters are assigned to the local election board to phone in returns in rotation. Then, extra people are put at Police Headquarters in case of disturbances.

In addition, knowing how crucial the South River atomic power plant may be in determining the outcome of this election, the city editor puts two reporters at Fire Headquarters with instructions to be on the alert for news of special precautions in and around the plant. This, of course, is just a hunch assignment—such things sometimes pay off.

What cannot be foreseen is the way the returns will come in. Nor does the voting on election day provide any clue to the outcome. All the *Leader's* reporters can say is that the turnout appears somewhat heavier than usual.

Stoddard has arranged for a stab at random sampling among the voters as they leave the city's polling places, but the results aren't enlightening. Those who participate in the opinion sampling appear to be evenly divided between the mayoral candidates.

The polltakers also find little enlightenment in what looks like an even split among Republicans and Democrats for the other two citywide offices on the ballot. On the Republican side, the controller, Josh Waybright, who is seeking his fifth term, turns out to be a top-heavy favorite among voters who are questioned as they leave the polling booths. However, Blackwell Feeney, a state assemblyman who is the Democratic nominee to succeed Bennington as council president, also seems assured of victory if the election day polltaking is to be believed.

That raises the suspense for election night as the polls close at 8:00 P.M. Although long lines of voters still are waiting to cast ballots at most inner-city polling places at that hour and have every right to be permitted to vote, KTLT-TV, the biggest and most competitive local station, already is on the air with a bulletin that an early count shows the race for mayor is close.

It's just an attempt to demonstrate that the station is on top of the news, as the press and wire service competition quickly realizes, and it seems to do no harm. If anything, it makes latecomers even more determined to vote.

The first genuine returns come over the Independent News wire under the by-line of Bob Timmons, a widely respected reporter, who begins his first lead:

> Central City (IN)—Mayor Reardon took a slight lead over his Democratic rival, Council President Bennington, in early and indecisive returns in their mayoral contest tonight.
>
> With 284 of 2,813 precincts reporting, the tally at the city Election Board gave:
> Reardon (R)—184,635
> Bennington (D)—161,421
> The lead for the mayor of about 23,000 votes was far from conclusive, however, representing only about 10 percent of the anticipated vote. . . .

That gives the enterprising KTLT-TV anchor, Jack Bleghorn, something solid to talk about and he makes the most of it. The home folks, waiting around their television sets, finally have something solid from KTLT-TV although it isn't much.

Within the hour, Timmons is back with two more leads that show the mayor and Bennington changing sides for the top spot as the returns continue to filter in. For more than three hours, that is the way the tally continues with Timmons putting out still another lead just before midnight:

> 4TH LD MAYOR
>
> Central City (IN)—Mayor Reardon and his Democratic challenger, Council President Bennington, were locked in a see-saw race for the mayoralty tonight.
>
> With almost every fresh announcement of returns in their contest, the lead changed. As a result, the outcome was likely to be in doubt for hours to come.
>
> However, Controller Josh Waybright, a Republican seeking his fifth term, seemed certain of reelection. On the Democratic side, Assemblyman Blackwell Feeney held what appeared to be a commanding lead as Bennington's successor as council president.
>
> With 1,122 of 2,183 precincts reporting, the local Election Board gave Bennington a lead of only a little less than 600 votes in this tabulation:
> Bennington (D)—700,635
> Reardon (R)—700,082
> That left Reardon, seeking reelection for a second term, trailing by 553 votes with the count about 40 percent complete. . . .

This is the way the election stood until the *Central City News* hit the street with its final edition, carrying a Bennington claim of victory in a banner headline. John Carbone, the *News*'s main political writer, signed the top story. It began:

> Council President Cory Bennington claimed to have turned back Mayor Henry Reardon's reelection bid at 3:10 a.m. today saying,
> "I am the next mayor of Central City."
> Although Bennington held only a narrow lead at that hour, with about 40 percent of the vote yet to be tabulated, he contended that the remaining districts were normally Democratic and would give him a sizable majority.
> In an interview with the *News*, he pointed to the sweeping victory of his running-mate, Assemblyman Blackwell Feeney, who will succeed him as council president. While Bennington acknowledged that Controller Josh Waybright had triumphed in his Republican bid for a fifth term, he said, "That was to be expected. Waybright is a first-rate public official and I like him."
> Returns from 1,684 of 2,813 precincts in the mayoral contest at that hour gave:
> Bennington (D)—1,095,482
> Reardon (R)—1,078,764
> This was a majority for Bennington of 16,718, the largest in hours of tabulating in which the lead see-sawed often. . . .

In the *Leader*'s newsroom, with its own first edition hours away, City Editor Stoddard and his political writer, Wilton, scanned the *News*'s account and shook their heads. "They're taking an awful chance," Wilton said. "I'm not at all sure that the outstanding precincts are all going Bennington's way."

Stoddard meanwhile had had reports from his people and commented, "Fenwick says the mayor's not going to concede and will demand a recount if necessary. And young Roberts at Bennington's headquarters tipped me at 1:00 A.M. that something was up because Carbone of the *News* was in a back room cooking up something with the candidate."

"Let's wait awhile," Wilton suggested.

But all the waiting didn't clarify the situation because the count still wasn't complete for the *Leader*'s first edition, even though Bennington was clinging to a narrow lead. Wilton's story began:

MAYOR

> Council President Bennington held a narrow lead over Mayor Reardon at 7:30 a.m. today in the closest mayoral race in Central City's history.

With about 90 percent of the vote tabulated from 2,813 precincts, the city Election Board gave the following totals for 2,521 precincts:
Bennington (D)—1,499,898
Reardon (R)—1,498,575
Bennington's lead at that hour was 1,323. At 3:10 a.m., he had claimed victory when he had a tabulated lead of 16,718 in 1,684 precincts. He said then that the remaining districts would assure his triumph but it didn't turn out exactly as he anticipated.

Mayor Reardon, upon learning of Bennington's claim, refused to concede and said, "Any way this vote goes from here in, I'm demanding a recount."

Controller Waybright, a Republican, was reelected to his fifth term and Assemblyman Blackwell Feeney, a Democrat, easily won the council presidency Bennington vacated to run for mayor.

The mayoralty vote tabulation see-sawed all night long. . . .

What finally happened in this complicated situation vindicated the *Leader*'s cautious approach. Although Bennington led in the complete tabulation by 832, the recount Reardon demanded ultimately gave him final victory by 137 after a lot of counting and successive court appeals by both sides. It took weeks to unravel all that happened on election night.

PART III
SPECIALIZED JOURNALISM

23

When Words Take to the Air

MANY NEWCOMERS TO JOURNALISM look for an easy way to fame and fortune which, they devoutly believe, will materialize almost overnight on network television. In a pinch, they lower their sights grudgingly to local television, cable, or even national radio for openers. Such is the dream.

Alas, the awakening comes as a shock. The gateway to electronic glory is narrow and the beginners who gain admission are very few and very specialized in the arts of journalism. Nor are they recognized at once as geniuses who can be trusted to ad lib furiously at the scene of the crime while turning their best profile to the camera.

The truth is that before words take wing on the air in broadcast journalism for any well-conducted news program, they are usually as carefully written and edited as they would be for print media. But the starting pay and hours may leave something to be desired.

The Status of Broadcast News

Although network news programs still are the most glamorous aspect of television for a young and inexperienced journalist, many a local station in America today provides comparatively better and more useful services for the people of its area. The position has been stated accurately and clearly by Joel Chaseman, president of the

Post-Newsweek stations, in an address before his fellow broad-casters:

> Some network newscasts have already lost their way. Instead
> of using their massive resources . . . to summarize the day and
> give shape to primary events and issues, they're wasting their
> time and ours on what I think are misguided excursions into
> touchy-feely trivia. . . . They try to personalize so much that
> they've gotten away from the central reason why people watch
> them and that's why [network] leadership is being threatened
> and even demolished.*

The difficulties facing network journalism shouldn't come as a
thundering surprise, however. With the rise of one- and two-hour
local news presentations and continual cable intelligence, the
twenty-two-minute network news summaries at the nation's dinner
hour are bound to suffer. And advertisers, always so defensive of
their own interests, may be expected to go where they will get the
most response for their dollar.

There is, after all, no law that freezes change in any undertaking,
including broadcast journalism. It is only a bit more than sixty years
ago that radio broke the news monopoly of print journalism. And
after World War II, television replaced radio as the first source of
news for millions of Americans and also forced a tremendous change
in newspaper reading habits. It was in this manner that the dominance of the evening newspaper was sharply curtailed and the
A.M.'s profited thereby.

However, radio and newspapers generally have survived by
adapting to changing circumstances. Indeed, daily newspaper sales
in the latter 1890s have actually increased to 64 million copies a
day as compared with an estimated 38 million viewers of network
news weekdays, and this has occurred despite the rise of great
newspaper chains and the sale, merger, or elimination of a number
of important dailies.**

It is, if an exaggeration may be permitted, a situation approxi-
mating the race between the tortoise and the hare. To illustrate, in
the summer of 1986 television jumped on an Atlantic coast hurricane
watch with typical ballyhoo that was bound to frighten a lot of peo-

*Chaseman is quoted in *Quill* magazine for September 1986, p. 42. He spoke at
the Broadcasting-Taishoff Seminars.
**Editor & Publisher International Yearbook*, 1985, Preface.

ple.* However, in this case, the big wind blew harmlessly out to sea, upon which a bystander remarked sourly when a microphone was thrust before him: "There was too damned much TV hype about this."

Despite the pictorial brilliance of the product and the professional qualifications of the top news people on the air, trustworthy researchers have raised other objections to the way events are presented on television. A respected survey of broadcast journalism has included this comment from a researcher: "Broadcast journalism during the past ten years has been going fast, sideways. We do not go up, we do not have depth, but we sprawl all over. We have more stations, more people, more money, but it does not add up to more quality. . . . We are not as well off, in many regards, as we were in the best days of radio. . . ."**

That pretty well says it: Relatively few changes have been made to improve the standards under which television news, both network and local, usually operate. Even in major markets where local broadcasters now are trying to tell national and international news before the networks do, the results leave a great deal to be desired.

Contrary to the gains in newspaper circulation in an era of change, quite the opposite result seems to have taken place among television audiences. The A. C. Nielsen Company, the source of most television statistics, has reported a decline of more than 13 percent in the average audience of all three network news programs between 1979 and 1986. For total network audiences between the 1980–81 and the 1985–86 seasons, Nielsen reported a drop of 11 percent.***

That appears to confirm the reported fragmentation of network audiences because of rival attractions such as cable, cassettes, and local programming. Such fragmentation is expected to continue.

Writing for Broadcast Use

Television news represents a unique blending of words and pictures, sights and sounds. In that sense, it is an art requiring something more than basic professional competence.

Sometimes, the pictures that flit across the tube call for language

*The hurricane watch was on August 18, 1986.

**Barrett and Sklar, "The Eye of the Storm," *DuPont-Columbia Survey of Broadcast Journalism, 1980* (NEW YORK: LIPPINCOTT & CROWELL, 1980), p. 103.

***Nielsen statistics are from Alex S. Jones, "The Anchors," the *New York Times Magazine,* July 27, 1986, pp. 13–14, and "Hard Times for the Networks," the *New York Times,* September 12, 1986, p. D-6.

shaped by dramatic sensitivity. On other occasions, one feels the need for skills that could produce a superior Hollywood script. And then, too, there are scenes of such quality that mere words cannot embellish them—that understatement or no statement at all is the best treatment.

Oh, yes, the text of a broadcast must be responsive to the needs of a mass audience—the short sentence, the familiar word, the clarity of understanding. But beyond that, whatever is put on paper must convey something more than the pictorial message of which it is a part. It must *fit*, just as a good lyric embellishes the music of a song.

There are mechanical requirements as well. Unlike news for print, most broadcast news other than anchor summaries is written in the present or present perfect tense. Whenever possible, the style ought to be personal as contrasted with the often impersonal manner of the average account in print. Most important of all, the timing has to fit the period allotted to the newscast—figuring one minute to a page containing about 170 to 180 words of typescript with three or four throwaway sentences at the end to avoid a runover.

Some of the journalistic procedures are different, too. The attribution in broadcast news nearly always comes at the beginning of a sentence, whereas it is often put at the end of a piece written for print.

As for figures, a necessity in many print stories, they either should be used sparingly and rounded off in the script or a separate tabulation should be prepared for pictorial use. As for strange names and terms that may be misunderstood or mispronounced, it is not considered demeaning to coach the anchor person or reporter to prevent horrible sounds from battering the ears of the audience.

Such precautions as these are second nature to Morry Gort, the veteran anchor at KTLT-TV, Channel 12 in Central City, and an experienced television reporter like Donna Kincaid. That's all to the good when they have to give the news about a freak tornado that wrecks part of Central City's suburb of Tiswell. Since it was settled by Polish immigrants in the last century, the news names there aren't the usual Smith, Jones, and Olson but Kosciusko, Wroclaw, and Szczecin.

Here is the script for the tornado coverage as Gort and Kincaid prepare it for the 6:00 P.M. local news on Channel 12:

VIDEO	AUDIO
Gort *(on camera in studio)* illustrating area of destruction in Tiswell from large map mounted	GORT (anchor): A freak tornado packing 90-mile-an-hour winds cut a quarter-mile path of destruction in

VIDEO

behind him. Areas hit are outlined and cross-hatched in red.

Camera pans on destruction in Tiswell in long distance shot from airplane. Then it comes in closer to show wrecked houses, felled telephone poles, downed trees, people wandering in a daze among the wreckage.

Camera points down some main streets to show how the twister leveled all in its path.

Woman walks about an overturned auto, stops and points to front part. Other people watching in background as she talks.

Woman moves about as she tells what happened. People follow her, listening.

Woman is seen wiping eyes with handkerchief. Camera pans from her to front seat of car and back again.

Kincaid (*OC*) now is seen walking along Wroclaw Avenue, a residential area, past overturned houses, trees, phone poles, twisted wires, a child's tricycle bent out of shape. As she moves along she tells what she sees of the tornado's destruction.

AUDIO

no more than 12 minutes today in the suburb of Tiswell. Three people were killed and 26 others were injured. Damage runs into millions. Donna Kincaid has our report. Donna.

KINCAID: What you see is all that is left of the central part of Tiswell after the tornado struck at 3:06 this afternoon. In just 12 minutes, this happened to a century-old community founded by an adventurous party of Polish immigrants. Portions of the main avenues—Kosciusko (*Kos-see-us-ko*), Wroclaw (*Verot-es-lav*), and Szczecin (*Sh-chet-sin*)—were destroyed. Store buildings and houses tumbled down like straw. It is a miracle that many more weren't killed.

WOMAN: My husband and I were driving home on Kosciusko Avenue in our car after shopping at the A & P. He is a mechanic, works nights, and he was driving. All of a sudden I heard a roar like a railroad train in the distance and I said, "Al, what's that?" Before he could answer, the car just seemed to roll over on its side. It was pushed over by the tornado, it was that strong. We were right there (*points*) and I was on top of Al and yelling for help. People came and pulled us out. I wasn't hurt bad but Al is in the hospital, broken arm. Thank God we weren't killed.

KINCAID: That was one of the survivors, Alice Valery of Tiswell. When I went to Bytow Hospital to see her husband, he asked right away how she was and was glad I could tell him she was okay. They were the lucky ones—the 3 who died and most of the 26 injured were badly hurt and you can see why as

VIDEO	AUDIO
Kincaid (*OC*) points to a wrecked house, then to a wrecked toy wagon.	you look around here. This was where Tad Polykarp lived with his wife and 6 children. He is dead, the roof fell on him when he was working on repairs in his attic. His youngest child, Isabel, 3 years old, was outside in this little red wagon
Kincaid keeps walking, stands before little wagon where the child was killed, then points to red brick house as camera pans to it.	and she was killed, too, when the branch of a tree fell on her. Mrs. Polykarp and the other 5 children have been taken in by neighbors, over there. The red brick house where they are staying now didn't even lose a shingle, which shows what a freak storm it was.
Now camera looks down a street lined with wreckage and Kincaid does a voiceover to wind up the report.	Yes, this pretty little suburb, a "bedroom community" as they call it, just north of Central City, was turned into a graveyard this afternoon. But tonight people here already are saying that they are going to rebuild. They have in them the spirit of the great Polish patriot, Thaddeus Kosciusko, one of
Camera looks down Kosciusko Avenue then fades out to distant sunset.	Washington's generals in the Revolutionary War, who never wanted to see the sun set on the country he fought to free. Nor will it,
Long shot of Tiswell from airplane at end of video report.	if the people of Tiswell have their way. Donna Kincaid in Tiswell for Channel 12.

There was a lot more to the Tiswell story on Channel 12 that night. It was not only the biggest local story in weeks. Because of the visuals that so dramatically illustrated the freakish nature of the storm, the network servicing Channel 12 lifted part of Kincaid's report for national use.

On the surface, once the script is completed, the job looks so simple that the beginner imagines all a reporter has to do is just walk around, microphone in hand, and keep jabbering.

That is part of the art of a first-rate television reporter. But in fact, Kincaid's work and that of the camera crews with her was anything but simple. It involved a mastery of electronic instruments with which television people work daily and on which they are dependent for the visuals that make the medium so compelling to a mass audience.

Even more important, Kincaid, as the chief reporter, had to keep thinking every minute she was on the job how to illustrate the effects of the tornado for the home audience. And at times, camera operators would come up with some good ideas, too.

In sum, this was no one-person feat of reportage. It was—and by its very nature, it had to be—a closely knit team operation in which everybody from Channel 12 worked as a unit. Yes, Kincaid took the bows—but in the newsroom everybody appreciated that she couldn't have done so well if it hadn't been for the people who gave her such strong and loyal support and the marvelous technology that has been developed for the ultimate benefit of many millions of viewers.

The operation would not be possible if *videotape* and the *minicam*, to name only two important elements, had not been developed for the narration of televised news. Videotape, as anybody who has ever been in an electronic newsroom knows, is magnetic tape that handles sight and sound so remarkably that it can be played back at once, even reused and stored indefinitely. It has almost completely replaced film in the television industry.

As for minicams, these twelve-pound instruments carried on the shoulder and their slightly heavier backpack of batteries are familiar to crowds wherever news is made. One or two minicam operators can accomplish very quickly and efficiently what a couple of the old three-member camera crews took hours to do because they had to transport an enormous amount of equipment. If necessary, through electronic relays, videotape exposed in minicams can be fed back to a studio directly from a news scene, whether it is in Moscow, Iceland, or South Africa.

That means a news director, even if far removed from a news locale, can maintain control over his ENG (electronic news gathering) operation through a computerized mobile telephone service if necessary. Naturally, that was the way Kincaid and other reporters with their photo crews handled the coverage of the Tiswell tornado.

Using Television in a Controversy

In working with a medium of such power over public opinion, the greenest recruit to television soon learns the truth of Justice Oliver Wendell Holmes's observation about free speech—it does not include the right to shout "Fire!" in a crowded theater. News directors, anchor persons, writers, reporters, and ENG operators alike must always remember the uses of restraint in covering a story that affects people emotionally.

Such precautions are mandatory, for example, when the Federal Nuclear Regulatory Commission announces that an atomic power plant may be operated. However, local authorities, fearful of political consequences, often hesitate to put into effect a safety plan that would evacuate people in a surrounding ten-mile area in case of danger. People in the mass may not know very much about nuclear power but they remember the near-disaster at Three Mile Island in Pennsylvania and the Soviet breakdown at Chernobyl.

Such feelings have delayed atomic power operations in this country, notably at Seabrook in New Hampshire and Shoreham on Long Island in New York State. Assuming the federal government gave a go-ahead to the reopening of the damaged South River atomic power plant of the Central City Light and Power Company, that would create controversy in the entire surrounding region and a problem for Channel 12. To sound an alarm would be unthinkable; to ignore the story would be impossible. The only possible way to proceed would be to do the story calmly, quietly, and concisely with attention to all sides.

Here is the beginning of such a script for Channel 12:

VIDEO	AUDIO
Long distance shot from the air of the closed South River atomic plant—zeroing in on the big sign CLOSED and the guards at the entrance.	GORT (anchor): The Federal Nuclear Regulatory Commission in Washington gave the go-ahead today to the reopening of the long-closed South River atomic power plant on the outskirts of Central City. But both Governor Farrow and Mayor Reardon announced they weren't ready to open the plant because an emergency plan for evacuation of a 10-mile surrounding area in case of trouble still hasn't been completed. For the mayor, that represents a change of front since his skimpy margin of reelection, during which he was attacked for favoring the reopening of South River. Donna Kincaid has been looking into this for Channel 12. Donna.
Camera zeros in on guard raising both hands in a warning gesture to keep visitors away.	
Kincaid (*OC*) outside the closed	KINCAID: The first thing you notice

VIDEO	AUDIO
South River plant, gesturing at the tall stacks, which are not in operation.	when you come out here to South River is that people wish the atomic plant would just go away. When I asked Cindy Ellery about the federal government's proposal to reopen South River, this is what she said.
Shot of Mrs. Ellery, with a baby in her arms, standing outside her home across the street from the closed plant. Kincaid holds the mike toward her and Buddy, the baby.	MRS. ELLERY: All of us who have to live next to this monster just wish it would go away, but that's impossible, I suppose. Anyway, I'd hate to see it reopen—I have Buddy here, he's only six months old, and I have two other small children. I don't like the idea of exposing them to atomic radiation. It's bad enough for my husband and me to be exposed to it.
Camera pans to Buddy and the baby smiles and waves when Kincaid plays with him.	
Camera shifts to Kincaid holding mike and asking a question.	KINCAID: But Governor Farrow and Mayor Reardon aren't ready with a plan to evacuate everybody in a 10-mile area. Isn't that reassuring?
Camera back to Mrs. Ellery and baby	MRS. ELLERY: Temporarily, yes. But what happens if the power company has its way and there is an accident and they start telling us to get out? How are they going to pull thousands of people out of their homes—and that means people right in Central City, as well—without confusion and danger? No, I don't see how it would work.
Shot of Mayor Reardon at his desk in City Hall, Kincaid heard talking off camera	KINCAID: This is the big problem for Mayor Reardon—how to provide for the city's future power needs and yet be sure that many thousands of Central City people like Mrs. Ellery and Buddy are protected. How would you respond to Mrs. Ellery, Mr. Mayor?
As mayor responds, camera shifts between him and Kincaid, across the desk from him	MAYOR: I want to assure Mrs. Ellery and all the people of Central City, not only those in a possible evacuation area, that I am not going to take chances with their safety or their lives. And everybody knows

VIDEO	AUDIO
Mayor goes to chart to show red outlined area to be evacuated in case of trouble at South River.	that I have gone out of my way to be fair to Central City Light and Power, which has invested so much money in this plant. But just look at the problem in this area here—and think of all the people we'd have to move in case of a breakdown at South River. Not only that. As we now know, air currents can carry dangerous particles hundreds of
Mayor leaves chart, shaking his head, and returns to desk.	miles beyond this. No, I'll not act very quickly in this matter and I am sure the governor won't, either. . . .

The newscast concludes with brief remarks by a spokesperson for the power company, giving assurance that South River is safe, and the governor, from the state capital, saying he isn't ready yet to give the city a go-ahead without a workable evacuation plan. The whole thing is done in very low key without dramatics or bluster.

It is very difficult, where great masses of people are involved, to give a fair display to arguments in favor of atomic power. Perhaps there might be more balance in the newscast if the chairman of the FNRC could appear on camera or, failing that, a key part of his statement could be read.

This is where newspapers continue to be invaluable. They have the space to devote to all sides (even if the statements aren't read by many subscribers). The press remains a much cooler and more open forum for the discussion of public problems of this nature. And radio news, although hampered by necessary brevity, also has a contribution to make.

Modern Radio Broadcasts in the United States

When a president of the United States takes the trouble to do a weekly radio broadcast to the nation, but cuts press conferences to the barest minimum, it says something about the continued use-fulness of radio in public discussion.* Although radio necessarily remains the principal medium of communication in developing nations all over the world, it has been reduced to third place behind television and newspapers in this country. To some extent, a news-

*This was the way Ronald Reagan operated in his two presidential terms, the second of which showed him to be the most popular vote getter in the history of the presidency, before the Iran controversy was exposed.

magazine such as *Time,* even though it is issued weekly, probably has more clout among its regular readers than any radio report. And yet, radio news often can be more immediate than even television because it is less hampered by complicated electronic controls and taboos.

The main reliance of radio newscasters for all but local news is wire service copy, particularly the special three-cycle radio wire (midnight to 8:00 A.M., 8:00 A.M. to 4:00 P.M., 4:00 P.M. to midnight).* Using a brief summation of the day's news, a radio announcer can break in almost any time with a minute- or two-minute report of developing events, although generally that isn't done except for overwhelmingly important news bulletins.

Here is the way some top stories would appear on the Independent News radio wire for use whenever a station wished:*

> Cape Canaveral, Florida—The shuttle *Orbiter* is on the launching pad with a crew of six for a major space flight.
> Washington—The Defense Department announces it is tightening border patrols in the southwest to choke off the flight of illegal aliens from Mexico.
> New York—The United Nations General Assembly has adjourned after a three-month session, leaving unresolved rival arms control proposals submitted by the United States and the Soviet Union.
> London—The British Admiralty says it is extending the search for a missing English Channel steamship, *S. S. Hallowell,* with 42 persons aboard. It was last heard from 24 hours ago while sending distress signals during a storm.

These bulletins then are expanded, usually to about one hundred or so words each, with concise reports that can be read over the nation's radio stations when convenient. It is an admittedly supplementary service in this country but a necessary one. The commuting public must be provided for, too, and radio is one way of reaching them.

---

*Of course, the radio wires are also open to TV stations but are usually used only as a backup service.

24
Sports Writing

THE WHOLE NATION TURNED into a televised baseball park in 1986 when the New York Mets defeated the Boston Red Sox, four games to three, in the World Series. It was a thriller from start to finish. The Mets rallied after losing the first two games to tie the Sox at two games all. Then, when the Sox won the third game and seemed on the verge of winning the fourth and the championship, the Mets came back in extra innings to save that one. And in the last and deciding game, when the Sox once again seemed to have victory within their grasp, the Mets pulled away to win an extraordinary sports contest.

The News Media and the Public

This kind of rivalry is the main reason for the enormous and continuing interest in sports in this country. Give your true sports fan something to watch, to hear, or to read about his favorite pastime whether it is baseball or football or tennis or almost anything else, and he (or she) will be satisfied. Oh, yes, television dramatizes the immediacy of the sports event; however, the newspaper and magazine literature of sports is still great and shows no sign of diminishing.

What has happened, in the area of sports at least, is that the media are complementing each other. There are certain aspects of sports, investigations for example, that television seldom touches. And print, of course, cannot approach the universality of television in photographing continuing action.

Earlier in this century, writers such as Bob Considine and Red Smith were able to dominate the field mainly because they could make the English language tingle to their touch. There even were separate schools of sportswriters. As described by the large and unkempt Heywood Broun, a northerner who affected a southern accent, the first and dominant school was the one typefied by the motto, "Ah, Wonderful!" The second, and more skeptical, enlisted under a darker banner that was enscribed, "Ah, Nuts!" Quite immodestly, Broun nominated himself as the outstanding exemplar of the former and put forward his mortal enemy, Westbrook Pegler, as the leading proponent of the second.

Then, too, there was Grantland Rice, the sainted "Granny," who once listened solemnly to a colleague, Frank Graham, insisting that one day he wanted to be buried in the infield at the Saratoga racetrack. As Red Smith described the conversation, Graham concluded his elegy to that particular country churchyard:

"If I behave myself maybe I'll be allowed to sit up about post time for the first race and see what's going on."

To which the horrified Granny exclaimed, "Post time for the first race? You'll miss the daily double."*

There were other famous journalists who began in sports and moved on to become dominant public figures and winners of Pulitzer Prizes, among them Ralph McGill of the *Atlanta Constitution* and James (Scotty) Reston of the *New York Times*.

For that matter, some who devoted their lives to the sports pages also won Pulitzers for their prose. Prominent among them were Red Smith of the lamented *New York Herald Tribune* and Dave Anderson of the *New York Times*. At least three Pulitzers also went to whistle blowers who exposed wrongdoing in the brave new world of sports heroes, the American equivalent of the Elysian fields of ancient Greece.

A Pulitzer for investigative reporting in 1981 went to Robert Lowe and Clark Hallas of the *Arizona Daily Star*, Tucson, for uncovering alleged irregularities in the financing of the University of Arizona football recruiting program. And, less recently, Max Kase of the *New York Journal-American* won a Pulitzer special award for producing the evidence of a basketball scandal that resulted in the conviction and imprisonment of several players.

One searches in vain for signs of similar activity by the knights

*From "The Best of Grantland Rice," Red Smith's lecture at the Columbia Graduate School of Journalism as reported in *Editor & Publisher, February 7, 1959.*

of the press box who represent television on fall Saturday afternoons and some weekday evenings as well. One of the best, Brent Musberger of CBS, has observed that it is "very unfortunate we are so hypocritical at the college level." He explained that he believed exposés of the benefits college recruiters offer to star athletes didn't do any good.

"They [the recruiters] are going to be back out there giving cars away, giving jobs to parents, because there is so much money at stake," he said. "It is an economic issue. They just ought to be honest with it and deal with it in some way."*

However, the issuance of even more Pulitzer Prizes to sports writers isn't going to solve the problem of what to write for the Sunday paper after television has thoroughly covered a major sports event. Telling the same story over again won't do it. No matter how elegant the prose, the melody isn't going to be different. The problem, in sum, has no solution.

Where the New Sportswriters Come from

Yet, the sports pages of the nation do not seem to be barren of young talent. The newcomers, some of them eager teen-agers, still pop up as stringers, copy boys, or copy girls in newspaper sports departments across the land. And there are literally thousands of high-school weeklies and college dailies that present necessary information for student bodies. In sum, not everything in sports is broadcast. The tube mainly glamorizes million-dollar athletes, but leaves the preponderance of sports events uncovered, even unmentioned.

In consequence, most modern sports pages teem with box scores and other statistics so dear to the devoted sports enthusiasts of all ages. There also are many more columns of newspaper comment than there were before the television age, for the sports public thrives on both opinion and argument. And, at least as far as most major dailies are concerned, there appears to be more space for the coverage of sports events than there was on the average fifty or sixty years ago.

True, the big money sports like football, baseball, basketball, horse racing, and, to a lesser extent, hockey, tennis, and boxing all are preempted at top level by network television and its big money

*From the *Proceedings of the American Society of Newspaper Editors*, 1982.

advertisers. But the appeal here for the public is mainly among the stars of professional standing aside from a few well-heeled, big-name college sports heroes. Except in Olympic games situations, however, television is blind to the attraction of track and field, rowing, and other purely amateur sports that also have a devoted, if smaller, following.

It is at this level that youngsters bitten by the journalism bug get their chance. Even at this late date, I can remember the thrill of riding in the University of Washington coaching launch as a beginning reporter to watch a championship eight-oared crew work out—a crew that later won an Olympic title. For me, that became the subject of a half-column account in a local paper. Today, a visual of the workout might be worth all of fifteen seconds on network television just before the crew won the Olympic championship.

Yet I suspect that television's exploitation of the top sports personalities and contests has increased public interest in sports in general. Moreover, the normal growth in our population has also tended to widen the audience for lesser-known amateur sports aside from college football. At any rate, the new recruits for journalism in general and the sports pages in particular still come from the same places—the high schools and colleges of the country.

There are differences, however.

The most important is that the field of activity for most newcomers to sportswriting is larger than it ever has been. Their opportunities, therefore, are also greater. Even the pay for box-score recorders and other sports stringers may have improved a little for the lucky ones. But the competition is also more intense and the pressure on youngsters, even more on women than on men, is unacceptably high.

In a perfect world, such an outlook for beginners in any field would be intolerable. But that is the kind of world we never have known and, in journalism particularly, we are unlikely to find even a trace of it.

Writing the Sports Story

Because so many sports reporters and commentators on television handle running play-by-play accounts in the vernacular, beginners are sometimes tempted to cheapen their writing. Some older journalists who should know better go a step further by advocating a "talky" style for the sports pages.

What actually follows, when such attempts are made, is the demeaning business of "writing down to the masses," as it is called sometimes by intellectuals. Or, to put it as Theodore M. Bernstein did in his advice to *New York Times* writers: too much liberalism with syntax risks "losing touch with the language of the literate."

In a parting thrust at the "write-like-you-talk" school of English prose, he gave this example of what could happen to a "talky" writer: "Whatever the people say is okay by me. The people speak real good."*

This scarcely means that the beginner should take the plunge into highfalutin' language in describing a basketball game between two high schools in Greenport, Long Island. There is no reason why sportswriters should bury themselves in clichés, pile up adjectives, and generally debase the English language on the theory that they are writing for an audience of morons.

When the English language is treated with respect, and used with grace and simplicity, it becomes a marvelously flexible means of communication. But when it is battered and bent on the theory that it must fit a mold suitable to the partly or totally illiterate, disaster can result. The outcome in that case may be literary anarchy and total confusion.

There is no reason, in short, for sportswriters not to follow the same rules as all other writers, in or outside journalism. It won't help them to set up in business for themselves.

Because of the nature of their work and the pressures of time that frequently result, many sports people become too technical and further handicap themselves as writers. The technicalities of the various sports alone are bad enough. But when they are combined with the technicalities of journalism, the resultant story may be well-nigh unusable.

To illustrate, consider some of the clichés that sometimes clutter the best of sports pages and delude young writers into using what amounts to rubber-stamp English:

In football, almost every game becomes a *clash*. And nearly any tackle is *bruising*. A quarterback does not merely pass the football; instead, he *rifles* the *pigskin*. And a receiver who happens to catch the ball, of course, has *glue on his hands*. If the offensive team is able to score a touchdown, it is called a *juggernaut*. But if the defense holds, then, of course, it is termed a *stone wall*.

The clichés in baseball are even more time-worn. It isn't enough to identify a pitcher. He has to be a *twirler* and he operates with a

*Theodore M. Bernstein, *Watch Your Language* (New York: Pocket Books, 1967) p. 3.

sphere from a *mound*. As for the hitters, they swing the *ash*, not a bat, and they seldom hit a ball; instead, they *put the ash on the horsehide*. And it is an offense to report that a batter hit a home run; rather, he is a *slugger* who *rounded the hassocks* after *hitting for the circuit*.

These illustrations may be spun out in sickening detail in describing the progress, or lack of it, in any game.

But consider now the added complications under which inexperienced writers labor when they must write three stories in whole or in part to report on a particular game for a newspaper. That still is done if the contest takes place during the publication of two or more editions of the paper.

This is a sample schedule:

The advance:—Such a story is prepared for use in an edition before the game is played. It is merely a space filler, a time-honored device that was used to reserve a section of a sports page for the real thing.

The running story:—On the news side, this would be called A or B copy—it often doesn't matter which. It is merely the play-by-play account as it develops from the beginning of the game. Even today, when a radio or television audience already knows the final score, some papers will continue to issue an edition either with an advance story or with a partial running story of the same game. Why? It is difficult to say; probably, it's just a tradition. But it is frustrating for the writer and often for the people who buy the paper as well.

The wrap-up:—Generally, this is a summary lead to condense the action into a few paragraphs that then are placed at the head of the running account.

If a young and inexperienced writer is presented with such a schedule and still hasn't broken the habit of writing in clichés or overstuffed language, the result can be painful. However, the whole business could be reduced to a workable routine by scheduling one story, simply and clearly written, once the game is over.

It would be so much less embarrassing to all concerned and it would dispose of the myth that newspapers can be competitive with television if both cover the same event from start to finish. What newspapers can do is to provide more statistics and, with better training for writers, more interesting pregame and postgame stories.

That doesn't seem to be asking too much. Looked at carefully, it even appears to make sense.

On Writing for a Local Audience

Except for special presentations, seasonal reviews, and similar set pieces, television reporting of sports events—locally and nationally—is based on minute-by-minute reporting as play progresses. This makes for public interest of a high order if the action is fast and the contenders are closely matched. But few narrations on television can be more boring and time-consuming than efforts by an announcer and commentator to make a dull contest interesting. It just doesn't work.

A sports crowd that has paid stiff prices for tickets to a much-ballyhooed contest that turns out poorly always can walk out—and many spectators do. In bars, motels, hotels, and at home, the disappointed viewers have an easier alternative—to switch off the television set and read about the whole sad business in the next day's newspaper. Even where there is a prepared script, rare in sports, no mismatch can be made lively.

But what of the newspaper account in such a situation? There really should be no pressure on the writer to make the contest seem to be a death-grapple between giants, something that television reporters are ill-advised to do on occasion. But often writers try to liven things up anyway.

Here, however, is an example of a newspaper account of a local contest that, to use a phrase associated with television's onetime favorite, Howard Cosell, "tells it like it is." It is the annual Thanksgiving Day football game between State University in Central City and State Agricultural College, the Aggies, also called the "Cow College," as the report is published some twenty-four hours later in the *Central City Leader*:

RAMS

   The Aggies' Ron Madlock, a 185-pound running back who hasn't played football most of this year, was the big man on the Rams' upstate campus today after scoring the winning touchdown against favored State U.

   Madlock did it in a pelting rain with one of the oldest plays in football, the "hidden ball" trick, when State U was looking for a pass. Not only that, but he also kicked the point after touchdown with a soggy ball and sent the State U Tigers home on the short end of a 7–0 score.

   The only score in an otherwise lackluster game at the Rams' Minot Field came in the second quarter. From then on, with the heavier Tigers slipping and sliding in the mud, the Ram defense stopped their foes on three goal-line stands.

"Don't give me the credit," Madlock said when it was all over. "That defensive line of ours played an inspired game. State U never had a chance to score."

The only real excitement in this rain-soaked contest came with the second quarter almost over and at least half the 50,000 spectators leaving for warmer and drier locations. Everybody was wet, even the local broadcasters in the open press box atop Minot Field, whose teeth were chattering like castanets on the glass neck of a whisky bottle between plays.

Madlock, who had been injured earlier this year and hadn't seen much action since, came off the bench at about the middle of the second quarter but didn't carry the ball right away. Instead, he kept faking around left end, pretending he had the ball held behind his back, and then laughing at his pursuers and showing he was empty-handed.

"He put on a good act," Coach Howie Armine said later. "It was a play we'd worked on a lot but I never really thought we'd surprise State U with it. Maybe the rain and the mud helped."

Whether it did or not, with only two minutes to go, Quarterback Nap Radnor ran to the right and seemed to be nursing the ball at one side as if he wanted to throw to three Aggie receivers who were plopping downfield in the rain, also to the right.

Meanwhile, Madlock was circling out to the left again all by himself in a leisurely way, his hand hidden behind his back. But this time, nobody chased him because the whole State U defense seemed to be shifting to the Rams' right, watching for the pass.

But, surprise! This time, Madlock actually had the ball and got around the left side of his own line without even a block being thrown for him. Next thing State U knew, he was across the goal line 42 yards away, holding the ball over his head with a big grin, then flinging it in front of him right in the middle of a mud puddle.

Even the Aggie crowd didn't believe it, however, until the six points went up on the scoreboard and Madlock added the extra point. Then the cheering began in the rain and kept up all through a dull and rain-soaked second half.

It was one of the happiest and wettest crowds of kids who ever knocked over the goalposts at Minot Field when the final gun sounded. . . .

So, the reader will say, what's so great about that? Great it is not. But it is honest. It is fair. It is accurate. And it does not exaggerate the importance either of the Aggies' surprise victory or State U's defeat.

That is the main point to be made when a newspaper story of a football game is published twenty-four hours after the event, after the broadcasters have given the play-by-play, after the rain-soaked crowd has gone home, after the season is ended.

It simply couldn't be written any differently for an evening paper that does not publish on Thanksgiving Day. So long after the event, it would have been the height of stupidity to try to pump up interest in a surprise victory in the rain, dramatic as it may have seemed at the time. The best that any writer could do was to tell the story simply, clearly, and without embellishment.

That is what the *Leader*'s sports editor wanted and that is exactly what was delivered to him. No false heroics, no slush, just a decent and unadorned account of two fairly average college football teams that had to play a traditional football game under miserable conditions.

Perhaps Cosell's old quote is worth repeating to sports writers, young and old, before the start of every football season. It wouldn't do any harm. Here and there it might possibly do some good.

As for the notion that television and the press are rivals in a scrambled news communications system, it doesn't hold up on close examination. What the American public has done, by supporting both, is to make them complementary in most developing news situations. This is especially true of sports, where television is bound to be first with the action. Therefore, for a major sports event, the whole nation becomes an electronic stadium, after which your true fan eagerly picks up the paper to read about what he has seen and agree or disagree with his favorite sports commentator.

This is the way it was before the electronic age and this is the way it still is, mainly because the public wants more than one source of information and pays handsomely for the extra safeguard.

25

Journalists as Experts

IT IS DIFFICULT FOR MANY in this country to accept the belief that journalists can be experts in covering a wide variety of specialized fields. And yet, of necessity in this complex era, that is one of the dominant trends in the profession.

It could not be otherwise. Without specialized knowledge and training, no journalist nowadays is likely to speak or write with clarity and understanding about a bewildering variety of subjects that are increasingly important to a large and discerning public. To identify only a few, such fields include science, medicine, education, farm problems, consumerism, religion, human rights, cultural affairs, and the environment.

It is conceivable that an old-time general assignment reporter might stuff himself with enough information to cover a major development in one of these areas. But in all areas, what if the writer is thrown into one or another at random? Sudden expertise would scarcely be possible.

How an Expert Functions

On January 28, 1986, Howard Benedict was working at an open telephone line to the Associated Press general desk in New York City from his post at Cape Canaveral, Florida.* He was then the

*This account is based on data from the *AP Log*, a publication of the Associated Press dated February 3, 1986, describing Benedict's role in reporting and explaining the disaster of the space shuttle *Challenger* to a worldwide audience.

aerospace expert of the wire service, having mastered his specialty through on-the-job training in the coverage of fifty-five previous American manned space missions. This was the big one—a space shot of the *Challenger* that was to carry six crew members and a New Hampshire schoolteacher, Christa McAuliffe, on a dangerous mission.

The weather was bad, with ice on the launching pad. There had been some concern about the equipment, too. but NASA—the National Aeronautics and Space Administration—had put all systems on go and life-off was expected momentarily. Benedict was dictating his story to the general desk, which was handling instant relays to the news media all over the nation and the world.

Lift-off occurred at 11:38 A.M., EST, and Benedict's first bulletin sped over AP's wires:

> PM-Space Shuttle
> BULLETIN⟨
> Cape Canaveral, Fla. (AP)—Shuttle *Challenger* rocketed away from an icicle-laden launch pad today, overcoming finicky weather and faulty equipment to carry aloft a New Hampshire schoolteacher as NASA's first citizen in space.
>
> -more-

> AP-NY-01-28-86 1138EST⟨

Within moments, general desk editor John Daniszewski heard Benedict saying, "Something is wrong. Something is terribly wrong."

Benedict later recalled, "Suddenly, without warning, there was a blazing fireball in the sky and the solid fuel booster rockets were spiraling crazily."

Daniszewski, in New York, saw the same thing on television sets facing the general desk. Benedict, who had been dictating details of the lift-off, stopped abruptly but Daniszewski didn't wait for him and typed this bulletin for the wire at once:

> PM-Space Shuttle
> BULLETIN⟨
> Cape Canaveral, Fla. (AP)—Space shuttle *Challenger* exploded today as it carried schoolteacher Christa McAuliffe and six crew members into space.
>
> -more-

> AP-NY-01-28-86-1141ES⟨

Once Benedict knew the second bulletin was on the wire, he added this with rapid dictation:

> PM-Space Shuttle, 1st add
> URGENT⟨
> Cape Canaveral⟨
> There was no indication of the fate of the crew but it appeared there was no way they could survive.
>   It was the first such failure in 56 such U. S. man in space missions.
> AP-NY-01-28-86 1143EST⟨

AP Network News at the Kennedy Space Center meanwhile had flashed a dread one-sentence alert over the broadcast wire:

NASA SAYS THE VEHICLE HAS EXPLODED.

Benedict had by now assessed the situation and resumed talking. As he later recalled:

"For the next two hours I was busy with the story. Too busy to think. When that time passed, the reality of what had happened hit me. I had witnessed the deaths of seven people I knew and admired. As I watched a slow-motion replay on television, I shed a tear or two. . . ."

In the anxious months that followed, America's space program was suspended. Investigators looked into all aspects of the *Challenger* tragedy to try to find out what had happened, why it had happened, and what could be done to prevent another such disaster at a most crucial time in our long and intense rivalry with the Soviet Union.

All through that difficult period, it was Benedict, as the AP's expert, who was responsible for much of the information that came to the American people clearly, quickly, and accurately. That was how a specialist in journalism was expected to perform and Benedict lived up to his responsibilities.

The Training of an Expert

Specialized reporting did not begin with Howard Benedict any more than it will end with him. One of the journalists whose expertise accelerated the trend earlier in this century was William L. Laurence of the *New York Times*—"Atomic Bill," as those of us among his contemporaries called him to distinguish him from his colleague on the *Times*, William H. Lawrence, otherwise known as "Political Bill."

"Atomic Bill" was small but husky and frighteningly dignified. He was striking in appearance, having the mild blue eyes of a dreamy poet and the bent nose of an unsuccessful boxer. But these and other personal characteristics didn't mean much when Laurence wrote about his speciality, the coming of the atomic age, which he foreshadowed in a story in the *Times* as early as January 31, 1939. It began:

> The splitting of a uranium atom into two parts, each consisting of a gigantic "cannon-ball" of the tremendous energy of 100,000,000 electron volts, the greatest amount of atomic energy so far liberated on earth, was announced here yesterday by the Columbia University Department of Physics. . . .

Laurence somehow was convinced that the development of atomic science would make a tremendous difference in our world. That was why he studied the subject with fanatical devotion and often wrote about it, long before most of us who competed with him realized what was going on.

He wrote in the *Times* on May 5, 1940, just five days before Hitler's blitzkrieg overwhelmed western Europe, that both German and American scientists were at work to develop enormous sources of atomic energy from a uranium isotope known as U-235. He followed up that disclosure with a sensational piece in the *Saturday Evening Post* on May 30 of that year entitled, "The Atom Gives Up." In the *Post* article, he came so close to tipping off American progress toward the development of an atomic bomb that the FBI took over as many copies of the magazine as possible. The agency also asked the editors to circulate no more of that issue and set up a plan under which it was notified whenever a request for a copy was made.

As for Laurence himself, he gave his pledge to the government not to write anything more about so sensitive a subject without proper authority. In return, he became privy to secret researches that changed the face of the world. But for the critical years when the A-bomb was being developed, what he learned went into a safe marked TOP SECRET. He became the government's own reporter in an arrangement made with the *Times* to obtain his services.

It was Atomic Bill's story that the government made public on August 6, 1945 about the birth of the atomic age—the same day that the first atomic bomb was dropped on Hiroshima from the B-29 *Enola Gay*. He had written:

> Mankind's successful transition to a new age, the Atomic Age, was

ushered in July 16, 1945 before the eyes of a tense group of renowned scientists and military men gathered in the desertlands of New Mexico to witness the first end results of their $2 billion effort. . . .

Laurence desperately wanted to go along on the *Enola Gay* to witness the destruction of Hiroshima, but he was put off. When he did go, it was in the B-29 *Great Artiste* on August 9, 1945. His story of the atomic bombing of Nagasaki was issued as an official War Department release to the nation. (It was only after World War II that the War Department became the Defense Department.) He had the satisfaction then of knowing that, in his own way as a journalistic specialist, he had contributed something to the successful end of the war. Japan surrendered six days after the Nagasaki bombing.

For his eyewitness report of the Nagasaki mission, as well as a series of articles he was permitted to publish later in the *Times*, he was awarded a Pulitzer Prize in 1946, his second as an expert interpreter of science to the American public. If Albert Einstein set in motion the vast government research on atomic energy with his 1939 letter to President Roosevelt, Atomic Bill Laurence became the first historian of the atomic age.

Many other journalists were to follow his example as experts in diverse fields, but none attained his importance both to his profession and his country.*

The Growth of Specialized Journalism

Most news organizations of consequence today include several reporters with specialized knowledge on their staffs. It could not have happened a half-century ago. But areas of news interest have broadened so appreciably that specialized reporters no longer are regarded as strange birds in the journalistic aviary.

They have proved their usefulness in many ways. For example:

A lengthy investigation of unsanitary conditions in American meatpacking plants by Nick Kotz of the *Des Moines Register* led to the adoption of remedial legislation, the Federal Wholesale Meat Act, as a protection to consumers.

A series of articles by Victor Cohn in the *Minneapolis Tribune*

*Much of this background is from Laurence's two Pulitzer Prize files in the Special Collections section of Butler Library, Columbia University. Some of Laurence's reflections will also be found in his book *Men and Atoms* (New York: Simon & Schuster, 1948).

pinpointed the relationship between overuse of tobacco and lung cancer at a time when tobacco companies were spending tens of millions of dollars on newspaper advertising. Cohn, as a pioneering medical reporter, did not let that dissuade him in his researches nor did his newspaper flinch from publishing is results. When the linkage was accepted long afterward by both the medical profession and large sections of the public, it became commonplace for writers to discuss the problem in the news media. But when Cohn broke the way, it took both superior medical knowledge and a great deal of courage.

The government's decision to bar a drug called thalidomide from the American market was based very largely on scientific researches that were described in fascinating detail by a medical reporter, Morton Mintz of the *Washington Post.* In a series of articles in that newspaper, Mintz was the first to disclose that the drug, widely used elsewhere, had been associated with the birth of malformed babies. The writer interviewed the scientists and researchers who had come up with these findings, explained them, and the government's ban on the drug was the result.

In one of the most unusual exploits of any specialized reporter, David Perlman of the *San Francisco Chronicle* was invited to accompany a scientific expedition that retraced the route of Charles Darwin in the Galapagos Islands off the coast of Ecuador. Wherever Darwin had gone in his ship, the *Beagle,* the twentieth-century explorers also ventured—among them botanists, entomologists, ornithologists, and others. What they sought was a new look at Darwin's evolutionary theories, and Perlman was the only journalist to interpret them to a lay audience.

Among many writers who have scrutinized damage to the environment in America, James Risser of the *Des Moines Register* stood out because he tackled a difficult subject. In the heart of the Midwest farm belt, he had the knowledge, the courage, and the editorial support to study damage to the environment caused by ordinary and accepted farming practices. It was scarcely the kind of publicity that made him popular in the farm belt, but he was not deflected from his central purpose.

Another of the journalistic specialists of our times, David Halberstam, formerly of the *New York Times*, devoted five years to a study of competing Japanese and American automobile manufacturers to account for Japanese successes and American failures. The book that resulted, Professor John Kenneth Galbraith wrote, was "an attempt, no less, to assess the whole post-war industrial and associated cultural, political, and larger economic history of Japan and the United States and the economic conflict that has arisen in consequence. . . ."*

Across the land there were by this time many hundreds of other journalists, working for both local and national media, who had specialized contributions to make to the public interest. It was a trend that would bear watching throughout the declining years of this century and the next as well.

Some Caveats

The era of specialization, without doubt, has improved our understanding of the society in which we live.

Most news organizations of consequence in every part of the country are usually able to assign qualified people to developments in national and international affairs, education and religion, the economy and the environment, housing and cultural affairs, science and medicine, and many other specialized fields. At the very top of the journalistic pyramid, there even are specialists who deal exclusively in news of the news media themselves.

It would be pleasant, therefore, to assume that whatever ills there are in the functioning of our society will come to public notice in a fair and objective manner. But it scarcely works out that way in practice because of the journalistic assumption that news more often than not is based on conflict.

The late J. Montgomery Curtis, the founding director of the American Press Institute (API), was fond of citing this example to the editors and publishers who so often consulted him on how to improve their product:

"We never seem to find any news in the daily routine of our schools, where teachers and students by the tens of thousands work together quietly and peaceably to further the educational process. But let one little boy throw a fit and slug a teacher in the sight of a policeman, and right away that school becomes news. It oughtn't to be that way, but it is."

It is true enough that we hear mainly of conflicts in the educational process, such as recent charges at the apex of government that some of our greatest universities aren't providing proper education in one respect or another.* But consider the whole panorama of American education in the latter years of the twentieth century:

New York Times, Book Review article by Professor Galbraith, October 26, 1986. Halberstam's book was "The Reckoning" (New York: Morrow, 1986).

*Secretary of Education William J. Bennett in 1986 criticized his alma mater, Harvard, in one of these governmental sallies against higher education.

A total of about 65 million students are enrolled in primary and secondary schools and colleges and universities at an expenditure of about $100 million a year of public funds alone. More than a million degrees are conferred annually upon those who have completed four years of higher education. Surely, this is worth more than passing notice. And yet it is the 5 million or so dropouts who attract the most attention when they get into trouble.**

The same situation is likely to exist in other important fields, notably housing, where the dissatisfaction of a part of a community reflects on whatever progress is being made to upgrade substandard living quarters. This is not intended to suggest that news sections should be edited in the spirit of chambers of commerce or that reporters ought to be cheerleaders. It is merely a mild plea for a better balance between controversy and accomplishment in so many areas of the news where we customarily judge content by the adversary formula—critics versus establishment, ins versus outs, and all the variations thereof.

Here, for example, is how a reporter following the adversary school of writing about public education would begin a story about a lawsuit critical of public school reading:

> A federal judge today told parents who want to protect Central City schoolchildren from "objectionable" reading that they didn't have to study books such as *Huckleberry Finn* and *The Scarlet Letter*.
> The ruling came from Judge Milman Pinder in a suit brought by the parents of nine children who are members of a religious group that objects to such books in school. Attorney Millicent Winkler, for the plaintiffs, argued, "Teen-agers will get objectionable ideas from reading books like that." . . .

Contrast this somewhat slanted account with an attempt by Mack Roberts, a State U graduate who covered the story for the *Central City Leader*, to produce a more balanced story:

> Federal Judge Milman Pinder ruled today that nine families could keep their children out of reading classes rather than have them exposed to "objectionable" books in Central City's public schools.
> The judge's decision came after a hearing without a jury of the complaints of nine Central City parents, members of a conservative religious sect, that their children were picking up "objectionable ideas" from some of the books that are required reading in the city's public schools.

**Statistics are based on Census Bureau figures, rounded off to the nearest large sum.

The Central City School Board's attorney, Linton Durward, announced the judge's decision would be appealed. "Under this ruling," Durward said, "we won't be able to have high school students read such American classics as Hawthorne's *The Scarlet Letter* and Twain's *Huckleberry Finn*."

Durward alluded to the contention of the plaintiffs' attorney, Millicent Winkler, that "teen-agers will get objectionable ideas from reading books like that."

In an interview after the court adjourned, Judge Pinder stressed that he was seeking only to protect the rights of the suing parents and their children for the free exercise of their religious beliefs under the First Amendment. "I do not intend that my decision in this case should be extended to all Central City's public schools or to all students in primary and secondary grades," he said.

A check with legal authorities indicated that this is the first suit of its kind locally in which dissatisfaction has been expressed with public school reading assignments for any reason. There are nearly a million public school students, about 70,000 teachers, and some 35,000 administrators and clerical employees in the city's school system. . . .

The objection to the first lead, although it is technically correct, is that it gives the impression of a general legal prohibition against two classic American novels. It is true that in the second paragraph the writer specifies that the only parents affected are those of the nine children at issue. Nevertheless, the lead amounts to sharp practice; even though it is a lot livelier than the second and more balanced account, it is weighted against the school board.

As a matter of experience, most journalists know that a slanted lead nearly always tops a slanted story. The second lead, which sticks to the facts and omits nothing, presents an account that is fair, which is the main reason for developing specialists to handle critical news accounts. It says something about a news organization if it permits objections by the parents of nine children to undercut confidence in a public school system covering nearly a million children in all.

The majority, in this case as in others, is also entitled to a fair shake.

26

Writing about Investigations

THIS IS THE CASE for investigative journalism, as stated in a recent national survey:

"Our survey suggests the public likes hard-nosed reporting and also values deeply the role of watchdog journalism. . . . The public actually shows how much it values independent reporting when so much of it watches '60 Minutes' and '20-20,' magazine [television] programs that make independent journalism their stock in trade. All recent Gallup opinion polls show that as long as journalism techniques used are honest and aboveboard, the public very much approves of investigative journalism. . . ."*

What Is Being Investigated

Modern journalists need little urging to participate in investigative journalism. The records of the Pulitzer Prizes show that more awards have been won by investigative reporters from 1917 to the present than for any other activity in newspaper work. As for television, the popularity of programs such as "60 Minutes" is sufficient evidence that the networks find it pays to investigate. So, for that matter, do local programmers who believe it a good way to win public approval, particularly through inquiries into complaints made by viewers.

All this has been going on for a long time, more than two and a

*Report on a Times-Mirror poll in *Proceedings of the American Society of Newspaper Editors,* 1986, p. 23.

half centuries on this continent, to be exact. It was foreshadowed in the acquittal of John Peter Zenger, the publisher of the *New York Weekly Journal*, in 1735, when a jury cleared him of seditious libel because he had printed the truth about arbitrary British rule in colonial New York.

In defense of Zenger's right to examine the acts of government and publish truthful information about his inquiries, his lawyer, Andrew Hamilton, addressed the jurors as follows:

" . . . It is the best Cause. It is the cause of Liberty. . . . That, to which Nature and the Laws of our Country have given us a Right—the Liberty—both of exposing and opposing arbitrary Power (in these parts of the World, at least) by speaking and writing Truth."*

To American journalists, it is still the best cause. The most cursory examination of their accomplishments, as described in the citations for Pulitzer Prizes, shows that most awards have been won for exposing corruption in government at local, state, and national levels.

The next most numerous prize category has to do with miscarriages of justice, that is, providing the evidence on which the guilty have been sent to prison and the innocent freed. After that, in no particular order, come a variety of inquiries that include nepotism in Congress and labor racketeering, violations of human rights and protection of the environment, financial frauds, and abominable prison conditions, among others.

Nor does the journalists' enthusiasm for conducting investigations appear to be running out. Succeeding generations of newspaper people seem to be stepping up their efforts to look into wrongdoing, rather than letting well enough alone. And in television, despite the controls exercised by the Federal Communications Commission, the investigators at times threaten to outdo their more experienced newspaper colleagues. There is no doubt, at any rate, that the public continues to approve of such efforts. The evidence consists of enlarged support for surviving papers with a record of investigative journalism as well as the high standing of investigative TV shows.

How Investigations Are Conducted

There is no approved way in which investigations begin, no set of rules by which they are conducted. The whole process is as wide open as blue skies. Moreover, successful inquiries are by no means

---

*A more extensive record of the Zenger case is in John Hohenberg, *Free Press/ Free People* (New York: Columbia University Press, 1971), pp. 38–43.

confined to old hands—veteran reporters who know their way around and have a solid background of achievement.

Woodward and Bernstein, of Watergate fame, were not the first beginners who became famous for cracking a tough case. One of the earliest and most spectacular of all Pulitzer Prizes went to two other beginners, Al Goldstein and Jim Mulroy of the *Chicago Daily News*, who were credited with solving the Chicago "thrill" murder of fourteen-year-old Bobby Franks. What the two cubs did was to develop much of the evidence on which two wealthy college students, Dickie Loeb and Nathan Leopold, were convicted.

To cite an accomplishment by an old hand at investigative journalism, Clark Mollenhoff of the *Des Moines Register* worked on and off for five years to break an exposé of racketeering. His target was the powerful Teamsters' Union and he produced the evidence on which one of its leaders, Dave Beck, was sent to jail. Like Mulroy and Goldstein, Mollenhoff simply followed the trail wherever it led him and never gave up when the going was tough.

But there have been martyrs to the cause, too. One of the earliest was Don Mellett, the editor of the *Canton Daily News* in Ohio, who was mowed down by gunfire while he was demanding a cleanup of municipal corruption. His newspaper persisted in avenging his murder, finally producing the evidence on which a top-ranking police detective and three ex-convicts were imprisoned as his slayers.

Two newspapers even smaller than the *Canton Daily News*, the *Whiteville News Reporter*, and the *Tabor City Tribune* in North Carolina, won a Pulitzer for taking on the Ku Klux Klan in their own state and putting it out of business. These two weeklies were the forerunners of many other efforts by the press to put down campaigns of hate and bigotry. As Editor Harry Ashmore wrote in the *Arkansas Gazette* of Little Rock when the federal government sent troops there to enforce a court-approved policy of school integration: "We are going to have to decide what kind of people we are—whether we obey the law only when we approve of it, or whether we obey it no matter how distasteful we may find it. And this, finally, is the only issue before the people of Arkansas. . . ."

That is the main issue, too, before the American people in supporting the administration of justice. Because Gene Miller of the *Miami Herald* believed it so implicitly, he entered upon a campaign to free two indigent black men who had been convicted of murder in Florida and sentenced to be hanged.

Miller was no starry-eyed do-gooder. He was a hard-nosed reporter who already had won a Pulitzer Prize for producing evidence on which two other people, in unconnected cases, had been freed of wrongful murder convictions. In the cases of the two black men, Freddie Pitts and Wilbert Lee, Miller believed their protests of innocence of the murder for which they had been convicted. And, by a seeming miracle, he was able to prove their innocence and set them free, but only after they had served twelve years and forty-eight days in jail through miscarriages of justice.

The record of investigative journalism in America covers much more than the Pulitzer awards. For every winner, there have been many whose patient and prolonged researches also entitled them to consideration by their peers.

One of the great ones whose work didn't win a Pulitzer, although other awards came to her, was the *Chicago Sun Times*'s Pam Zekman. As an investigative reporter, she and her colleagues on the paper ran the Mirage Bar in Chicago to prove how stolen goods are sold in such places.

Television people, not being eligible for Pulitzers, had to be content with the plaudits of their colleagues and some electronic awards. That, for example, was the case with David Andelman's investigation of space weaponry for the "CBS Evening News."

The credibility of the Pulitzers was tested in the extreme when an award went to Janet Cooke of the *Washington Post* for a story about an eight-year-old heroin addict who, it turned out, didn't exist. To the *Post*'s credit, the paper's own executives exposed the fake. They returned the prize after questioning the reporter extensively about fabrications in her résumé that raised eyebrows at the Associated Press. Over the long run, the hoax did not do permanent harm either to the prizes or to the practice of investigative journalism.

Yet, despite the substantial record of accomplishment among the press's investigative reporters, the national survey quoted at the head of this chapter was not particularly reassuring about the press's credibility as a whole. On this point, the survey said:

> Over 60 percent of public reasoning as to why the press does not live up to standards is explained in part by [its] dependency . . . on commercial pressure, interest group pressure, government news management, and advertiser pressure.
>
> Only about a quarter of public reasoning concerning reasons for public perceptions of press failure deals with things other than the dependency issue—bias in the reporters themselves, budgets not sufficiently large, incompetence of news people

and the like. In a way, the public sees the press as led astray by its dependency on the power structure, advertisers, and audience. . . .*

Other surveys over a considerable period suggest that so censorious a public view of the press as a whole does not encompass all newspapers, particularly the standouts on a regional basis. Nor do the bulk of such surveys show that other parts of the national news media—the newsmagazines and radio and television news reports—are as severely judged as are newspapers.

It follows that we may not have a thorough understanding of the reasons for such apparently contradictory public views of the news media. For one thing, we do not know the extent to which public opinion of the press is affected by political partisanship—the feeling, for example, of President Nixon and his devoted White House aides in the Watergate cover-up that it is "us against them." For another, we also have no substantial indication of how many readers are turned off by what is published that goes contrary to their political, economic, and perhaps even their religious beliefs.

No matter. From all indications, the movement is not likely to dry up and blow away. Most practicing journalists agree that it is stronger today than ever before.

That, however, does not mean that journalists as a whole are complacent about their public image. Speaking for newspapers alone, Robert P. Clark of the Harte-Hanks Newspapers concluded his term as president of the American Society of Newspaper Editors by saying: "I would urge that we not have a blind spot about credibility. No one is suggesting that we slack off on quality journalism or hard-hitting reporting. We simply have to be tuned in better to the needs and feelings of the public."**

Handling an Investigative Assignment

Mack Roberts, who is concluding a month on rewrite at the *Central City Leader,* has just received an assignment to check on complaints from subscribers that sellers of illegal narcotics are operating openly on the State U campus. The city editor, Joe Stoddard, has instructed

*Proceedings of the American Society of Newspaper Editors, 1986, pp. 22–23. There are many sources for Pulitzer Prize material, all of which is available at the Butler Library at Columbia University.
**Proceedings of the American Society of Newspaper Editors, 1986, P. 65.

him to draw whatever funds are necessary from the *Leader*'s cashier to buy the drugs.

"And keep a careful record of what you buy, when and where you buy it, a description of the seller and, of course, the product itself. And don't go using any of it!" the city editor adds with a grin.

Roberts, being a recent graduate of State U, takes him seriously as to the last. "I got sick on pot once at my fraternity house and that put me off the stuff," he says. "Don't worry about me destroying the evidence."

"I'm only kidding," Stoddard says. Then, as Roberts turns to go, he calls the youngster back. "Oh, and don't take any chances with those dope peddlers. They can be damned mean."

Roberts feels strange as he returns to the State U campus as an investigator. After leaving his car in a big public parking field near the main entrance, he is not sure how to begin. Does he walk around aimlessly, watching for a dope pusher? Or does he look up some fraternity brothers in search of a lead?

Like many another reporter at the outset of an investigation, he has trouble making up his mind. And because of his uncertainty, he hangs around the parking field to assess the layout before him. It is familiar enough, but now almost everything he looks at has a different meaning.

Take for example that dull red brick building over there. As a student, he recognized it as the home of the business school. But now he thinks of it only because he knows it faces on a back alley where a dope pusher might be waiting. And in that once friendly fraternity house across the way, he now recalls that there are a lot of careless youngsters who will try almost anything for kicks—easy marks for a pusher.

In his pocket, Roberts has $1,000 with which to make his own buys. What does he want? Almost anything, to prove a point. But in the main he's after cocaine and its expensive and harmful derivative, crack. As he speculates on whether to make his first move into the alley behind the business school, a prosperous-looking middle-aged man parks a shiny new car a short distance away and waves to him.

Roberts waves back for no particular reason. He's never seen the fellow before. But soon enough the stranger makes his business known. He wants to be sure where a certain fraternity house is because he has a package to deliver. And, as luck would have it, the place is the one just across the way with the crazy kids who'll experiment with almost anything.

On reporter's instinct, Roberts walks beside the stranger, making conversation, on the off-chance that the delivery he is making will be worth investigating. That is how it turns out.

In the package are individual glassine packets of crack for the fraternity brothers. And are there others available for another customer? Of course!

It is in this manner that Roberts makes his first buy on the public campus parking lot, out where anybody can see what is going on. The money and the package of crack, produced from the trunk of the peddler's car, change hands. And Roberts remembers to take down the license of the peddler's car as he drives off for another delivery.

After that first buy, the young reporter realizes that there is no point to skulking around in back alleys. The traffic in illicit drugs is so well-established on this campus, as elsewhere in town, that the pushers take few precautions.

In fact, as the morning's work goes on, Roberts makes buys on a pleasant campus sidewalk while State U police cars pass by on traffic assignments. And just off campus, later in the day, he finds a pusher who makes a deal with him while two city police are parked in an official car not too far away.

So it turns out, on his first day as an investigator, Roberts exhausts his $1,000 and has several packages wrapped in brown paper to show for it. He also has learned that dope pushers aren't necessarily the sleazy-looking, shifty-eyed characters portrayed in the movies and on late-night television. Most of them turn out to be affable, quietly dressed business types out for a quick buck at little risk.

Joe Stoddard listens to the report Roberts presents late in the day, approves the expenditure of another $1,000, and tells him to continue on the job. This goes on for more than a week in much the same fashion, with only the personalities and the locale changing. But the prices seem to be standard, the business is uninterrupted, and the customers at State U seem inexhaustible.

Finally, at the end of the inquiry, when Roberts has established beyond question that the campus is a thriving marketplace for illicit drugs, he is told to summarize his evidence for the benefit of the university administration and the local police.

There are two reasons for this. First, the *Leader* isn't out to sandbag the university. The newspaper's executives want to show that the inquiry is no mere circulation-building stunt but has been conducted in good faith. And second, the reporter does need official comment on his findings, reactions that may indicate what, if anything, will happen as a result of his work.

Naturally, in tipping the results of an investigation ahead of publication, there is always a risk that there will be an adverse break before the story is spread before the public. But that is a chance the *Leader*'s executives are taking. In Roberts's case, everything turns out favorably for him. The first story of his series about crack sales on campus begins:

CRACK

Crack, the harmful and expensive cocaine derivative, is being sold openly to students on the State U campus.

The price runs from $50 to $100 for a small packet. The social damage is incalculable.

During ten days of investigation on campus, a reporter for the *Leader* bought $2,500 worth of illicit drugs, much of it crack of a particularly dangerous variety, from drug pushers who operated openly.

Sometimes, the purchases were completed within the view of passing campus and city police cars.

While the reporter was making his buys, he saw several pushers with whom he had dealt previously delivering packages to various buildings on the campus.

The *Leader* has made known the results of its inquiry to both the State U administration and the local police, together with whatever identification the reporter was able to give of the men who sold the drugs. An analysis of the purchases he made, conducted by the Folwell Chemical Laboratories, Inc., showed that one lot was merely sugar but the rest consisted of crack, heroin, and a little marijuana.

President Edgar Braintree, at his office at State U, expressed surprise and shock at the *Leader*'s findings. "We'll make every effort to see that this traffic is stopped and stopped fast," he said. "If we find evidence of collusion to protect these dope peddlers, I promise immediate prosecution of offenders."

Police Chief Langston Howell gave similar assurances, promising to put more city police on campus to work with the undermanned university guards. "We'll put these gangsters out of business," he said.

As for the students, few were surprised to learn of the results of the *Leader*'s investigation but none wanted to be quoted directly. One student, a 22-year-old senior who is headed for law school, said:

"You'd have to be deaf, dumb, and blind not to know about the drug traffic on campus. It's been going on for all the four years I've spent here and, after this blows over, it'll keep right on going because there are a certain number of students who want drugs and can pay the price. And there are pushers around who have access to a supply at all times."

The student refused to be identified saying, "It's none of my business. I'm just an innocent bystander and don't want to get involved. . . ."

Although the story bears Roberts's signature and he was the reporter who bought the drugs with the *Leader*'s money and on a regular news assignment, he is instructed not to write his story in the first person. This is the usual practice in publishing the results of such inquiries, although it makes little sense to the public.

However, the old print prejudice against glorifying the reporter still hangs on despite current practices on television.

27

The Writer as Public Advocate

SOME CALL THEMSELVES DIGGERS, which is a part of the job. Others think of themselves as campaigners, which they most certainly are. But by whatever name they are known, they are men and women with a cause in American journalism.

More than that—whether they are beginners or veterans, and whether their work involves investigation or some other aspect of journalism—the nature of their undertaking makes them public advocates. The scornful may ask in derision, "Who appointed *you?*"

To that, Eugene Patterson gave a proper answer in his newspaper, the *St. Petersburg Times* in Florida: "When a strange new force imbeds itself clandestinely in this community and sets out to harm people who raise questions about it, a newspaper has a particular duty to resist intimidation itself and inform citizens fully of what is going on."*

It was the ultimate justification for the press in public service.

The Challenge and the Response

The challenge could not be ignored. A group of intruders who righteously clothed themselves in the First Amendment by calling themselves the "Church of Scientology," set up their headquarters in nearby Clearwater in 1975.

*Patterson's statement in the *St. Petersburg Times*, December 16, 1979.

Bette Orsini, a reporter for the *St. Petersburg Times*, began making inquiries about the newcomers in Clearwater, their backgrounds and their purposes. For this, she became the target of abuse, as did her superiors on the newspaper. Snooping, prying, and terror were the weapons the invaders used in an effort to beat down opposition.

Had the newspaper been interested merely in profits amassed through providing the populace with entertainment, very likely the Scientologists would have become the dominant organization in Clearwater and the owners of some of its most valuable property. But the response was quite different.

The paper chose to fight.

First of all, Mrs. Orsini was reinforced with other newspeople, notably Charles Stafford, then the chief of the paper's Washington bureau. Next, the paper undertook a series of court actions that were as extensive as the investigations Mrs. Orsini and Stafford undertook.

After four years, nine of the leaders of the Scientology group were prosecuted on various federal charges in Washington, D.C., and convicted. After the successful prosecution, the Federal government's spokesman commented:

> The crimes committed by these defendants are of a breadth and scope previously unheard of. No building, office, desk, or file was safe from their snooping and prying. No individual or organization was free from their despicable conspiratorial minds.
>
> "In view of this, it defies the imagination that these defendants have the unmitigated audacity to seek to defend their actions in the name of 'religion.' ... [It] adds insult to injuries which they have inflicted on every element of society.*

The Press in Public Service

The twin concepts of the writer as public advocate and the press in public service are in the American tradition. If radio and television have not been as quick to develop a public conscience, it may be attributed in part to the Federal Communications Commission's control of the airwaves.

In colonial America, the much more stringent controls exercised by the British governors and their allies resulted in the jailing of some of their violent press critics, among them James Franklin, the older brother of the redoubtable Ben.

*As quoted by Charles Stafford in an article in the *St. Petersburg Times*, December 16, 1979. Mrs. Orsini and Stafford were awarded a Pulitzer Prize in 1980.

Indeed, Ben, upon taking over from his imprisoned brother, announced in their weekly, The *New England Courant* of Boston, that his main design would be to "entertain the town with the most comical and diverting incidents of human life." The cautious young Franklin remembered full well that the first newspaper in the colonies, *Publick Occurrences*, had been suppressed in Boston in 1721 after a single issue and its publisher, Ben Harris, had been jailed for circulating news embarrassing to the authorities.

Young Franklin was too smart to be caught in that spot, even as a teen-ager, but what he did do was to pick up part of a tract from a London newspaper that precisely expressed his true notion of what journalism ought to be:

> Without freedom of thought, there can be no such thing as wisdom; and no such thing as public property, without freedom of speech: Which is the right of every man, as far as by it he does not hurt and control the right of another; and this is the only check which it ought to suffer, the only bounds which it ought to know. . . . Whoever would overthrow the liberty of a nation must begin by subduing the freedom of speech; a thing terrible to public Traytors.*

Young Franklin gained courage when he moved to Philadelphia and began putting out the *Pennsylvania Gazette* in 1729. Six years later, in a letter to the editor in which he posed as an elderly citizen, he called for better fire protection including a battalion of volunteer firemen and licensing of chimney sweeps. "An ounce of prevention," he wrote, "is worth a pound of cure." And so it turned out when his reforms took hold.

Encouraged, Franklin next demanded better police protection but he also advocated something very unpopular then as now: more taxes on business to pay for an enlarged force. That didn't work as well as some of his other crusades, but his example was followed by journalists in other colonial cities. In effect, therefore, he became the first successful crusading journalist in America and thereby the founder of a useful tradition.

It was understandable, however, that many thoughtful citizens, then as now, would be troubled when the press, in its pursuit of the public good, seemed to be defying the law. It wasn't merely the Alien

*Franklin impishly attributed these sentiments to his mythical character, Silence Dogood. Actually, it was part of an essay published by two London newspaper men, John Trenchard and William Gordon, under the pen name of "Cato." Pen names were not a very reliable cover for staying out of jail then.

and Sedition Laws of the administration of John Adams, our second president, that aroused public concern. A number of journalists went to jail for flouting these strict statutes, which intensified journalistic conflicts between the First Amendment and other precepts of our basic laws. That created an adverse opinion, as well as partial approval, for the role of the press as a public advocate.

A Classic Press-Government Conflict

Differences between press and government about what the people ought to know have continued into our own time. Until the *New York Times* obtained the Pentagon Papers and began publishing them although they bore a top-secret classification, just how and why we went to war in Vietnam remained a disturbing mystery. Even so, the government fought in the courts to keep this vital information from the public.

This was a major conflict between a free government and a free press. Future generations should make no mistake about that when they read about this "dirty little war." The administration of President Lyndon Baines Johnson was determined from the outset to make it appear that the forces of Communist North Vietnam and their allies in the south, the Vietcong, were being defeated by the South Vietnamese with American supporting troops.

Unfortunately, it didn't turn out that way. But the government insisted to the end that the press was lying, although the Pentagon Papers, had they been promptly released, would have proved exactly the contrary was true.

The Supreme Court at last had the final word in the press-government controversy. It ruled 6 to 3 that the press was right in publishing the Pentagon Papers, with Justice Hugo L. Black writing: "Only a free and determined press can effectively expose deception in government. . . ."*

The Anatomy of a Campaign

Most public service campaigns are local in nature and essentially undramatic in character, as contrasted with the heroics of the press-government conflict in the Vietnam War. Nor can the writing have the compelling urgency of a war correspondent's dispatch directly

*The *New York Times* won the Pulitzer Prize gold medal for public service in 1972 for publishing the Pentagon Papers.

from a foreign battlefield. In fact, because of legal complications, the local campaigner has to be extremely cautious in handling such campaigns.

Sally Ward's experience with an investigation of four deaths at the Central City plant of the Dependable Gas Company is fairly typical of the routine, although the case itself turns out to be unusual. It begins without fanfare—a note to the newspaper from a woman complaining that her husband has been killed in a subbasement of the gas company plant but nobody will believe her. She blames a strange gas.

Sally, of course, is neither an investigative reporter nor a campaigner. As a specialist covering science and medicine for the *Central City Leader,* she is probably a poor choice for the assignment. And yet, the city editor, Joe Stoddard, has no alternative. Nobody else on the staff would know a poison gas from pure oxygen except after inhaling one or the other.

Sally is resigned to a lot of running around and telephoning with little chance of any newsworthy result. She visits the widow of the gas company employee who wrote the note, Mrs. Lydia Pengborn, a middle-aged mother of four children in a run-down section of town. On the surface, it doesn't seem to be much of a story. The facts are these:

Simon Pengborn, fifty-two, employed for twenty-eight years as a laborer at the Dependable Gas Company plant, was stricken with a heart attack while at work in a subbasement and died in the company's emergency medical quarters. There is a death certificate giving the relevant circumstances and dates, signed by a company doctor, H. M. Letterwort, M.D.

The only other circumstance, Mrs. Pengborn adds, is that Matty Miltree, her husband's friend and co-worker, who was with him at the time, also died in a city hospital, St. Gotthard's, several days later of a congenital lung disease. As a matter of routine, Sally calls on Miltree's widow, a person in much the same circumstances as Mrs. Pengborn, and finds corroboration in the death certificate there.

Sally is about to conclude that a brief note to the city editor will dispose of the matter. She is standing at the door when Mrs. Miltree says she has heard that there have been other deaths in the subbasement, but she has no specific information.

When Sally returns to the office she calls the Health Department of the city, and learns that two more deaths of laborers have occurred in the subbasement in the past few months. A city inspector has checked all four cases and found nothing of a suspicious nature.

Still, four deaths in the same place in a gas company plant does

seem a bit peculiar to Sally. And as she summarizes her findings
to the city editor, he agrees that she ought to stick with the story
for another day at least.

Now, clearly, she must visit the gas company plant herself but
she knows perfectly well that management isn't likely to be very
pleased to receive her. She has two choices as an investigative reporter (no campaign is in sight as yet). The first is to go skulking
around, only she hasn't the faintest idea where to start. The second
is to take the direct route and go to the top. For lack of anything
better to do, she arranges for an interview with the company's general manager, Jameson Esterfelt.

In a businesslike way, he confirms everything Sally has learned,
expresses his regret over the four deaths, and says, "It was just one
of those things. We've done the best we could for the men's families
and we're sorry that Mrs. Pengborn complained to you. We thought
we'd given her a good settlement."

Settlement? Sally wonders about the use of that particular term
but doesn't say anything. Instead, she asks if she can see the subbasement where the deaths had occurred. Again, there is cooperation, with Esterfelt accompanying her.

The place is spotless. As the general manager explains, the job
of cleaning out excess lumber, bricks, and debris, on which the four
men had worked, has since been completed by others who suffered
no ill effects.

There is only one thing that really bothers Sally now. As soon as
she enters the subbasement, she detects the faint odor of rotten
eggs, always something to be concerned about in a gas company
operation. In the presence of sufficient oxygen, the gas may not be
permanently harmful. However, if the oxygen supply is limited and
the space is enclosed, as is the case with the subbasement, it could
mean that she and the plant boss are breathing a form of gas that
is debilitating in some cases, deadly in others.

When she asks Esterfelt about the odor, she catches him by surprise. Momentarily he shows annoyance, then affects a careless
laugh. "The blowers aren't on," he says, and snaps an order to a
small, frightened man who has been tagging along behind them.
Quickly, there is a rush of fresh air in the subbasement from two
blowers, which causes Esterfelt to dismiss the seeming problem
with a wave of the hand. But Sally takes it more seriously. Through
the mail next day, she gets a scrawled note without signature that
reads: "The blowers were out of order when the four men died."

Now Sally knows that will be difficult to prove, even if it is true.

After a conference with the city editor, then the higher-ups in the *Leader*'s structure, everybody concludes that this is a matter for the district attorney of Central County.

Sally, much relieved, presents what she has learned to District Attorney Homer Clough. After a preliminary check, during which Clough interviews some gas company employees and begins to suspect a cover-up, he decides to call witnesses before the grand jury. That is when the *Leader* breaks its story—and it has to be very carefully done to skirt the possibility of libel. Sally begins:

GAS

The recent deaths of four workmen at the Dependable Gas Company plant here have prompted District Attorney Homer Clough to order a grand jury inquiry beginning today, the *Leader* has learned.

Among those under subpoena to testify are Jameson Esterfelt, general manager of the company, and relatives of the four workmen.

District Attorney Clough acted on the basis of information given to him by the *Leader* and a preliminary investigation that was conducted by members of his own staff.

"There is no suspicion of foul play here," Clough said. "But after hearing from certain people in the plant and relatives of the four workmen, I want to be sure that no negligence was involved in this case."

Clough emphasized that he had warned all witnesses to be called before the grand jury to observe the secrecy governing its operations. It is up to the 23 members of the grand jury to decide whether or not action is justified.

If an information or indictment is returned, then the case will go to trial in the appropriate court. If not, it will mean that the prosecutor is satisfied that no negligence was involved in the deaths.

Esterfelt, speaking for Dependable Gas, said, "We are fully cooperating with the authorities. We have nothing to fear."

The four workmen who died on different days and from different causes after cleaning a subbasement at the gas company plant, according to their death certificates, are: . . . "

The opposition newspaper and the electronic media ignore the story at the outset—too slight and too dangerous. So Sally alone is preoccupied with the case for much of the following three months under these circumstances:

After an extended inquiry, the grand jury returns an indictment charging the company and its top executives with criminal negligence in the four deaths. But at the subsequent trial, the state has difficulty in proving that the fatalities were caused by exposure to toxic gas.

The prosecutor contends that the gas, inhaled while the men were working in the subbasement, aggravated preexisting physical conditions. The defense stands on the medical testimony in the death certificates, supported by the physicians who signed them. Even a sensational witness like Mrs. Pengborn, who screams on the witness stand that the company has murdered her husband, cannot change the complexion of the trial.

Then, all of a sudden, a surprise witness pops up at the conclusion of the state's case and Sally has her story. She begins that day:

GAS

A 64-year-old electrician testified in Superior Court today that his bosses at the Dependable Gas Company were indirectly responsible for the deaths of four workmen.

Rising from the witness stand and pointing at Jameson Esterfelt, the company's general manager, Cleon Minzer said in a trembling voice:

"That man told me not to worry when I warned him the blowers weren't working in the subbasement and bad gas was making people faint."

District Attorney Homer Clough asked, "You told Mr. Esterfelt more than once?"

Still standing, the witness replied, "Yes, sir. I told him first when Simon Pengborn and Matty Miltree were cleaning the subbasement. I said the motor that ran the blowers was burned out and had to be replaced."

"And did he tell you to replace the motor?"

"No, sir. Then Simon and Matty died and later, before the other two went in there to clean up, I reminded Mr. Esterfelt about the blowers not working and he just laughed and said to forget about it. And the other two died."

There was a commotion in the courtroom as the witness finished his testimony. On cross-examination, when the defense asked why the witness had never before told his story, he flared up saying,

"I told the *Leader* about it. I wrote a note about the blowers not working."

Shortly afterward, the state rested its case. . . .

Now Sally remembers Minzer, the witness, as the frightened little man who had followed her in the subbasement when she inspected the place with Esterfelt. Reflecting on the unsigned note she had received about the blowers, she blames herself for not having guessed that he held the key to the case.

But that's the way it is with many a campaign that winds up in the courts. Whatever the reporters and their newspapers may do, it remains for the officials charged with the administration of justice to determine the extent of the crime, if any, and the punishment. And that process is often painfully slow.

In Sally's campaign, the jury brings in a guilty verdict with a heavy fine for the company and a jail term for Esterfelt. In consequence, the widows of the four victims sue for damages and are successful. But by that time, Sally is off working on an entirely different story and the *Leader* pays only cursory attention to the epilogue to her campaign. As for the opposition, which laid off the *Leader*'s campaign at the outset, all had to recognize the importance of the story at the end.

It assured more attention to safety for people working under potentially dangerous conditions. And that, while essentially undramatic, was nevertheless an accomplishment.

28

Personal Journalism

ARTHUR KROCK, ONCE THE GOOD GRAY DEAN of Washington journalists, often observed with a gentle smile that many a funeral had been held for personal journalism in America but it had never been obliging enough to die.* Krock was perfectly right. As one of the most respected of personal journalists, he was sufficient reason in himself to keep the art alive.

It is significant that individual points of view are still of enormous importance in American journalism. At a guess in the closing years of this century, there probably are more columnists, commentators, and news analysts at work in this country now than ever before. And once television overcomes its timidity and grants its talented people the liberties that have always been theirs in print, the nation will be the better for it.

The Influentials in Television

I have always been deeply concerned over Edward R. Murrow's warning about misusing television:

"During the daily peak viewing periods, television in the main insulates us from the realities of the world in which we live. If this state of affairs continues, we may alter an advertising slogan to read,

*Krock is quoted in Marquis Childs and James Reston, eds., *Walter Lippmann and His Times* (New York: Harcourt, 1959), p. 83.

252

'LOOK NOW, PAY LATER.' For surely, we shall pay for using this most powerful instrument of communication to insulate the citizenry from the hard and demanding realities which must be faced if we are to survive."*

Murrow's entire career as the best and still the greatest of television reporters and commentators is a testimonial to the direction in which television eventually must move unless it is to be a willing captive of special interests. What an older generation still remembers best about his work is his service as CBS's wartime watchman in London when Hitler's bombs were falling on the British capital. From the darkened rooftops, night after night, this brave reporter continually reassured millions in America that the British were still in the battle of a lifetime, that—in his words—"London can take it."

Why haven't there been others, given all the talent that exists today in television's American newsrooms, to follow Murrow's much-admired example of personal courage and personal conviction? It is difficult to say. But scanning the well-nigh limitless horizons of the tube's influence, all we do know is that—barring the weekly talk shows in the Sunday morning ghetto of electronic journalism, and noncommercial television—there are precious few regular programs that permit journalists the right of personal observation and comment as well as factual reportage.

For the networks, still the most important factor in American news communication as far as the public is concerned, we can count on Mike Wallace and his colleagues in "60 Minutes" on CBS and Barbara Walters and her associates in ABC's "20-20." There are a few others, here and there, who sometimes are permitted to give us their personal views, both on network and local news presentations, but not as a regular thing. We do not, therefore, benefit from a diversity of opinion on television that is so necessary in a democratic society if truth is to emerge.

It is a mistake, I think, to expect our three network anchors of these times—Tom Brokaw of NBC News, Dan Rather of CBS News, and Peter Jennings of ABC News—to carry the whole burden of managing and reading their nightly news presentations and also commenting on them. True, we do have capsule network commentaries now and then from John Chancellor, Bill Moyers, and others but these are scarcely of a piece with the scope of opinion available in the print media.

*Murrow's speech was on October 15, 1958 in Chicago before a meeting of broadcast news directors.

The point is beyond argument. We cannot, as citizens, permit television to continue to be a mere money-making machine; if that is all the tube is to be used for, then we are the poorer for it as a nation. We may well ask ourselves the key question, "If we do not use our constitutional privilege of freedom of speech, if we are content not to hear opinions of all kinds over the electronic media as well as to read others in print, will we not ourselves be undercutting the First Amendment?"

That is the potential danger.

For the new generation of journalists, then, the objective is clear. It isn't sufficient that many leading local news stations now devote as much as one to two hours a day to news programs. How much of this period is given over to investigative journalism, to commentary, to the exposition of an editorial point of view that varies from city to city, state to state? From my own sampling as I move about the country, even if local television generally is opening up to a diversity of views, network television still is skittish unless a program involving commentary soars in the ratings.

Ratings ought not to be the standard for journalism in these times when no particular brand of opinion, liberal or conservative, can claim ultimate authority over our affairs. What we require is a more open television as a proper forum for the free discussion of the issues that confront us as a people and as a nation. To continue to close the tube to the new generation of journalists of talent and conviction is to disregard once again Murrow's warning. We cannot, in all good conscience, wait much longer for a thorough-going reform in the way American television conducts its public responsibilities.

The Influentials in Print

Under current circumstances, when there is an argument about the course of government, whether it is Republican or Democratic, the burden of talking back to a president has to be borne in large part by the print media. And this is—make no mistake about it—a heavy responsibility, especially when a president is as popular as Ronald Reagan was during his first six years in office.

Haynes Johnson, a columnist for the *Washington Post*, did not blame that president or any other for the rising tide of criticism of the press when he examined the position. But, after reflecting on how strongly his mail showed antipress sentiment, he wrote as follows:

"There should be no need to belabor the point about the dangers inherent in such a climate of opinion. Events at home and abroad are generating deep concerns and fears, coupled with a yearning for security and stability, among American citizens.

"The administration shows strong impulses toward further restricting the free flow of information. The smell of censorship is in the air.

"We do not need, in the relations between press and government, more secrecy. We do not need, in the relationship between press and citizen, more hostility. We do need a better understanding of the process by which press and government function, and an appreciation of the proper roles of each. Most of all, we need to remember why a free press was established in America. . . ."*

It may be vain to hope for a greater understanding by a censorious public of the role of the press as a watchdog over government operations. The forced resignation of President Nixon for his Watergate cover-up did not endear the watchdog press to a public that witnessed, but scarcely cheered, its alertness and its power. Nor did that same press win plaudits for revealing weaknesses in the administration of President Carter, the Democrat whose four years were sandwiched between the respective years of the Nixon, Ford, and Reagan administrations.

Scant wonder that the masters of commercial television hesitated to relax their tight rein on personal journalism and the uncertainties of unrestricted commentary either about government or anything else! But then, no one with the slightest knowledge of American journalism ever suggested that all personal journalism would be popular, ever-rewarding, and without risk.

The proprietors of the press, both newspapers and newsmagazines, have even more cause than the owners of television to be concerned about taking on the government in any issue. That is because, basically, the fundamental nature of the American press has changed in this century from a largely family-owned status of individual publications to the growth of ownership concentrated in massive chains—Gannett, Knight-Ridder, Newhouse, Los Angeles Times-Mirror, and Cox, to name some of the dominant groups.

It is this concentration of press ownership that now must face repeated challenges, in and out of court, that seek to make inroads

*Haynes Johnson's column was published in the *Washington Post*, November 27, 1983, p. A-3.

on what should and should not be published in a newspaper. A typical case was that of *Tornillo* v. *Miami Herald*, in which a candidate for public office invoked a Florida "right-of-reply" law to force the *Herald*, a Knight-Ridder newspaper, to publish his statement responding to the paper's criticism of his candidacy.

When the *Herald* carried the case to the Supreme Court, the ruling was 9 to 0 in its favor with Chief Justice Burger writing for the court:

> The choice of material to go into a newspaper, and the decision made as to limitations in the size of the paper, and content, and treatment of public issues and public officials—whether fair or unfair—constitutes the exercise of editorial control and judgment. It has yet to be demonstrated how government regulation of this critical process can be exercised consistent with First Amendment guarantees of a free press as they have evolved to this time. . . .*

It remains to be seen how long the bulwark of the First Amendment, as interpreted by the courts, will hold back the rising tide of government and public disapproval of the press's watchdog role. Meanwhile, it is a safe bet that those who still believe in personal journalism will exercise their rights in the public interest, except on television.

The Scope of Personal Journalism

It should not be imagined that the exercise of personal journalism is confined to criticism of government. Indeed, its role is far broader than that. This useful convention of journalism makes possible, first of all, a breadth of emotion and personal expression in our writing for immediate publication that would not be possible if there were tight restrictions on freedom of the press.

Consider what could have happened to the news media when the *Challenger* exploded at lift-off at Cape Canaveral and thereby endangered both future appropriations and development of our missile program. A government with the power to curb coverage and commentary could very well have choked off all information to the public once the tragedy occurred in full view of a national television audience.

*Tornillo v. *Miami Herald*, 418 U.S. 258 (1974).

But that is not what happened. And because it did not happen under our protective basic law, Jules Loh of the Associated Press wrote an unforgettable account of the tragedy and its effect on the people closest to one of the seven victims, Christa McAuliffe, the schoolteacher who went along for the ride. Loh was there, observing her parents, Ed and Grace Corrigan, her husband, her children, and her children's flag-waving little friends. The AP account concluded:

> When the explosion lit the TV screens and the sky, the assembled watchers cheered, thinking it was the scheduled separation of the shuttle from the boosters. Almost immediately, it became clear it was not. A voice said so on a loud speaker but the Corrigans did not comprehend this or would not.
> A NASA official approached them and said, 'The vehicle has exploded.'
> 'The vehicle has exploded?' Mrs. Corrigan said.
> The official nodded, and led them away. A sorrowful nation wept with them. . . .*

Then, too, the function of commentary makes possible a broad exploration of local and regional problems that might not otherwise be possible. Jim Minter, editor of the *Atlanta Constitution and Journal,* demonstrated what personal journalism could do to illuminate a grave problem for rural Georgia, caused by government action at the state level. What had happened was that the state of Georgia had proposed a tax-free subsidy to an Irish dairy to enter the overcrowded market in Macon County where thirty-five local dairies already existed. Minter wrote:

> A lot of Georgia dairy operators are spitting mad over a deal they consider grossly unfair to them. Yet, there is a lure of 900 new jobs (offered by the Irish dairy in a state where bankrupt farmers are looking for jobs, and where 20,000 jobs have vanished in the textile industry.
> The Macon County story, Catch 22, dramatizes just how truly desperate rural Georgia is for economic opportunities. The size of the problem can be simply stated by remembering that 90 percent of the state's population still lives outside the thriving Atlanta metropolitan area. . . .**

What if the Minters of the nation are forbidden to speak and write in protest against what they believe to be demonstrably unfair actions of government? Considering what was happening to mid-

*Jules Loh, "America Mourns Christa McAuliffe," in the AP file for January 29, 1986.
**Minter's column in the *Constitution and Journal*, April 13, 1986, p. D-2.

western rural areas as well as in the South in the 1980s, any weakening of the right of fair comment would scarcely have been in the best interests of the people as a whole.

As for the injured feelings of partisans of this or that popular figure in government when they believe that their hero—or heroine—is being unfairly criticized, they often overlook the extent of the sympathetic treatment such politicians receive in many publications.

Consider, for example, how a rather restrained Hugh Sidey handled a piece for *Time* magazine after President Reagan let his temper boil over and plastered newspeople with a familiar expletive within their hearing:

> As might have been expected, Reagan knew just what to do once his SOB got loose. . . . Only a couple of hours went by before White House spokesman Larry Speakes was explaining that the President had no recollection of letting out an SOB. He had just remarked to [David] Packard, 'It's sunny and you're rich.'. . .
>
> But Wednesday morning about 50 of the best SOBs crowded into the White House State dining room for a scheduled breakfast with Reagan. No smiles, no T shirts, only tape recorders and ball points.
>
> Reagan brought a T shirt, a yellow number that he unfurled over his chest. Big black letters read SOB. There was only a halfhearted gurgle from the avenging crowd. Then Reagan flipped the shirt— 'Save Our Budget.' He had not only SOBed them, he had defeated them. Those SOBs applauded, which is almost enough to get you thrown out of the brotherhood. . . .*

The chances are, in any confrontation between a popular president and the press, that the press is always at a disadvantage. And the president knows it. However, the Republic is not likely to be saved if presidents continue to use all the power of their high office to create a favorable press for themselves at the cost of sidestepping or even ignoring the First Amendment altogether, as could be possible at some future time. That way lies disaster.

Much more to the point would be to open wider the gates of diversity of opinion by persuading television to permit its professionals to handle comment with the same freedom that they are given to report the news.

When Explanations Are Required

Straight news often can be misleading. Consider the problem faced by the *Central City Leader* when Governor Farrow goes before the legislature to propose a state-run lottery to finance ex-

*Sidey's column, "The Presidency: Son of a . . . ," *Time*, March 17, 1986, p. 28.

panded state programs of education, transportation, and social welfare.

A straight news story manifestly must make the governor's point that a state-run lottery will avert a probable rise in the state's already large income tax. But what such a story cannot do is explore the basic question of whether a state-run lottery is really necessary and, if so, whether it is the best way of meeting the state's financial problems. Here is the proof, a straight news piece by Independent News, a wire service, on the governor's program:

> Midland (IN)—Governor Farrow called on the legislature today to enact a state lottery to raise needed funds for education, transportation and public welfare.
>
> The governor said a lottery that may raise as much as $75 million a year will avert the need for a boost in state income taxes. He said he was opposed to a tax rise.
>
> Although the Republican-controlled legislature applauded the governor's proposal, the Democratic minority leader, State Senator Minor Garside, charged the lottery proposal was a "sell-out to big business interests."
>
> "Many of the largest corporations in this state don't pay taxes now and they'll continue to get away with it if the lottery plan is adopted," Garside said.
>
> Here is how the lottery would be run, under the governor's program, with a million-dollar top prize to be given every month. . . .

However, the management of the *Central City Leader*, even though the paper has generally supported the governor, asked its chief political writer in the state capital, Loren Wilton, to do a news analysis as a sidebar to the wire service story. Wilton had no instructions except to describe the situation as he saw it and explain what the chances were for enactment of the lottery.

Here is how Wilton begins his sidebar:

ANALYSIS - with LOTTERY

By Loren Wilton

Midland—Governor Farrow's proposed state lottery won't get through the legislature without a fight.

Mainly, that is because of the opposition of the state's United Church Council.

Its president, the Rev. Dr. J.C.D. Bartholomew, pastor of the Evergreen Baptist Church, said immediately after hearing the governor's special message today:

"We'll have to look this proposal over very, very carefully. On the basis of experience elsewhere with state lotteries, most of the money supporting them comes from the heads of families least able to afford to gamble and lose. And the losers then come to the churches for help. No, I wouldn't say the governor's proposal is an unmitigated blessing."

Some of Dr. Bartholomew's doubts were echoed by Republican legislators, but they didn't want to be quoted by name. One said, "I'm just not sure. There are a lot of angles about this lottery thing that I don't like."

In any case, the assumption that anything a Republican governor wants will get through the Republican legislature may not prove valid this time. Although the Democratic opposition is outnumbered in both houses, some sources here estimate that if as few as ten senators of the majority party either abstain or vote no, the governor's lottery plan could go down the drain.

However, the alternative, boosting the state income tax, is even less appetizing to legislators. And, as an important legislative source commented after listening to both the governor and Dr. Bartholomew,

"Farrow's put the Republican party in this state in a terrible position because he wants to run for president and wants us to be his cheering section. If we go for the lottery, the churches are going to be after us. And if we raise taxes, everybody's going to be after us. I'd say it's one hell of a note. . . ."

The points made in Wilton's news analysis are valid and well-documented except for the material that was given to him on background—that is, not for attribution. But it would be unthinkable for a veteran political commentator of his standing to manufacture mythical opponents for the governor, especially in a paper that has supported the state's chief executive in the past.

Contrasting the straight news story with the analysis by a reporter who has complete independence to write the truth as he sees it, there can be little doubt that explanatory material can sometimes put an entirely different face on what looks like a valid program worthy of speedy enactment. That is what happened in the case of the lottery plan. It has often happened to other seemingly useful programs upon closer examination.

While it is the function of the journalist to ask questions, he expects little thanks for it. About the most a reporter of Wilton's professional competence may receive after years of faithful service is a prize of some sort and good wishes from his colleagues. A conscientious journalist, unlike a mere entertainer, can't afford to play to the galleries. It doesn't work that way.

29

Critics and Editors

WHEN BROOKS ATKINSON WAS ASKED to define his standards as a critic, his usual reply was, "I like it or I don't like it."* That is a practical attitude for both critics and editors of newspapers and magazines. And it applies, as well, to news directors for the electronic media and the relatively few critics and editorialists who are given the right to voice their opinions over the airwaves. In the restricted areas in which American journalists are expected to express their convictions, their responses should be prompt and vigorous. No critic or editorialist can attract an audience by dancing sedately on the head of a pin.

The Uses of Expert Criticism

The British journalist and historian, H. G. Wells, often said, "What I write goes now." That's the way it is with critics. When the curtain comes down on a play, when a concert is over, when a new book has been read, the newspaper critic must repair to his typewriter and bat out a quick opinion. Whether the critic is right or wrong, that's the way it is done.

When Atkinson was asked how he could justify doing a thirty-minute wrap-up (and sometimes a destructive one) of a show that

*Atkinson, who was for many years the drama critic of the *New York Times*, frequently lectured on his specialty at the Columbia Graduate School of Journalism.

had taken months to produce at a very high cost, he would patiently respond, "How else can it be done for a daily paper?" And the book critic, Lewis Gannett, when asked how he could speed-read so many books and produce so much rapid-fire criticism, was equally candid: "Why, that's how I make my living." He might have added that a certain amount of good taste and education helped.

Magazine critics have a little more time for their essays on the arts, while the relatively few television critics usually have less. However, the problem for all of them, if they are honest, is to have something to say that is interesting—and to be quick about it. Tardy critics miss deadlines—and paychecks.

However, not all publishers and broadcast executives want critics with opinions. They ask instead for "reviews," by which they mean a mere report that a performance took place and will continue. The notion may be that it isn't good business to offend potential advertisers. (But it is even worse business to offend a much larger audience by not giving people an honest account in discussing an artistic event.)

Then, too, some critics are more ferocious than others. Although it is the current fashion to go easy on amateur theatricals or academic presentations of various kinds, no holds are barred when it comes to professional performances—especially on Broadway. Even though today's Broadway isn't what it used to be (and some believe that Broadway existed mainly in the imagination of Grandma and Grandpa), the critics can be merciless.

To quote a Pulitzer Prize critic, Walter Kerr,* slamming a new musical called *Going Up*: "It had its charms but not enough of them." And his estimate of Samuel Beckett as a dramatist was equally devastating: "Beckett had a message. The message was that there is no message." Of a new dramatist who wrapped his offering in a lot of sexy goings-on, the critic demanded: "At what point did the contemporary world, enlightened as it is, come to regard sex as poison, deadly no matter what the dosage?" And as for the revival of a play by the classic French dramatist, Molière: "When you've seen one *Tartuffe* you haven't seen them all." But he wasn't as respectful of the ancient Greeks, for he wrote in a review of Mickey Rooney in *Sugar Babies*: "The sketches . . . go right back to Aristophanes, although Aristophanes was slightly more lyrical and decidedly dirtier."

Kerr could be kind, too, when he liked a show. For example, after

*Kerr, who reviewed for *Commonweal* magazine and two New York newspapers in a long and distinguished career, won his prize in 1978.

seeing the long-running *Fiddler on the Roof* when it starred Zero Mostel, he was all admiration: ". . . In *Fiddler*, Mostel is playing Sholom Aleichem's Tevye, Tevye the dairyman with all those daughters to marry off sensibly; Tevye, the intimate of God with whom he is candid but to whom—as he points out—he never complains. ("After all, with Your help, I'm starving to death.") Wryness, yes. But crossed eyes, cap and bells?

"The professional fool intercepts the great actor, the role the actor is playing inhibits the fool—somewhat. And you can, as a reviewer, point out the contradiction, the quarrel of styles. What you will not have done is account for the effect Mr. Mostel imposes on the yielding Winter Garden stage. . . ."*

The larger newspapers and the more profitable magazines in America go in heavily for cultural news, so-called, and all forms of criticism. Almost anything that attracts public attention may be the subject of a critique in these rarefied areas. At a current sampling, in addition to the usual standbys of theater, film, books, and television, there are critiques of such subjects as "new age" music, modern art, cassette recorders, ballet, and Monday night football. It is safe to say that nearly all newspapers try in one way or another to critique, review, or do straight news stuff on current films and television programming because those are in the forefront of popular tastes. The worst-covered field, sad to say, is music (except for the pop variety).

But all in all, because of the breadth of the field, the audience for news and views of cultural affairs in this country is second only in size to the millions who avidly follow sports. For that reason, it is well worth the attention of the newcomer to journalism, who brings both freshness of view and literary skill to bear on public offerings of the arts.

Younger audiences today are quite different from others earlier in this century. Few older critics to date have been able to make a sufficient adjustment to talk to them or write for them in terms of this audience's own experience and background.

In Matters of Style and Content

In style and content, critical writing in America varies today with the type of publication, the size and sophistication of the audience, and the professionalism of the writer. Some excellent critics may

*The *Fiddler* review and others are from Kerr's Pulitzer Prize exhibit.

pop up in unexpected places—small-town papers and "little" magazines, for example—and some overrated ones still hang on in metropolitan centers. Very few television critics show distinction.

There is really nothing new in all this. Times of transition in a nation's cultural life, such as we are undergoing in the closing years of this century, are likely to reflect the changing tastes of a society from top to bottom. All that can be said with certainty of the present is that it is by no means the age of Henry James, Eugene O'Neill, George Gershwin, and Robert Frost. But perhaps George M. Cohan, the old-time Yankee Doodle Dandy, might find himself back in critical favor and popular esteem. Perhaps he understood the fundamental character of America better than most of the more serious artists of his time.

To illustrate the wide swings in critical writing in America, here is an excerpt from a brief television review of a new program in the mass circulation *New York Daily News*:

> David Rappaport, the star of the CBS comedy adventure series, "The Wizard," may be a small fellow but not when it comes to ratings. . . . The show about a toy maker with magical powers pulled in a whopping 16.0 rating and a 28 percent share, easily wiping out the competing NBC with its movie, *Going Ape*, which came in second . . . while ABC's second installment of *The Winds of Bore*, oops, I mean, *The Winds of War*, continued to falter. . . .*

Here, by contrast, is an excerpt from a critique of so-called new age recordings by a *New York Times* music critic:

> . . .The music is simple and even restful, full of unashamed beauty and evocations of folk music, exotic ritual and meditational calm. This is just what the new-agers do, yet their music is routinely dismissed by rock and jazz critics (the people who pay most of the critical attention to it) as simple-minded schlock. . . . Some music challenges, other music entertains, still other music relaxes, and new-age music is merely the latest label to be applied to relaxing background music with pretty tunes. . . .**

Finally, this is an excerpt from a review in a smaller newspaper in Tennessee, the *Knoxville News-Sentinel*, of a college dramatic performance (toward which professional critics are traditionally gentler than they are to professional work):

New York Daily News, September 11, 1986, p. 84.
**New York Times*, June 22, 1986, p. H-25.

> *Beyond Therapy*, the opening show in the University of Tennessee's Carousel Theater this year, is a hilarious spoof of human foibles and, at the same time, a sad look at people's deep need to be loved and wanted.
> Christopher Durang successfully combines slapstick comedy and the pathos of loneliness as he outlines several ways people cope with life. . . .
> The play is funny and well-executed. Those who find explicit sexual references unsettling, however, might prefer to stay at home.*

The style and content in all three cases are predictable, which is to be expected. What the writers are doing, and they are quite honest about it, is adjusting to the character of their audiences and tempering their views accordingly. There are more serious faults in critical writing, particularly when a critic completely misjudges an audience and writes a piece that is either insufferably vague or downright insulting in a patronizing way.

Guidelines for Younger Critics

Newcomers to criticism often ask in near despair, "But how do I start? What do I do after I finish reading a book or come back to the office after a performance of one kind or another?"

Professional critics seldom offer satisfactory guidance in such matters. Brooks Atkinson sometimes paced up and down just outside the newsroom for no particular reason before grappling with a theatrical critique under deadline pressure. Lewis Gannett, after reading a book, would stretch, pet the dog, annoy his wife with a burst of nonessential conversation, then call for a messenger to take his copy to the office. Having thus pressured himself, he had to write the review at top speed.

Younger critics offer little more solace. But what they all seem to have in common is the ability to concentrate on a job that most journalistic outsiders would find impossible.

In my own case, I have always adhered as closely as possible to Lewis Carroll's prescription in *Alice in Wonderland,* which proposes: "Begin at the beginning, go through to the end, then stop." The procedure may not guarantee either wisdom or excellence, but the job will get done by adhering to it.

Here are a few helpful hints, which may be safely disregarded if

Knoxville News-Sentinel, October 26, 1986, p. B-8.

writers have firm notions of procedure that make them feel more comfortable in deadline critiquing:

Regardless of subject matter, newcomers to critical writing ought to remember that the purpose of the exercise is twofold: to provide information on a cultural work or performance of interest to the public, and to evaluate it for potential audiences.

One way to begin would be to tell what is being critiqued and why, then touch on an evaluation of the work in a sentence or two. Necessarily, a brief description of the play, movie, book, music, art, or whatever ought to follow.

Thereafter, the writer ought to develop the evaluation of the work as effectively as possible, giving credit or blame wherever due as the case may be. But the whole thing should not run to excessive length and it oughtn't to be too detailed unless advance provisions have been made for adequate time and space. Nor should the writing dribble off at the end, where most critics like to emphasize the judgment with which they began.

It seems so easy to set these things down, but they aren't easy to do. If there are any rewards for such performances, it is that critics have achieved greater respect today than was possible earlier in this century. And better pay in most cases.

The Uses of the Editorial Mind

The editorial mind, too, has advanced in value both professionally and materially. It is surely no accident that editorial page editors at two of the greatest papers in the land, the *New York Times* and the *St. Louis Post-Dispatch*, have been elevated in recent years to the editorial management of their respective newspapers. Max Frankel, having advanced through the ranks from campus correspondent to chief Washington correspondent and later editorial page editor of the *Times*, took over as executive editor from A. M. Rosenthal. And at the *Post-Dispatch*, William F. Woo moved up from the editorial page to succeed Joseph Pulitzer, Jr. as editor.

The recognition of the power of proper editorial direction in the public interest does not stop there, however. The editorial board of the *Miami Herald* has won great respect for its defense of civil liberties, notably a successful campaign against the detention of illegal Haitian immigrants by federal officials. And Meg Greenfield, one of the editorial page editors of the *Washington Post*, has also been singled out for commendation in this and other areas.

Nor does the rising approval of those who make and execute important editorial policies for the press end with the great newspapers of the land. A number of smaller ones, too, have been widely recognized for their achievements in their respective communities. Horance G. Davis, Jr. of the *Gainesville Sun* in Florida was credited with a major role in the peaceful desegregation of Florida schools. John Strohmeyer of the *Bethlehem Globe-Times,* Pennsylvania, was no less prominent in campaigning for a reduction in racial tensions in his city. And the editorial page directors of the *Reno Evening Gazette* and *Nevada State Journal of Reno* took on difficult peacekeeping tasks that some police wouldn't touch in that gambling-crazed city.

Contrast such developments in the American press, despite all the criticism it has had to absorb, with the dizzy cost cutting among the entertainment-oriented networks in the latter 1980s and there is cause for wonder. For years, most major polls have given public confidence in television (not merely television news) an advantage of 10 percent or more over the printed press. And yet, when the economy began to tighten, it was CBS, NBC, and ABC that plunged into what one *New York Times* critic called "the wild rush of change."*

Said the critic: "The aim is to shrink the glamorized television bureaucracies so that the networks can survive what many deem a crisis in the marketplace, with its declining advertising revenues and rising costs."

To be sure, in the long consolidation process through which the American press has passed, some great newspapers have gone under in the past quarter-century—the *New York Herald-Tribune, Washington Star,* and *St. Louis Globe-Democrat* among them. But there was never a question about the survival of any key element of the industry even though television had long since become the first source of news for most Americans.

However, when hard times hit and new forces took over the networks, change hit them much harder than it had their colleagues in print. What Laurence A. Tisch and others in control at CBS did was to cut at least thirteen hundred jobs in fifteen months, a total duplicated by the new Capital Cities Communications management at ABC. And General Electric, the new boss at NBC, was committed to reduce the size of the force at that network by at least 5 percent.**

It would seem in retrospect that the uses of the editorial mind

---

*Peter J. Boyer in the *New York Times,* under the heading, "Trauma Time on Network TV," November 2, 1986, p. F-1.
**Ibid.

had done more to keep newspapers in the forefront of American life than the money men of television had been able to accomplish for their own business.

Perhaps, too, it says something about the usefulness of the American newspapers' public policies as compared with those of the tube. This is not to suggest that the American press consists wholly of knights in shining armor, ever willing to take on the dragons of special privilege. We know that isn't true. Despite the achievements of the few, there remain human frailties among the many in newspaperdom.

What *is* beyond question relates to the leading role the press has taken to combat the shortcomings of government in this century during nearly every major crisis from Teapot Dome to Watergate. However, the masters of the electronic media, once they became enchanted with the clink of the tube as a money-making machine, seldom took such long chances, preferring to plead their fears of the regulatory Federal Communications Commission.

I think it is important that the editors of the nation's editorial pages, in large part, had something to do with taking risky positions in the public interest. It is not that they pushed publishers to do their duty; in some instances, the publishers had already made that determination for themselves. But the demonstrations of editorial courage and responsibility, as expressed on the editorial pages, were what made the impression both on Congress and the public along with the disclosures of the investigative reporters.

It is for this reason, primarily, that newcomers to journalism ought never to ignore the editorial comment of the smallest of American dailies and weeklies. Throughout our history as a nation, they have been the weather vanes that pointed to a necessary course of action and gave warning when a storm was in the offing.

The notion that editorial pages are dominated by worn-out former reporters who dutifully point with pride and view with alarm never had much substance in American journalism. It doesn't now. One of the signs of continuing progress is the sight of young men and women, relatively new recruits in journalism, handling some of these key responsibilities in a democratic society.

However, it will not do to look for any master plan for developing an editorial conscience. There is none. The editorial page, being the heart and soul of the American newspaper, has a vitality all its own. And the following two articles, Pulitzer Prize winners both, illustrate that.

The first is Meg Greenfield's appreciation of the presidency of

Gerald Ford, published in the *Washington Post*—a newspaper that was one of his toughest critics. This is it, in vital part:

> "At no point has he shown a keen or impressive grasp of the complexities of hard questions. Pedestrian, partisan, dogged—he has been the very model of a second level party man. It is no accident that over his quarter century of unremarkable service in the House, he has never been put forward for the Presidency."
>
> So we spoke in this space a little over three years ago upon learning that Gerald Ford was about to ascend to the office of Vice President. We do not cite our respondent appraisal because we think it was on the money, but rather because we think it was not. Having been forced to replace his Vice President, and being in not-so-secure condition in office himself, Richard Nixon had just informed a waiting world that Gerald Ford was the one. Frankly, it did not occur to us that Gerald Ford was the right one.
>
> But we were wrong. He was. The President who will leave office this week brought precisely the needed temperament, character and virtues to the high office he has temporarily held. These qualities are regularly subsumed under the familiar general heading of "decency," a word that does indeed fit the man. . . . Our point is that Gerald Ford brought to the White House an open, unsinister and—yes—decent style of doing things that altered the life of the city and ultimately of the country. . . .
>
> We will leave it to others to tote up the pluses and minuses of the Ford administration in strict program and/or policy terms. We can frankly do without reviewing it ourselves. We think it is enough to point out that Gerald Ford had an all but impossible assignment—and that he did a hell of a job. . . .*

The other editorial is a classic, a relatively short piece written by William Allen White of the *Emporia Gazette* in Kansas to reassure a reader who feared the consequences of freedom of thought, of speech, and of the press in America at a time when all three were in desperately short supply in America. White's argument is the ultimate defense of liberty of action for a free press. Here it is, as he wrote it:

TO AN ANXIOUS FRIEND

> You tell me that law is above freedom of utterance. And I reply that you can have no wise laws nor free enforcement of wise laws unless there is free expression of the wisdom of the people and, alas,

---

*"Decency in the White House" by Meg Greenfield, published in the *Washington Post* January 16, 1977 and awarded a Pulitzer Prize in 1978. Reprinted with permission.

their folly with it. But if there is freedom, folly will die of its own poison, and wisdom will survive. That is the history of the race. It is the proof of man's kinship with God. You say that freedom of utterance is not for time of stress and I reply with the sad truth that only in time of stress is freedom of utterance in danger. No one questions it in calm days because it is not needed. And the reverse is also true; only when free utterance is supressed is it needed, and when it is needed it is most vital to justice. Peace is good. But if you are interested in peace through force and without free discussion, that is to say, free utterance justly and in order—your interest in justice is slight. And peace without justice is tyranny, no matter how you may sugar-coat it with expediency. This state today is in more danger from suppression than from violence, because in the end, suppression leads to violence. Violence, indeed, is the child of suppression. Whoever pleads for justice helps to keep the peace, and whoever tramples on the plea for justice, temperately made in the name of peace, only outrages peace and kills something fine in the heart of man which God put there when we got our manhood. When that is killed, brute meets brute on each side of the line.

So, dear friend, put fear out of your heart. This nation will survive, this state will prosper, the orderly business of life will go forward if only men can speak in whatever way given to them to utter what their hearts hold—by voice, by posted card, by letter or by press. Reason has never failed men. Only force and repression have made wrecks in the world.*

Thus the editorial writers, from White's time to Meg Greenfield's, which is our own. They and their colleagues had something important to say to the American people, and still do. And whether the people agree or not, they still understand, support, and respect the right of free expression. And that, finally, is what America is all about.

*Published July 27, 1922 in the *Emporia Gazette*, winner of a Pulitzer Prize in 1923.

30

Writing about National Affairs

WHEN GOVERNMENT IN AMERICA FALTERS, the electorate usually is quick to vote for change. And vast changes are possible, which adds to the challenge of writing about national affairs in these closing years of the twentieth century. In the sometimes violent swings in public sentiment between liberalism and conservatism, nothing can be taken for granted.

Consider, for example, what has happened in the fifty years since Franklin Roosevelt won reelection as president in 1936 by forty-six states to two in a great Democratic victory.

In 1984, Ronald Reagan led the Republicans to an even greater triumph in his own presidential reelection campaign by taking forty-nine of the then fifty states. And yet, only two years later, when key parts of the nation were in recession, the Democrats came back to win control of Congress despite Reagan's best efforts.

The Main Problem in Washington

It follows that every national administration is tested almost at once for its credibility. And sooner or later, the main problem emerges—an almost continual tug of war between government and the news media over the shape and meaning of important news. For the newcomer to journalism who is fortunate enough to land a berth in

Washington, this can be puzzling, even dismaying. But it is something that has to be endured.

One would expect, under the circumstances, that the public would have a vital interest in the claims and counterclaims that are made about governmental successes or setbacks. But in all except the rarest of cases, such as Teapot Dome or Watergate, most people are disinterested in press/government conflicts.

If anything, public sentiment generally tends to favor the White House over the news media when it is a case of believing one or the other. Nor is there a great tendency to be more suspicious of government when there are charges of doctoring the news at the State Department, the Pentagon, or lesser government offices.

Of all the nonissues in Washington, this one is usually near the bottom of the dismal list. Even home offices often have to be coached by their Washington correspondents before the journalists' side of the argument can be fully understood.

Under the circumstances, newcomers to the capital can't be blamed for puzzlement. "What's it all about?" many a beginner asks. And, of course, the inevitable, "Why should I get myself involved in something like this?"

The principal witness whose testimony is worth considering, Theodore Roosevelt, had this to say about the problem:

"I have a very definite philosophy about the Presidency. I think it should be a very powerful office, and I think that the President should be a very strong man who uses without hesitation every power the position yields; but because of this fact I believe that he should be watched sharply by the people . . . and held to a strict accountability by them."*

So spoke one of the strongest and most successful of all our presidents who boasted, after one of his greatest triumphs, "I took Panama." Which is exactly what he did, in order to build the Panama Canal.

But if T.R.'s warning is to be taken at face value, who is to watch the president? In constitutional theory, that assignment supposedly is the responsibility of the coordinate branches of government, Congress, and the Supreme Court. But in practice, in recent years, it has fallen by default mainly to the far weaker private organization known as the White House Press Corps. This may be unfair but, as President Kennedy reminded the nation on occasion, "Life is unfair."

*Roosevelt's statement is in Henry F. Pringle, *Theodore Roosevelt* (New York: Harcourt, Brace & World, 1931; 1956), p. 377.

The result, to any impartial observer, is that reportorial prestige in Washington has steadily declined for some years. The remarkable part of this phenomenon is that it has occurred during the period of the Watergate exposé, the downfall of Richard Nixon's presidency, and the loss of the Vietnam War and the Iranian affair. That mythical expert, the Man from Mars, might have expected, in view of the exemplary conduct of journalists in all these cases, that they would be hailed as American folk heroes. However, quite the opposite has occurred.

Today, with few exceptions, newspaper correspondents and a few from the newsmagazines are generally viewed with suspicion at the nation's capital. Very often, government news impresarios try to set up rivalry between them and the television reporters on the dubious theory that the tube will be kinder to government, being beholden to the Federal Communications Commission, than the press.

Sometimes this ploy works, but not often. Television correspondents like Sam Donaldson of ABC and Daniel Schorr of National Public Radio are not easily influenced, to say the least.

In any event, the governmental tendency developed in the 1980s to cut down as far as possible on presidential news conferences and depend more on direct presidential statements to the nation, to Congress, to meetings of selected journalists who may be more malleable, and to outright attacks on the most troublesome correspondents. In sum, White House insiders in recent administrations were inclined to agree with the battle cry of the besieged Nixonians in their last days, "It's us against *them!*"

It has thus become difficult for the White House Press Corps, on all but the most important occasions, to study the day-by-day conduct of the presidency in the manner proposed by Theodore Roosevelt. It is one of the consequences of having permitted the growth of what the historian, Arthur Meier Schlesinger, Jr., has called, in the title of one of his most important books, "The Imperial Presidency."

The Information Gap

In the latter half of this century, there is no doubt that an information gap has existed between what our national government has said and what it actually did in some crucial instances.

To illustrate, without public warning of the growth of a major crisis, President Kennedy moved us to the brink of atomic warfare with Russia in the tension over the discovery of Soviet missiles in

Cuba in the 1960s. In the 1970s, through the Tonkin Gulf resolution which President Johnson carried in his pocket while waiting for a provocation, we were plunged into the Vietnam War when North Vietnamese gunships attacked two American destroyers in Asian waters. In the next decade, there were questions about the Reagan administration's conduct involving either the legality or the propriety of the invasion of Grenada, the bombing of Libya, and the shipping of arms to Iran in exchange for hostages.

These were all demonstrations of the hard truth that presidential decisions, of which the public had little or no advance knowledge, could cost the nation dearly in the long run. Certainly, it has been demonstrated all too clearly that the journalists cannot make such disclosures on their own without powerful assistance. Some have not, sad to say, been able to convince most concerned citizens that they are covering the news in the nation's capital fairly, honestly, and decently. The average reporter's posture toward government— all aspects of government, both the good and the bad—simply does not sit well with public critics.

One such critic, Vermont Royster, a former editor of the *Wall Street Journal*, observes that otherwise sensible journalists seem to lose their senses when they question a president in a news conference. Their queries, Royster maintains, seem all too often to be less those of journalists seeking information than public prosecutors examining a witness. He argues, therefore, that presidents and their people cannot be blamed for taking defensive measures and replying in kind.*

A leading White House correspondent, Jack Nelson of the *Los Angeles Times,* has argued, however, that the situation in the modern White House means that reporters will have to work harder to get at the crux of the news. "Press oversight of the Executive Department falls far short," he conceded, "especially in the case of a popular and powerful president who unabashedly runs the government as though it is a corporation and he is the chairman of the board."

To Robert H. Giles of the Gannett Newspapers, the editor of the *Detroit News,* a lack of trust has grown up between the White House and its press corps. As he put it: "What is missing is trust. Neither side trusts the other. And in the absence of trust, newspaper readers and TV viewers are deprived of clarity and understanding. I suspect the problems between president and press have been years in the making."

*Vermont Royster's views were in the *Bulletin of the American Society of Newspaper Editors*, April 1984, p. 44.

Nor are television correspondents as a whole jubilant because they sometimes are given advantages over their press colleagues. The NBC legal correspondent, Carl Stern, observes, "The present system leads to media managers who are disdainful of the press and manipulative. Reporters, in turn, feel called upon to beard these lions in their den, match wits with them. The result is often an embarrassment to both."*

In sum, no solution to the problem as Theodore Roosevelt presented it to the nation at the turn of the century has yet developed. No doubt the closing of the information gap, if ever it is to be accomplished, will be left to future presidents and the new generation of journalists.

Government Information by Leakers

Even when newcomers recognize the difficulty of obtaining news in the nation's capital if the government is reluctant to issue as much negative material as exists nowadays, there is always an expectation that someone will leak the bad news. Alas, beginners ought not to depend on it and professionals seldom do.

At the time an official named Daniel Ellsberg was supplying various correspondents with copies of the Pentagon Papers, there was great jubilation among some Washington reporters. They coined the saying, "The ship of state is the only vessel that leaks at the top," and it was widely accepted by the uninformed.

As a result, a pleasant delusion lingers on, particularly among the younger and more ambitious reporters in the nation's capital, that somewhere in the various cabinet departments and regulatory agencies there will always be a righteous government servant who will uncover rascality by leaking the Big Story. If only it were so!

The inconvenient truth is that leaks such as those in the Pentagon Papers and Watergate stories occur infrequently. It is also a lamentable truth that most leakers are notoriously undependable and that government by leak is an impossibility. It has happened, too, that incautious reporters who accept leaked information at face value have gotten themselves and their news organizations into expensive and prolonged legal actions.

As all but incorrigible romantics can easily see, it is far healthier for cabinet officers and regulatory agencies, as well as others, to

---

*The views of journalists were in letters to me: Jack Nelson, December 29, 1984; Robert H. Giles, December 6, 1984; Carl Stern, November 30, 1984.

deal directly with the top people at the White House rather than with some reporter who will be there today, gone tomorrow. For one thing, not all reporters are uniformly reliable even in Washington. And for another, the powers of the presidency are formidable, especially when they are directed against the news media.

It is a matter of record that the Nixon administration tried to intimidate and punish its critics. Until Vice-President Spiro Agnew's financial troubles forced his resignation, he was turned loose against the correspondents on several occasions. Then, as the *Washington Post* was following the Watergate trail, challenges suddenly arose against license renewals for two of its television stations.

Nor was Nixon the only president in this century to strike back at reporters who badgered him. John F. Kennedy pressured the *New York Times* to tone down a story that would have tipped off the "Bay of Pigs" invasion against Castro's Cuba. Lyndon Johnson, too, never suffered adverse journalistic criticism of his Vietnam War policies in silence. And even Franklin Roosevelt wasn't above plastering an uncooperative reporter with ridicule by handing a Nazi Iron Cross medal to one and telling another to put on a dunce cap.

The leak may be a time-honored device when all else fails a determined reporter, but it cannot be a permanent solution to the troublesome relationships between presidents and press. The world has become a far too dangerous place for tit-for-tat journalism—or politics, either, for that matter.

News Sources in Congress

Some newcomers, repelled by the obstacles that can inhibit White House news coverage, expect that reporting on Congressional affairs will be a lot easier because almost everything is in the open there. It is true that Congress is the second major source of news in Washington and that some correspondents prefer to work out of the Senate and House press galleries. But as for being easier, no, it is not.

It is helpful, of course, to have covered a state legislature before coming to Washington. But the complexity of national affairs, and the sheer numbers of open sources on the Hill, make for a lot of study and maneuvering before a word is ever typed on copy paper. As the Congressional Directory shows, there are 435 members of the House and 100 members of the Senate to begin with, each of whom has a constituency, an office staff, and special interests. Beyond that, there are a number of important committees, headed by chairpersons; interested government officials on almost every issue; and hordes of lobbyists plugging private interests.

Then, too, the Congressional Record must be watched. Nor can the wire services and the other competing correspondents, print and electronic, be taken for granted. At almost any time the vice-president, as the president pro tempore of the Senate, and the speaker of the house may have something important to announce.

And once a bill passes House and Senate, that is by no means the end, for differences between the two versions of the same measure have to be reconciled, then reapproved, before the bill goes to the White House for signature. Moreover, if there is a presidential veto, and an effort is made to override, the whole difficult business has to be repeated.

Months can pass in consultations, maneuvering for advantage and debate on such complicated matters as taxation and budget making, Social Security legislation, problems of unemployment, consumerism, and the like. For large news organizations, this may not be difficult.

But for small bureaus, in which it isn't possible to specialize on issues as far apart as national defense and revision of immigration laws, to mention only two, the mere process of keeping up with the steady flow of legislation becomes a serious problem. As an additional factor that is sometimes bothersome, Congressional sources often decide to go on background, that is, to have unattributed news conferences so that they may keep their options open on some types of sensitive legislation.

In many ways, therefore, reporting from the Hill can be as complicated and as full of surprises as coverage of the White House, but in a quite different way.

Writing about National Defense

Although the State Department beat traditionally carries the most prestige for a journalist after the coverage of the White House and Congress, it is national defense that usually provides the most closely watched domestic news among the various departments and bureaus in the federal government. To enter the Pentagon and be accredited for the first time, however, is an unnerving experience for a newcomer.

It is difficult enough to conceive of separate news operations for DOD, meaning the Office of the Secretary, Department of Defense, and the secretaries of the Army, Navy, and Air Force plus the military commanders of each service and the Marines.

The separate offices of the chiefs of such special functions as "Star Wars" research and of arms regulation and reduction, for example, are always capable of producing the top news of the day. And in the event of a test malfunction, as was the case when the *Challenger* exploded just off its launching pad, worldwide news is made instantly.

The process of getting the news out, however, isn't always simple. It isn't as if all a reporter has to do is to talk to a mayor or police chief, then phone the office. In the Pentagon, much of what goes on is classified and subject to clearance. Then, too, interservice arguments may develop about critical matters such as funding, to single out only one trouble spot in the news. And the rival public relations officers of the separate services sometimes may have differing accounts of the same event, usually given to reporters on background.

This is why the whole subject of national security often becomes difficult for journalists to translate into terms that a mass public can readily understand. Advance briefings by experts are always helpful. But nothing is quite as important as detailed knowledge and experience on the part of correspondents who are charged with responsibility for writing or broadcasting the news of national defense.

The Diplomatic Beat

The coverage of the State Department actually involves what amounts to an oversight of foreign affairs, as viewed from Washington. In the hush-hush atmosphere of "Foggy Bottom," as the State Department is known because of its site in the nation's capital, what happens in a whole range of foreign lands, from Nicaragua to South Africa, can become of major importance in the development of foreign policy. The way such matters look in Peoria isn't at all the way they appear to the secretary of state and his press people.

To the nation at large, there have been so many crises in our relations with the Soviet Union since the end of World War II that most writers have a general notion of how to handle additional newsbreaks in that area, from summit conferences on down. But it is quite different when there are terrorist outbreaks in Europe that involve Americans or if American hostages are seized by small, and usually unidentified Arab groups. For if the masters of Foggy Bottom are confused by such things, it may well be imagined that the dispatches of the correspondents will reflect it.

Of all the public affairs offices of government in the nation's capital, the one at State is often either among the last to know what is to be done about a sensitive development abroad or the last to be briefed on what to say to the always demanding correspondents. It may not be the best way to conduct foreign affairs, but it sometimes helps the government to stay out of trouble by not making too many snap judgments.

Other Sources in Washington

There are so many other important sources of news in the nation's capital that only the greatest news organizations in the land can afford to maintain regular coverage of all of them. Merely to name some of the beats, not necessarily in the order of importance, the news of the day may come quite unexpectedly from the Treasury or the Department of Justice, Agriculture, Commerce, Labor, the Interior, or any of the rest of the great offices represented in the president's cabinet. And sometimes, the various subordinate bureaus and agencies, the CIA and the FBI to single out only two, demand first priority among the Washington press corps for the newsbreaks they may be able to announce.

In fact, on any given day in Washington, it is a fairly good bet that more important news is being formulated by the government than it is able to make known to the public across the nation.

Writing about the Supreme Court

The most difficult beat on the Washington scene is the great edifice in which the Supreme Court, the nation's highest tribunal, hands down its judgments. The court meets annually from the traditional first Monday in October, when its sessions begin, until late June or early July of the following year.

The impact of the chief justice of the United States and the eight associate justices, all appointed for life by the president with the concurrence of the Senate, has been enormous throughout our history. And so it continues under Chief Justice Rehnquist, who was appointed by President Reagan.

It is possible, perhaps, for relative newcomers to Washington to cover a number of important assignments with very little formal training or academic background. But at the Supreme Court, it is well-nigh hopeless to expect someone without a decent background in both the issue to be decided and legal procedure in general to write for a mass audience about a major decision.

The Court's positions on such matters as civil rights and associated issues, for example, have played an often decisive role in the history of our country. And as for the key element in the whole edifice of constitutional law, the First Amendment, it would not retain its present strength were it not for the decisions of the high court over a century or more.

To assign a reporter to cover a Supreme Court decision of major importance, therefore, is not something that Washington's bureau chiefs take lightly. They pick the best and most adaptable people who are available and then, if they are realists, mutter a prayer that no misunderstanding will create a foul-up in the coverage.

Some day, perhaps, it may be possible for the public to participate directly in such decision making at the highest judicial level in the country through television, but that time is not yet. In many other courts, yes, the red eye of the camera doesn't blink. But the Supreme Court makes its own rules.

31

Writing from Abroad

FOR MANY IN THE NEW GENERATION OF JOURNAL-
ISTS, the great adventure in the profession is a foreign assignment.
To those with stars in their eyes, it does not seem to matter that the
field of action is impossibly large and often dangerous. Nor are they
deterred by the knowledge that probably less than 1 percent of the
eighty to ninety thousand professionals in the American news media
live and work abroad. The dream persists, even though the American
people as a whole still remain indifferent to all but the most critical
developments in world affairs.

On Becoming a Foreign Correspondent

Newcomers to journalism who want to become foreign correspondents someday know quite well that they should be able to speak a
language other than English, and preferably two. They are advised
time and again to make themselves familiar with the background,
history, economy, and social conditions of a particular region or
country. Moreover, they are warned not to expect rapid promotion—
to be patient—to await their turn at taking the long career route in
a major news organization.

All this is very sound. It is utterly correct and painfully honest.
But the aspiring journalist knows quite well, all the same, that few
international relations majors in our universities wind up as foreign

correspondents. The majority, instead, go for governmental or commercial foreign services, teaching, or a variety of nonrelated occupations that are steadier, safer, and relatively better paid.

How, then, are foreign correspondents made? Like so much else in journalism, it is a matter very often either of stubborn-minded persistence or of being in the right place at the right time. Call it luck, accident, or what you will. Blame it on economy-minded managements that would rather pick up a youngster right at the scene of great events instead of assigning someone from home base at much greater cost. Denounce the system—or lack of it—as an affront to intelligence.

But that isn't going to change reality.

To be sure, there are career foreign correspondents of great competence in the field today, as always, who represent some of the largest and most powerful news organizations in the land. And there also are able wire service professionals the world over who maintain the basic backup news budgets daily that cover the bulk of the American news media. However, that has never stopped an adventurous youngster with some background in journalism from taking a chance and going abroad.

I well remember traveling to Vietnam for the first time in 1964, more than eleven years before the South Vietnamese surrender to the triumphant North Vietnamese and Viet Cong, to find that the people working for the American news media consisted of a small, devoted knot of young men and a few dedicated and courageous young women. As usual, the larger and wealthier news organizations had assigned their own people but others had come in mainly because they were available—and they filled a need.

What, for example, was *Newsweek* magazine to do when its first Vietnam correspondent, François Sully, fell out of favor with the American embassy and couldn't continue to file from Saigon? Instead, Beverly Deepe, a recent graduate of the Columbia Graduate School of Journalism, was in Saigon, available and ready to work— and took on the temporary assignment. Later, she represented, in turn, the *New York Herald Tribune* and the *Christian Science Monitor* with such competence that she was nominated for a Pulitzer Prize. And at the end, she was able to escape to safety, among the last Americans to leave Saigon.

By that time, of course, the situation had completely changed. In the intervening years, with the American troop buildup, the corps of correspondents had expanded to about six hundred—and most of them had never before heard a shot fired in anger. Yet, they covered the disheartening story, told the truth as they saw it, and cut through the frequent government announcements of glorious victories that had no basis in fact.

It was a midwestern free-lancer, Seymour Hersh, who single-handedly uncovered one of the worst tragedies of the war—the My Lai massacre. He was thirty-two at the time, a graduate of the University of Chicago, and a former Associated Press correspondent at the Pentagon. Acting on a tip and a hunch, he journeyed to various places to seek out eyewitnesses to the massacre in the Vietnamese village in 1968. He confirmed the U.S. Army's participation, then broke the story a year later by writing a series of articles and submitting them to thirty-six newspapers.

A Pulitzer Prize jury voted him the 1970 award for foreign correspondence in these terms:

> In the face of disbelief and disinterest on the part of many newspapers, and operating with limited resources, Hersh showed initiative, enterprise and perseverance to break the My Lai story—a story that shook the nation and had vast international repercussions. In pursuing his story to the point that the topmost officials in the United States, South Vietnam, Great Britain, and other countries became publicly and directly involved, Hersh's performance met the highest journalistic standards for which Pulitzer recognition is traditionally granted.*

It was by chance a veteran, Keyes Beech, a World War II war correspondent for the *Chicago Daily News,* who radioed the last dispatch of the Vietnam conflict to his paper from an American warship in Asian waters: "My last view of Saigon was through the tail door of the helicopter. Tan Son Nhut [the Saigon airfield] was burning. So was Bien Hoa. Then the door closed—closed on the most humiliating chapter in American history."**

If anything should disabuse the new generation of the notion that foreign correspondents are trench-coat types who swagger around Parisian bistros, the Vietnam experience ought to do it. But probably it won't.

Yes, the dream is very pretty. But the reality all too often is made up of heartbreaking effort, dirt, tragedy, and the smell of death on foreign battlefields. No one can possibly mistake that for glamor—and no one should.

*From the Pulitzer Prize records at Butler Library, Columbia University.
**From the *Chicago Daily News,* April 30, 1975.

The Development of Foreign Correspondence

Efforts to interest a larger share of the American public in international events are of comparatively recent origin. But outside the largest cities such as New York City and Los Angeles, Chicago, Washington, and Miami, comparatively little progress has been made. Despite all the dark portents of the atomic age, with missiles and laser beams in process of development as weapons of destruction, there is scant evidence that the traditionally isolationist mood of the American public has begun to change to any marked degree.

This is the primary reason for the reluctance of American news organizations, with the exception of some of the richest and most powerful, to devote as much time and space to foreign news as the subject merits. The long cold war with the Soviet Union, and the depressing outcome of the Korean and Vietnam Wars, have served to sharpen the characteristic mistrust of large sections of the American public toward what conservative opinion still calls "foreign entanglements."

Barring some unexpected and as yet unlooked-for catastrophe, that is unlikely to change.

Yet, there can be no denying the deep involvement of American interests in the world at large. The very large share of the American automobile market that has been captured by our former enemies, Germany and Japan, is noticeable on every American highway and byway. The American dependence on foreign oil supplies and its effect on our own oil producers, too, is noticeable in the ups and downs of the economy in our Southwest. Even a farm crisis in the Midwest has its roots, at least in part, in the slackening of foreign demand for our products.

All this is bound to have an effect on our employment, the growth of our national debt, and the interest rates that both our government and our national banking system are able to pay. However, since such matters don't make for easy reading and are difficult for a mass public to understand, the news media on the whole seldom devote much time and space to them. How, after all, can you sum up the decline of the value of the dollar against certain foreign currencies in thirty seconds of a network newscast? Or a lively three hundred words in a wire service report?

It just can't be done for a mass audience. The *Wall Street Journal*, however, has jumped to more than 2 million circulation a day because of its specialized reporting for the investment-minded segment of the public. That and kindred publications, plus the news weeklies and some of the austere monthlies on international affairs constitute the principal recourse for the 1 to 2 percent of the American people who *do* want to know.

In a sense, the unsophisticated beginnings of American foreign correspondence still influence what is covered in the mass media and how it is presented. Until World War I, what our relatively few foreign correspondents covered tended to flatter the American ego. It was probably an extension of the all-conquering mood created by the easy American victory in the war with Spain, the start of our rise to world power. And as long as there was a flag-waving aspect to the news of American involvements abroad, editors assumed it would be read.

The change came at the outset of World War I. It was then that Richard Harding Davis and his colleagues dwelt from the outset on German atrocities—the burning of the great library at Louvain, the violation of Belgian neutrality, the execution of Nurse Edith Cavell by a German firing squad, the shock of unrestricted German submarine warfare on the high seas. No one prompted the few American writers who cabled their dispatches from war-torn Europe. No one had to. From the outset, their sympathies were with the Allies. Relatively few Americans even bothered to stay in Berlin because of the heavy restrictions the German authorities put on what the correspondents could write.

These circumstances, together with the effective use British and French propaganda made of German war policies, set the stage for America's entry into the war in 1917. And with it came the creation of the first effective American organization for war propaganda and censorship. Because this also was a winning war, the complaints of correspondents didn't count for much and were quickly forgotten.

In the wake of that conflict came the first real attempt to interest the American public in larger aspects of foreign news. Ambitious young men thronged to London and Paris, hoping to catch on with one news organization or another as foreign correspondents. What they sought to tell, in the main, was the shaping of a brave new world, which was being created as a result of the "war to end all wars." It was, alas, a delusion fostered mainly by lazy evenings at the Dôme and the Select and the Ritz Bar—the homes away from home of many an American newcomer to Paris.

But with the rise of Adolf Hitler to power in Nazi Germany, it soon became evident that the Reich would march again. And when it did, majority American opinion this time did not recoil against all the horrors of Hitler's military dictatorship. Until the shock of the Japanese attack on Pearl Harbor, the American public clung to neutrality. And then, everything changed. But once again, because this was a winning war, the controls exerted over American correspondents did not seem to matter.

It was, however, a sign of future developments when the postwar world settled down to a frightfully intense contest between the United States and the Soviet Union: as the years rolled on, it was self-evident that no correspondent could help being affected by the pressures that each side exerted to try to sway public opinion at home and abroad. The breadth and sophistication of both the American and Russian propaganda efforts dwarfed anything that had been attempted previously. The stakes were very high. And despite the surface calm of an occasional summit conference at the Big Two level, nobody was fooled. The conflict was not to be settled that way.

Both sides fought with every device at their command. The Soviets, both directly and through their Cuban allies, aided a Communist regime in Nicaragua against an American-supported insurgency. And the Americans, on their part, made sure that the Soviet occupation of Afghanistan would undergo harassment in the Vietnam manner by guerrillas who were supplied through Pakistan.

There seemed to be no limit to the battleground. The Soviets used surrogates, mainly Cubans and East Germans, to fight some of their battles in distant African and Asian lands. Where the Americans could, they stimulated resistance. And so the struggle continued.

Inevitably, it had an effect on every part of the world. In the Middle East, for example, Syria played Moscow's game if it seemed advantageous at a time when Israel, Saudi Arabia, and Egypt remained firm to their American commitment. The lineups may have varied in the Far East, in South Asia, Latin America, and southern Africa but there were fewer and fewer neutrals as time passed. Now and then, mild protests developed in some western European countries against extreme American tactics but the alliance, nevertheless, remained unshaken.

The conduct of the American government toward its own news media changed. While Washington never did take the dictatorial line that Moscow took toward its own Soviet press and television, there was less patience in the capital with traditional American news procedures that put the government at a disadvantage.

Sometimes, it seemed as if the American government changed its position toward the American news media to suit particular situations. A special team of the Federal Bureau of Investigation was formed, for example, to track down and expose sources that leaked certain types of information to the press and television.

But when the CIA seized a Soviet employee at the United Nations as a spy and the KGB in Moscow countered by arresting a longtime American correspondent, Nicholas Daniloff, the American government at once demanded Daniloff's release. However, when the Russians agreed to exchange their American captive for the Soviet citizen who had been held in New York, the Reagan administration agreed to the deal but all the while argued that it wasn't a deal.

This became very confusing, as may be imagined. To illustrate, here was a commentary by William F. Woo, the editor of the *St. Louis Post-Dispatch*:

> Let us examine the situations [of Daniloff and the FBI action against leaks] to see what thread connects them.
>
> The Daniloff case is not as simple as it may seem. Yes, a reporter imprisoned in and later confined in Moscow is back in America. Any policy that achieves that result cannot be considered a failure. But neither is it something to praise uncritically. Despite the gloss that the administration has put over the release, and despite the diverting speculation about who blinked, the fact is that Daniloff was exchanged for a Russian spy.
>
> Implicit in that is the administration's willingness—to be sure, perhaps compelled by circumstances—to consider journalists and secret agents equivalent commodities. That will help neither individual reporters, whom the Kremlin will consider fair game for snatch-and-trade maneuvering, nor the press at large, which must not be perceived as an accomplice of government.
>
> The fact that government officials will try to stop information leaks is hardly news. The creation of what you might call a federal police hit squad is worth some thought, however. That might be better than a government burglary ring, which was Richard Nixon's solution to leaks. But not very much. Why?
>
> The answer is that the point of the FBI exercise is political. It is not to prevent dissemination of sensitive or secret information. That stuff is given away every day by the highest officials in government, either to promote their own policies or to frustrate their adversaries'. What the Reagan administration wants stopped, and what previous administrations wanted stopped, is the leakage of information that does not serve their purposes. Another way of putting it is to say that the administration wants to be the judge of the news that's fit to print, and that it is willing to use the intimidating power of the FBI to achieve its ends. . . .*

*"When Government Poisons the Well," *St. Louis Post-Dispatch*, October 5, 1986, p. F-2.

All this was very logical. But what the free press of America often has not taken into account is that the government, in its increasingly dangerous and difficult contest with the Soviet Union, sometimes is forced into a wartime position toward the American news media despite a technical state of peace. This may not justify the government's course. But it does serve to explain how and why the White House has reacted as it so frequently has.

On Presenting Foreign News

It should not be assumed, however, that the bulk of news affecting American foreign policy stimulates such conflicts. Whenever an American is in trouble abroad, the public is instantly attentive whether or not the government takes action. Presidential journeys around the country and to foreign lands, too, are closely followed. And summit conferences with foreign leaders, especially the Russians, often are likely to be turned into publicity circuses plus weeks of fruitless discussions thereafter about who won and who lost.

The problems having to do with public understanding are concerned mainly with arcane matters. Among these are such difficult concepts (even for professionals) as arms control, the observance of international treaties, and American participation in the affairs of the United Nations and its specialized agencies.

In these and kindred areas, the manner in which the news is presented by the government to the news media and by the news media to the public makes considerable difference in the assessment of American foreign policy at home.

The great newspapers and magazines, of course, use expert commentators and editorialists to explain such developments to audiences of more than average sophistication. For the mass public, however, it is not so easy to interpret them except when television devotes its resources to the presentation of a documentary (usually on noncommercial stations).

Otherwise, editors and news directors who can't count on staff specialists either use whatever wire service material they have or devise ingenious local expedients; sometimes both. In developments on arms control, for example, comment might be solicited from academic authorities in and around the community. Now and then, such experts also can be located abroad, sometimes as members of important American negotiating teams.

This technique, when it works, serves to "localize" the story. And in most cases, it produces a gratifying local response. It is so much easier for a newspaper to interest a local audience in foreign affairs when the leading figures include someone who has lived among them.

Let us assume, for example, that the *Central City Leader* has just received a short bulletin and add from Geneva via Independent News:

> Geneva (IN)—The Soviet Union's delegation today walked out of a negotiation with the United States on arms control.

-more-

> Add BN GENEVA
> Wilson Gearing, chief U.S. negotiator, said the secret talks broke down when the United States rejected a Soviet draft treaty. "We'd have signed away our entire national defense," Gearing said. . . .

It turns out, on inquiry, that Gearing is the former dean of the School of International Affairs at State U, in Central City, and a longtime local resident. At the request of Joe Stoddard, the city editor, Sally Ward, the paper's science editor, telephones Mrs. Gearing, then contacts her husband by telephone in Geneva. He is both friendly and forthcoming, the result being the following local story:

GEARING—WITH ARMS

By Sally Ward

"They'll be back."

That was Wilson Gearing's assessment today of the Soviet walkout at arms negotiations with the United States in Geneva.

The former dean of the School of International Affairs at State U, now the chief United States arms negotiator, gave this estimate of the situation to the *Leader* by telephone from the Swiss capital.

"We have to expect these ups and downs in international negotiations," Gearing said. "But I don't take the walkout as anything more than Soviet strategy. You see, the chief Soviet negotiator phoned me only a little while ago at my hotel and proposed to talk things over with me privately at dinner tonight. Of course, we'll accommodate him."

Gearing regretted that he could not make public the terms of the Soviet proposal he rejected. He explained that both sides still adhered to a prior agreement, despite the break, that negotiations will remain secret until a complete report is issued simultaneously by the State Department in Washington and the Soviet foreign office in Moscow.

"But I can say this much," he commented. "If this draft treaty had

been accepted, we'd be back in the same position we were in 1922 when
we agreed, quite mistakenly in London, to sink the main part of our
navy. Only this time, we'd also have dismantled our air force and our
missile strength in return for a Russian promise not to attack us. It
was an impossible proposal." . . .

This is what is known as enterprise journalism. It is often used
at home to try to maintain local interest in abstruse national and
international affairs, provided a local source of consequence is
available. However, it seldom works in situations where visiting
foreign speakers, especially those from the United Nations, try to
explain points of view that run contrary to American interests. Such
lectures seldom are received in the American heartland with anything other than polite but chilling reactions.

The UN, for all its promise after World War II, has fallen on trying
times.

32

Ethics in Journalism

WHAT ARE THE RESPONSIBILITIES of newspapers when they are offered ads for pornographic films and other objectionable material at regular (or even premium) advertising rates?

Even more important, what are the responsibilities of television networks or stations when they are offered political commercials that are blatantly deceptive and even untrue, especially when the rates involved are very high?

These are among the most troublesome ethical questions the profession faces today. They transcend in importance, for the time being at least, the ethical shortcomings of individuals, such as they are. Managements all too often take the position that they have the right, even the duty, to sit in judgment on others but that the First Amendment excludes them from inquiry. As the old song had it, "It Ain't Necessarily So."

The Sins of Management in Journalism

Newspaper managements *are* vulnerable to public judgments of their ethics, or lack of them. Such was the position taken by editors and guest experts in a broad survey of journalism's ethical problems by the Ethics Committee of the American Society of Newspaper Editors (ASNE).* This view was not lightly taken.

Proceedings of the American Society of Newspaper Editors, 1986. This and subsequent material on press ethics is spelled out at greater length on pp. 364–368.

John Finnegan, editor of the St. Paul newspapers and chairman of the committee, led off the Society's 1986 discussion of this issue by pointing to the case of a newspaper publisher in the South who was dismissed because he had lied about his military record and the paper's owner found out about it. Such performances, Finnegan acknowledged, were bound to raise questions about the press's credibility.

"All of which suggests," he added, "that we had better get the publisher, the general manager, the advertising director, the production director, and the circulation manager into our ethical discussions."

Laura Nash, director of the Best Practices Project at Harvard's Center for Business and Government, was quick to agree. She pointed out that other ethical problems may occur when editors and publishers "play the market rather than do the hard-hitting story that ruffles feathers." She also warned against economies in newspaper work that reduce editorial staffs and result in less in-depth reporting and research.

Another participant in the ethics discussion, Deni Elliott-Boyle, a member of the faculty at Utah State, put the position of management in these blunt terms: "Ethics start at the top. If you are not ethical in top management, you will either lose your good people or corrupt them."

The self-examination at ASNE, however, should not stop with a survey of the personal shortcomings, where they exist, of members of top management. Some of the less ethical practices of the press itself deserve a public airing, too, a point that was frequently made to editors who attended sessions of the American Press Institute (API) by its late director, J. Montgomery Curtis.

Curtis would ask, for example, how ethical it was for a newspaper to accept money for an X-rated movie ad or an ad for a massage parlor and then run editorials denouncing pornography in all its forms.* The question has been raised from time to time since without a satisfactory answer. For one thing, the defenders of management would argue that few newspapers are guilty of such practices; for another, they would contend that the First Amendment protects the right to advertise almost anything as long as the thing advertised is legal.

The trouble with both arguments is that the public doesn't buy them. It does not require a Ph.D. in philosophy to point out that such defensiveness goes contrary to everything that a free press

*I often heard Curtis make this crucial objection both in public lectures and private conversation while API was located at Columbia University.

should advocate—honesty, fairness, and objectivity among others. Moreover, it is precisely these issues that are raised against the press in America in most public opinion polls that continually show little confidence in the nation's newspapers.

Since the same polls indicate that public confidence in television news is almost as low as that of the press, what is one to make of the electronic practice of flooding the tube with questionable political advertising at election time?

It is to the credit of CBS News, among others, that the periodical embarrassment of television was openly and honestly discussed on election night, 1986, in a rare exhibition of frankness with the public. The reporter, Mike Wallace, usually seen on "60 Minutes," told of analyzing more than three hundred television ads during that fall season, some of them false and others carrying wildly exaggerated charges against political opponents. Taken together, as the discussion indicated quite clearly, they constituted one of the dirtiest campaigns in recent political history.*

It is fruitless to discuss who is to blame and why. A finding of guilt, justified or not, will scarcely resolve the situation ethically or serve to prevent a recurrence at subsequent elections. To cite one instance exhibited by Wallace as one of the worst in his survey: a group of actors pretending to be politicians sat in a smoke-filled room laughing when someone objected to lying about an opposition candidate. The tag line was given by the apparent chairman as follows: "By the time we get done with him [the object of the smear], his own mother won't vote for him." [Sign-off amid much laughter.]

Aside from the dubious persuasiveness of such ads, it is worth asking how some television managements can accept very large sums of money for such trashy commercials while wringing hands in the process and agonizing publicly over the display. Certainly, one way to improve the public's trust in both newspapers and television news in this country is to solve such ethical problems at the management level—and promptly.

The Sins of Staff People in Journalism

The ASNE editors who sat in judgment on their staff people listed these matters as serious ethical violations: plagiarism; the use of unpublished information for financial gain; accepting discounts for

*The Mike Wallace survey was shown nationally on the CBS election night broadcast November 4, 1986.

personal purchases at places where staffs also have a business or professional relationship.

The editors appeared to have less serious objections to social contacts between staff people and their sources and picking up material from opposition sources without thoroughly checking it.

Out of my own lifelong experience in journalism, I should list the following ethical matters in addition as worthy of the deepest professional concern: invasion of privacy; violations of confidence; taking the public for suckers; misrepresentation; unbalanced reporting; making up quotes, faking interviews, or both; and stealing documents and pictures for exposés.

Evidently, the editors were worked up mostly about plagiarism. One in every six who participated in the findings said they had encountered evidence of plagiarism over a three-year period. However it was attempted—and within my own experience, youngsters sometimes think they can get away with lifting a paragraph or quote without detection—it is a stupid breach of professional conduct. It assumes that deskpeople don't read and are ignorant of current literature, which is part of their job. Also, it shows a lamentable lack of confidence in the culprit's own ability as a writer. Rather than to plagiarize, it might be better for those with the urge to leave journalism at once instead of being rendered unemployable.

As for the various dodges that are used to profit by inside information, freebies, or sharp dealing, a few people may get away with it for awhile—and it can affect editors as well as reporters—but eventually the practice catches up with them. What often happens is that the supposed victims of such transgressions become dissatisfied with the journalist's efforts to accommodate them with free publicity and tip off management to what amounts to a shakedown. The outcome may be serious for individuals involved; in addition to losing their jobs, some have been tried and convicted on criminal charges.

It is the basically journalistic violations of ethics that concern me most, especially as they apply to beginners. Many a newcomer is under the illusion that sharp practices, even though openly condemned, are secretly encouraged by editors and news directors who still admire "The Front Page" school of journalism. To those who have never seen the play, the basic statement it makes to the uninformed is that anything goes when you're after a story. That might have been just fine in Chicago in the not so good old days—I know that it worked in New York City on the tabloids and their opposition—but the nature of American journalism really has changed for the better over the years.

I do not contend that the profession is now peopled exclusively by Sunday school characters. However, it is an observable truth that most working journalists do have an innate sense of decency; otherwise, they would not merit the respect of their sources. Professional conduct cannot in all instances be spelled out in published codes of ethics, although a lot of them are around these days. But at the very least, professionals know through experience what not to do.

The fault that is mentioned most in public complaints of which I have knowledge is invasion of privacy. To illustrate, this sometimes has to do with a reporter's efforts to gain immediate access to relatives of a person who has been kidnaped, hijacked, seriously wounded, or killed in a spectacular news event. People quite rightly sympathize with a family's desire to protect its loved ones at such times or to grieve privately over a death. There are, of course, numerous other occasions when it does no good to come charging in with tough questions on a person or a group, but good sense and good judgment ought to be exercised by journalists in all such situations.

Probably the most difficult of ethical judgments are made in cases involving violations of confidence. Here, an experienced reporter needs more than anything else the support of management because judgment calls by sources who cry "Foul!" almost certainly carry an element of self-interest. To be specific, charges of such violations arise most often when there is a misunderstanding about the ground rules for an interview or news conference.

My own observation is that an experienced professional on a regular beat takes extreme care in such cases not to be caught off base, but if the resultant story is embarrassing, the source sometimes tries to disavow it. The trouble generally arises when either the reporter is inexperienced or the person involved doesn't know the difference between talking on background or going off the record entirely.

A good rule for all to follow is to back out in case of doubt with this disavowal: "If it's off the record, I don't want it." The point is that reporters should not let themselves be tied up. The same news may develop elsewhere, issued on background, which means that only the identify of the source has to be withheld.

That, however, cannot entirely resolve the ethical problem involved. The fact is that so much unsourced news now is used both in the press and on television that a very large section of the public has serious doubts about its validity. Indeed, I have heard perfectly sensible people—government officials with a long record of dealing with the press—contend that a lot of unsourced news is actually made up by irresponsible reporters. Therefore, when a real hoax does come to public notice, such as a *Washington Post* reporter's story about a mythical child drug addict, it serves to reinforce doubts about all reportorial credibility.

I do not know how to resolve the ethical objection to unsourced material in the day's news except to continue to try, as most professionals do, to get more of it on the record. However, in view of the increasing tendency of government people at all levels to use background announcements, the struggle will go on, seemingly, without end. One final caveat in the matter: this is not a situation for amateurs.

As for the ethical problem of misrepresentation, that is much easier to handle. I do not know of any circumstance in which a journalist is justified in posing as someone else. To put one's self under a false identity is a needless and completely unjustifiable risk. I have never done it in a long and active career as a journalist and I don't know of anybody else who has done so. Of course I have heard of youngsters posing as gas meter readers or delivery men to gain access to a home or office, but I have never understood what can be gained by such maneuvers. To steal documents or pictures and offer them for publication or television use is the height of irresponsibility. (Anyway, most of the supposedly purloined stuff that becomes public is leaked, not stolen, and always for a deliberate purpose.)

It is even more inadmissible to encourage people to act in an unwise and injudicious way for the benefit of television or still cameras. Or, for that matter, to help reporters looking for a story. I do not have in mind the silly business of television game show hosts encouraging a captive audience to cheer and applaud people on stage or to *ohh* and *ahh* when prizes are shown. But when a political demonstration is deliberately created for the sake of a spectacular camera shot, that is something else again. It is a chilling reminder of Hitler at Nuremberg—the little corporal on his rise to power over the Reich and the waging of a war that took millions of lives.

For newspaper or magazine reporters, the line should be just as sharply drawn on principle. To illustrate, no one can object if a reporter by accident witnesses a lawyer's attempt to reconcile a couple in the middle of a divorce suit. But if the reporter in such a situation mischievously advises the couple not to settle (because the story is so juicy), that is what is known as sandbagging people. It is manifestly not the business of a journalist to interfere in any situation, personal or not, for the sake of a story.

Sandbagging, in many ways, is even more reprehensible than

stealing. It just isn't done, mainly because a person's life and well-being are a lot more important than any news story.

The same observation may be made about unbalanced reporting. Here, however, the newcomer to journalism all too often assumes that a particular interest, cause, or political party ought to be favored in the news columns because the editorial page signals that this is the publisher's desire. The same assumption may be made by new-comers to television, based on the sympathies of dominant adver-tisers and/or stockholders.

Here, once again, a professional judgment should be made. Eth-ically, the approved practice in reporting any contest—whether it is in sports, politics, international affairs, or anything else—is to lead with the results, then give a fair and equal summation to the positions of the contenders so far as possible. No one can reasonably object to such balanced reporting. To tell the story as the stock-holders or the publisher may want to see it assumes that anything goes in shaping the news. Only—it doesn't.

The Organization of Self-Restraint

Where a nation's laws protect the principle of free speech and a free press, it is obvious that a certain amount of restraint has to be practiced by the news media. In societies such as those in Britain and the Scandinavian countries, that policy has taken shape in the form of self-policing journalism organizations—the British Press Council for one and the so-called Courts of Honor in Scandinavia for another. Every attempt to introduce such organizations in the United States, however, has failed, even though professional jour-nalists of the highest caliber have been at the helm of such projects. The fear of regulation that is implicit in any such organization, vol-untary or not, is what killed the movement in this country.

In Britain, the story was different. Despite the recommendations of two Royal Commissions, beginning after World War II, the bulk of the British press resisted the notion of a self-policing organization and the British Press Council staggered along with little support for its first fifteen years. But in 1964, when the press was under legal assault through a barrage of libel actions, the council was given a chance. In an effort to divert complaints from the courts to the council, where aggrieved people had to agree to abide by its decision instead of seeking hard-cash settlements, some of the British press lords changed course. The council was reorganized under a distinguished former judge, and nonjournalists were taken on the board as it embarked on a new course.

Now, its purpose was to look into complaints from the public against the press and return a verdict in each case. However, the organization still had no real power to enforce its decisions, which was why the masters of Fleet Street decided there would be no harm in the experiment. Almost anything seemed better at that juncture than more antipress judgments in the courts and more pressures from a fearful and censorious government.

The turnabout in Britain was what revived interest in the United States in the press council notion, which had been tried in various guises without attracting more than passing attention within the profession. However, in 1972, the Twentieth Century Fund and the John and Mary Markle Foundation financed the creation of the National News Council as an American counterpart of the British organization. Its purpose, to quote the original prospectus, was "to receive, examine, and report on complaints concerning the accuracy and fairness of news reporting in the United States, as well as to initiate studies and reports on issues involving freedom of the press."

There were a few cheers, fainthearted and distant, mainly from small organizations without much power in the field. But there was even more grumbling and all kinds of objections were raised, including one that the United States was too large for the self-policing action of a free press. Finally, the *New York Times* struck what turned out to be the decisive blow against the National News Council. The *Times*'s publisher, Arthur Ochs Sulzberger, argued that the council "would encourage an atmosphere of regulation in which government intervention might gain public acceptance." That did it. The bulk of the press simply declined to give the council a chance.

Nevertheless, in its first four years, beginning in 1973, the council received and investigated about a hundred complaints a year against the press. For that reason, primarily, the Gannett Foundation, the organization supported by the largest chain of newspapers in the land, came up with the fresh financing, and Norman Isaacs, a former president of the American Society of Newspaper Editors, took over as chairman. What Isaacs did was to expand the council's agenda to include the defense of the press against threats to its freedom.

Television, which had been sitting this one out, now showed signs of interest. William S. Paley, chairman of CBS, pledged his cooperation "including reporting by CBS of any council findings adverse to CBS News." But that didn't help much. One news organization that had been on the losing end of a council verdict even called upon it to disband. It didn't right away, but eventually it died an unmourned death.

What remained of the self-regulating notion in the United States was an occasional sentry for fair play, called an "ombudsman," after Swedish practice, whose purpose was to investigate complaints against his newspaper. Charles B. Seib, the *Washington Post's* ombudsman, was perfectly honest about his role, saying: "Self-monitoring is the same as saying let Congress monitor itself or let the White House monitor itself. But it's better than nothing."

Even at the height of the movement for self-regulation by a small section of the American press, there were—at a guess—no more than two dozen ombudsmen serving newspapers of fifty thousand or more circulation.*

To conclude, the problem with ethics in American journalism is that everybody is for ethical conduct but there is no uniformity about defining it or deciding what should be done about it. And yet, there is no doubt that journalists of integrity and good conscience are an essential ingredient in a democratic society.

They do not help their cause by being fearful of both self-regulation and detailed public scrutiny. At this juncture in American history, they must know that they never will be loved and that their service to society, for the most part, will be taken for granted. And yet the work is there to be done now as always—the difficult daily effort in large part to represent the acts of government to the people and the situation of the people to the government. If the journalist does not do it, most assuredly no one else will.

The responsibility is there. The journalist has a right to be proud when it can be fulfilled with courage and honor and truth.

*I have discussed the problem at greater length in my *A Crisis for the American Press* (New York: Columbia University Press, 1978), pp. 263–270.

APPENDIX
Checklist for Writers

THE FIVE-PART CHECKLIST that follows is based on common errors that are made by most newcomers to journalism in their written work. It is by no means a complete writers' guide; however, if regularly consulted, it may help the beginning journalist over some rough spots.

Spelling Checklist

Here are some of the most misspelled words in the English language:

accessible	carrousel	discernible	indispensable
accommodate	changeable	dissension	ingenious
acquit	claque	ecstacy	ingenuous
all right	colloquy	embarrass	innocuous
analogous	commiserate	eying	inoculate
appall	consensus	fulfill	judgment
appendicitis	council	furor	kimono
arraignment	counsel	gaiety	liaison
ascendant	curlicue	glamor	likable
assassin	defense	guerrilla	marshal
bettor	deity	hemorrhage	mien
buses	dependent	hygiene	mulct
canoeist	dietitian	impeccable	naphtha
carousal	diphtheria	incompatible	nickel

ninety	saxophone	under way	withal
ophthalmologist	supersede	vein	wrack
Portuguese	timbre	vilify	yield
queue	transcendent	weird	yours
renege	ukulele	whisky	zephyr
sacrilegious	unctuous	wield	Zwieback

Conciseness Checklist

In the following list, overworked and incorrectly used words and phrases will be found under the column headed DON'TS and proposed substitutes will be listed directly opposite under DO'S. For example, the phrase, "at the present time," is listed under DON'TS and the word "now" is directly across. There are a lot of others but these are among the worst offenders.

DOS	DON'TS
afterward	afterwards
all round	all around
because of	due to
before	before in the past
big	big in size
biography	biography of her life
body	dead body
bridegroom	groom
broadcast	broadcasted
combined	combined together
consensus	consensus of opinion
departed	checked out
different from	different than
dinner	banquet
doesn't (does not)	don't (do not)
do as I say	do like I say
effort	college try
farther (for distance)	further (for distance)
further (for everything else)	farther (for everything else)
forward	forwards
hanged (for people)	hung (for people)
hung (for pictures, etc.)	hanged (for pictures, etc.)
if	if and when
incumbent	present incumbent
matinee	matinee show or performance
monopoly	entire monopoly
more than (meaning in excess of)	over (meaning in excess of)

DOS	DON'TS
now	at the present time
principal (the main one)	principle (the main one)
principle (a general truth)	principal (a general truth)
proved	proven
rearing (referring to children)	raising (referring to children)
reason is that	reason is because
received injuries	sustained injuries
repeat	repeat again
registered	checked in
St. James's (the palace)	St. James (the palace)
Scots (the people)	Scotch (the people)
Sahara (means desert)	Sahara desert
Sierra (means mountains)	Sierra mountains
strangled	strangled to death
tonight at 8	tonight at 8 P.M.
toward	towards
unidentified person	unknown person
unique	very unique
virtually	practically
whether	whether or not

Checklist of Grammatical Errors

Here are illustrations of some of the most common grammatical errors and how to avoid them:

Nouns

   Collective nouns—Examples like corporation, company, legislature, council, and Congress are singular, and pronouns and verbs must agree in number. ("The *council is* meeting for *its* first executive session.")

   Plural nouns—Examples like data, police and fish are plural, and pronouns and verbs must agree in number. ("The *police are* taking their time.")

   Gerund—This is a verb used as a noun that takes a possessive modifier. ("The crowd groaned over the *favorite's running* last.")

Pronouns

   Pronoun used with antecedent—The pronoun that refers to an antecedent, a noun, or noun equivalent, must agree in number with the antecedent. ("The *people* will have *their* way.")

   That and which—*That* introduces a limiting clause, *which* a parenthetical clause. In brief, if the clause could be omitted without distorting the meaning of the sentence, start it with *which;* otherwise, with *that.* ("Long Island Sound, *which* is usually calm, was rough last night." Or, "It was unusual last night to see *that* Long Island Sound was rough.")

Who and whom—*Who* is the *subject* of a clause or sentence, *whom* is the *object.* ("*Who* goes there?" "He knew to *whom* she referred.")

Adjectives

Dangling participle—A participle is a verb that is used as an adjective. If it isn't in direct contact with the subject modified, it is said to dangle and make no sense. ("*Looking* up at him, *her lips* smiled," is an example of a dangling participle. It should read: "*Looking* up at him, *she* smiled.")

Verbs

Active voice—Writing is usually more forceful if verbs are in the active rather than the passive voice. ("The accident *occurred* when the two cars *crashed.*" Instead of, "The accident *was blamed* on the collision of the two cars.")

Sequence of tenses—The rule of parallelism usually is preferred here. ("Ruth *said* she *enjoyed* the show.") In this case the sequence is in the past tense.

Subjunctive mood—It is used when a clause is contrary to fact. ("George felt *as if he were* nine feet tall.")

Will and shall—This is the distinction: In the simple future tense, shall is used in the first person, will for the rest. ("*I shall* see the show tonight. *They will* go, too.") But in a forceful situation of command, the order is exactly opposite. ("I *will* fight. You *shall* help me.")

Misused verbs—The use of *chair* as a verb is incorrect. (Instead of, "She *chaired* the meeting," use *presided.*) The use of *claim* as a verb also is incorrect. (Instead of, "He *claimed* he was out of the city when the shooting occurred," use *said.*)

Adverbs

Incorrect modifier—Splitting an infinitive is bad enough. To insert an adverb between the split is indefensible. (Instead of: "He decided *to gradually approach* the darkened house," use: "He decided *to approach* the darkened house *gradually.*")

Prepositions

At end of sentence—They can be awkward. (Example: "English was what she took her degree in." Better: "Her degree was in English.")

Conjunction

Not only—Once again, the rule of parallelism should be followed. In the following example, note that *not only* and *but also* each precede a verb. ("The Iran-Iraq War *not only exhausted* both sides *but also endangered* U.S. oil supplies from the Middle East.")

Exclamations

Use sparingly or not at all—These make for artifical, hopped-up prose that creates a false sense of excitement. All too often, these make writing sound amateurish.

Checklist for Punctuation

If sentences are reasonably short and uncomplicated, there should be little use for punctuation except for periods, an occasional comma, and semicolon or colon and quotation marks. Too much punctuation is the mark of an unskilled writer. Some observations on the utility of punctuation follow:

Periods

The most useful punctuation mark in American jouralism. It should be used freely and often.

Periods end declarative sentences. Where a sentence is enclosed in parentheses, the period goes inside the final parenthesis. It should also be used with abbreviations (Ave., St., etc.) but not after percent.

Quotation Marks

They cause more errors than all other punctuation marks put together. There isn't much that can go wrong with opening quotation marks, particularly when they begin a paragraph. But at the end, the writer sometimes forgets to put either a comma or period *inside* the concluding quotation mark. Another source of error is failure to leave the quotation open if a new paragraph continues the same quotation. Double attribution, single quotation marks within double quotation marks, should be used sparingly to avoid confusion.

The only kinds of punctuation that follow the concluding quotation mark are colons and semicolons.

Commas

Use commas sparingly to clarify meaning; also, to separate qualifiers before the last in a series. [Note: Unlike editing for book publication, all forms of editing for journalism omit the next to last comma in a series of three or more modifiers. Thus, "The flag is red, white and blue."

Semicolons

Mainly, they're used at the end of a phrase containing commas and in addresses and sports scores.

Colons

Use sparingly except to introduce statements and resolutions, in the calculation of time and in scriptural readings.

Apostrophes

Principally, these are to indicate possessives and appear between a singular noun and the added *s*. Also, they are necessary where words are contracted, such as *I'm, I'll, we'll*, etc., and at the end of plural possessives, such as *his sons' children*.

Question Marks

Except after a direct question, use with great care.

Hyphens and Dashes

Dashes indicate an abrupt change of thought, hyphens form compound words. If in doubt, the best rule is to look up a fuzzy case in the dictionary.

Checklist for Copy Editing

The following editorial directions for copy editing are followed by the symbols most editors use:

DIRECTIONS	SYMBOLS
Start paragraph	⌐
No paragraph	NO ⌐

DIRECTIONS	SYMBOLS
Spell out word	Ga.
Contract into abbreviation	Georgia
Spell out figure	5
Contract into figure	Twelve
More on next page	More
End story	30 or XXX or end
Capitalize	long island
Use italics	Manhattan
Overscore letters	n̄ m̄
Underscore letters	u w
Use lower case	Jungle
Transpose	Canitser
Separate	New Jersey
Insert	We ∧worried
Eliminate space	for ever
Period	⊙
Comma	⁄
Quotes	∧ ∨
Center	⊐ ⊏
Indent from left	⊐
Indent from right	⊏
Instructions to printer	set agate

Tired Words and Phrases

Not every newcomer to journalism can write in fresh, original terms with compelling style. What all *can* do, however, is to avoid using tired words and phrases. A selection follows (and no doubt the list could be extended for pages more):

> *A shot rang out.*
> *At one fell swoop*
> *A goodly number*
> *A man after my own heart*
> *Get down to brass tacks.*
> *Blushing bride*
> *Budding genius*
> *Busy as a bee*
> *Cool as a cucumber*
> *Dull thud*
> *Don't beat around the bush.*
> *Don't rest on your laurels.*

Don't rush in where angels fear to tread.
Fair maiden
Fast as a jack rabbit
Great beyond
Green with envy
Hits the nail on the head
Gamboling on the green
Knows the score
Last but not least
Method in his madness
Sadder but wiser

INDEX